BRITISH PROCESS SERVERS GUIDE
The Ultimate Guide for the Professional Process Server

By
Stuart Withers | Helen Withers
Jorge Salgado-Reyes

BRITISH PROCESS SERVERS GUIDE
The Ultimate Guide for the Professional Process Server

Published by: Indie Authors Press
e-mail: publishing@salgado-reyes.com
www.salgado-reyes.com

Copyright © Stuart Withers, Helen Withers, Jorge Salgado-Reyes 2012
All Rights Reserved

The moral right of Stuart Withers, Helen Withers & Jorge Salgado-Reyes to be identified as the authors of this work has been asserted in accordance with the Copyright, Designs and Patents Act of 1988.

No part of this publication may be reproduced, stored in a retrieval system, or transmitted, in any form or by any means, electronic, mechanical, photocopying, recording, or otherwise, without the prior written permission of the publisher, nor be otherwise circulated in any form of binding or cover other than that in which it is published and without a similar condition being imposed on the subsequent purchaser.

A CIP catalogue record for this book is available from the British Library

Law is stated as at August 2012

Edited by Dr Cyrus Mansouri, Mansouri & Son Solicitors, 37a – 37b High Street, Croydon, CR0 1QB.

Photography by Jorge Salgado-Reyes.

Book Cover Design by Madison Paige.

Every care has been taken to ensure the accuracy of the contents of this guide. No responsibility for loss occasioned to any person acting or refraining from action as a result of any statement in it or using any precedent in it can be accepted by the authors or publishers.

The British Process Servers Guide is reproduced under the terms of Crown Copyright Policy Guidance issued by HMSO.

ISBN: 978-0-9569486-4-9

1st Edition

BRITAIN'S PREMIER PRIVATE INVESTIGATIONS ORGANISATION

Provides a comprehensive national and international service to Lawyers, commerce, industry & the public.

Nationwide Investigations Group provides a professional and comprehensive private investigation service. With almost five decades of practical experience in conducting investigations on behalf of lawyers commerce industry and the general public into all types of civil, criminal and personal matters. Our private investigation services have been retained by Princes, Presidents, Politicians and Personalities, as well as International Corporations, Government Agencies, Police Forces, the Press and Broadcasting Media. Our experienced, qualified and professional private investigators have extensive and practical knowledge of law and are fully conversant with the many aspects of private investigation including;

- Financial investigations and asset searching
- Tracing missing persons
- Personal injury investigations
- Criminal defence investigations
- 'Locus Quo' sketch plans and photography
- Process serving
- Internal fraud and theft investigations
- Product counterfeiting and trade-mark fraud investigations
- Employee screening investigations, due diligence and background checks
- Investigating fraudulent insurance claims
- Matrimonial prenuptial and alimony investigations
- Forensic science facilities including DNA Profiling
- Photographic and video image enhancement
- Handwriting and fingerprint analysis
- Mobile Phone and Computer Examination
- Polygraph examinations "lie detector"
- Computer-related fraud investigations
- Electronic Sweeps/De-Bugging

CENTRAL LONDON AND HEAD OFFICE: +44(0) 20 7649 9415
ALPHA HOUSE, 100 BOROUGH HIGH STREET, LONDON SE1 1LB
FACSIMILE: 020 7649 9416 EMAIL: INFO@NIG.CO.UK WEB: WWW.NIG.CO.UK

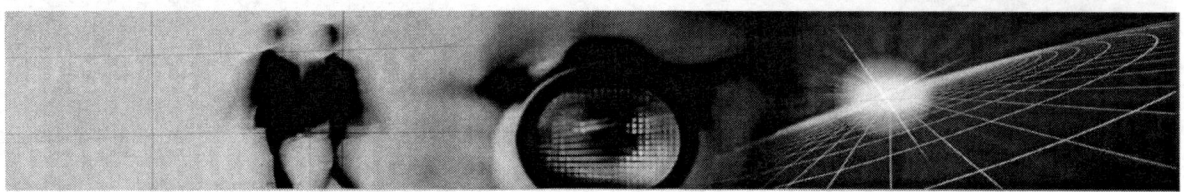

WORLD WIDE OFFICES
With offices in the UK, Ireland and internationally, **Priority Investigations** is your "local" international private investigation service

DNA PATERNITY TESTING
Priority Forensics, part of the **Priority Investigations Group,** is the exclusive UK and Ireland agent for a world leading forensic laboratory.

Members of WAPI and other Professional Associations
Ethically & Legally Compliant

HEAD OFFICE:
PO Box 266 Belfast BT5 4AQ UK
T: 028 9442 8284 - F: 028 9442 8370 – M: 079 7064 5420
US ONLY: 240-205-7897
E: HQ@PILimited.com www.pilimited.com
http://www.youtube.com/watch?v=AOKwCcb5IAw

UK Registered Company N139707
DPA Notified Z6032379

UK – USA – EU – AND WORLDWIDE SERVICE

"52 YEARS OF INVESTIGATING FROM OCTOBER 1960 TO 2012"

OBTAIN AN OFFICIALLY RECOGNISED QUALIFICATION IN PRIVATE INVESTIGATION

- An officially recognised Edexcel BTEC qualification in Advanced Private Investigations Level 3 Diploma

- Putting you in the elite category of Qualified Professional Private Investigator

- No other distance learning course provides this qualification

VISIT OUR WEBSITE
www.pi-academy.com
or Call: 01444 441111

Academy of Professional Investigation
The Priory, Syresham Gardens, Haywards Heath, West Sussex, RH16 3LB
E-mail: sales@pi-academy.com

DON'T DELAY ENROL TODAY!

The World Association of Professional Investigators

'UNITED BY VOCATION'

ACTING IN THE BEST INTERESTS OF THE PROFESSION

For an application form please contact

The General Secretary, World Association of Professional Investigators,

212 Piccadilly, London, W1J 9HG

Tel: 0870 9099970 Fax: 0870 9010209

Website: www.wapi.com E-mail: enquiries@wapi.com

CONTENTS

Acknowledgements P.1

Introduction P.3

Section 1 - Introduction to Process Serving P.5

       Glossary of Terms P.6

       National Occupational Standards P.9

       The English Court System P.13

       Civil Procedure Rules (CPR) P.19

       CPR Part 6 Service of Documents P.21

       Practice Direction 6a - Service within the United Kingdom P.38

       Annex - Service on Members of the Regular Forces P.42

Section 2 – Claim Forms, Companies Act 2006, Possession Claims, Admiralty, Crown Proceedings, Orders To Obtain Information From Judgment Debtors, Third Party Debt Orders, Charging Orders, Stop Orders And Stop Notices P.47

Section 3 – Witnesses And Depositions - CPR Part 34 .... P.65

Section 4 – Insolvency Proceedings P.69

Section 5 – Family Court Proceedings P.135

Section 6 – Magistrates & Crown Court Proceedings P.156

Section 7 – Scottish Process Proceedings P.165

Section 8 – Foreign Process Proceedings (Hague, EU Convention & Informal) P.173

Section 9 – Affidavits, Statements and Certificates of Service P.221

Section 10 – General Observations & Notes P.295

About the authors P.301

Afterword P.305

Index P.307

ACKNOWLEDGMENTS

The British Process Servers Guide has been written and compiled by practising professionals, whose vast accumulated experience, skill and in-depth knowledge acquired over 110 years, provides a wealth of vital information and procedures.

Including all the latest relevant legislation and the Woolf Reforms, it is the essential guide to the successful completion of all legal process.

There have been some people who have assisted greatly in the design, writing and proof editing of this guide. To them all I extend my thanks and if you spot any errors, they are entirely my responsibility.

I would like to thank Madison Paige for her book cover design who has devoted her time and expertise free of charge.

My thanks to Ian Withers of the World Association of Professional Investigators for his direction, assistance, and guidance and in taking my Skype calls sometimes in the middle of the night.

I also wish to thank "Finvarra" from the Law Forum www.swarb.co.uk, who wishes to remain anonymous.

Special thanks should be given to my Facebook friends who helped me in many ways and in particular to my business partner Neil Sheppard who kindly offered to proofread this guide.

Finally, words alone cannot express the thanks I owe to Zwide Holder, my sweetheart, for her encouragement and assistance in these difficult economic times.

~ **Jorge Salgado-Reyes** ~

INTRODUCTION

This guide has been rewritten and updated to reflect the changes made to the Civil Procedure Rules and Court Procedure since the highly successful and original Process Servers Guide 2000 was written and published by Nationwide Investigations Group.

The Civil Procedure Rules (CPR) was introduced in April 1999 following a report on the state of civil justice carried out by Lord Woolf. Formerly practice in the High Court was governed by the Rules of the Supreme Court (RSC) and practice in the County Court by the County Court Rules (CCR). The CPR incorporates one code of civil practice for both the High Court and the County Court. However, many differences in practice between the High Court and the County Court have survived the introduction of the CPR. This is because large chunks of the RSC and the CCR have been re-enacted as schedules to the CPR. The surviving parts of the RSC have been re-enacted as Schedule 1 to the CPR. The surviving parts of the CCR have been re-enacted as Schedule 2 to the CPR.

The two most commonly used practitioner texts on the Civil Procedure Rules are "Civil Procedure", familiarly known as "The White Book" and published by Sweet & Maxwell, and "The Civil Court Practice" familiarly known as "The Green Book" and published by Butterworths.

The Civil Procedure (Amendment) Rules 2011 came into force on the 6th April 2011. This guide has been updated to reflect those changes in the CPR. Amendments to Part 6 that allow service of documents on a solicitor acting for the defendant, where the business address for service of the solicitor is in Scotland or Northern Ireland, came into force on 1 September 2011.

This guide will be further amended as the rules change in the future.

As a practising process server, I have always wished to have a ready reference to the rules on my iPhone. For this reason, The British Process Servers Guide will be published in electronic format (Kindle) for easy reference on your Kindle, Kindle app (iPhone/iPad2), Kindle for Android, Kindle for PC & MAC as well as published as a paperback and hardback on www.amazon.com.

~ **Jorge Salgado-Reyes** ~

SECTION 1

INTRODUCTION TO PROCESS SERVING

Process Serving, other than that carried out by the Court office, is the personal delivery by hand, of a legal document, by a person acting as an agent for a party to a legal action, on one or more of the parties involved in a court case.

The serving of Process is governed by strict rules that you as a Process Server should adhere to at all times. Your conduct has to be impeccable in the eyes of the law and this will be assisted by your personal approach to the matter.

Interestingly, the Civil Procedure Rules makes no stipulation as to age for a Process Server. Nor is there a rule which states that service is prohibited in a Place of Worship i.e. Church, Mosque or Synagogue. I would keep service in a Place of Worship to a last resort. Nor for that matter is there a rule or law that prohibits service in a Court of Law or the Houses of Parliament. However, you may be found in Contempt of Court or Contempt of Parliament, should you try. **Also see page 51 of this guide.**

An example of this occurred in 1993, in ALEXANDER BARON v GERRY GABLE AND OTHERS, where Baron felt himself to be libelled and issued a Writ against Gable and others. He attempted to serve the Writ on Gable inside the Houses of Parliament. A newspaper, the Jewish Chronicle in December 31st issue printed the following story;

COMMONS WRIT SERVER IN CONTEMPT by Jerry Lewis

A writ served on the editor of an anti-Fascist magazine as he gave evidence to a top-level Commons committee has been ruled "in contempt of the House." But MPs have decided to take no further action against the server of the writ, which was handed to Searchlight editor Gerry Gable as he appeared before the Home Affairs Select Committee on racism. The man was questioned by police and removed from Parliament. The Writ was said to concern material published in a recent issue of the magazine. In a report, the committee ruled that "what occurred was a contempt of the House," but declined to take further action.

A Process Server is much more than just a glorified postman. The hand delivery of a document ensures that the person whom it concerns actually receives it. If Process Serving was simply a case of just pushing the document through the letter box (except in exceptional circumstances) there would be a possibility for the recipient concerned to use any one of a number of excuses to deny having received the document in time to appear in Court. The Process Server, therefore, exists in order to prove receipt of documents by the person for whom they are intended.

In most cases instructions originate from Solicitors. The Solicitor instructing you will normally represent the party issuing an action. This person may be termed the Applicant, the Claimant or the Petitioner, depending on the type of case involved. The person you may be directed to serve will be termed the Defendant or the Respondent respectively, and sometimes where a third party is involved, the Co-Respondent or Second Respondent. There are other terms but in the main the above are the most usual.

GLOSSARY OF TERMS

ADVOCATE	One who pleads the case of another. (e.g. Barrister-at-Law)
ADULTERY	Sexual infidelity within the confines of marriage.
AFFIDAVIT	Written statement sworn on Oath.
APPLICANT	One who applies.
ARTICLE	Clause in contract.
BANKRUPT	An insolvent person unable to pay a due debt on demand and/or has no resources to meet due debts in a Bankruptcy Court.
BANKRUPTCY	State of being or being declared Bankrupt.
CLAIMANT	Person who commences an action in a Court of Law
CLAIM FORM	The commencing document in a civil High Court or County Court case.
COMMISSIONER FOR OATHS	A person appointed by the Lord Chancellor with power to administer oaths or take affidavits. A Commissioner for Oaths can include Notary Public, Solicitor, Barrister, Legal Executive, Licensed Conveyancer.
OATHS	An oath is either a statement of fact or a promise calling upon something or someone that the oath maker considers sacred, usually God, as a witness to the binding nature of the promise or the truth of the statement of fact. To swear is to take an oath, to make a solemn vow.
AFFIRMATION	A declaration made by and allowed to those who conscientiously object to taking an oath
COMPLAINANT	Normally the victim of a crime reported to Police.
CO-RESPONDENT	A joint Respondent, especially in a Divorce case.
CO-DEFENDANT	A joint Defendant, against whom an action is commenced.
COUNSEL	Legal adviser, more commonly used to describe a Barrister-at-law.
DEFAULT	Failure to appear or plead in court case.
DEFENDANT	A person against whom an action is commenced.
DEPONENT	One who makes a statement on Oath.
ENDORSE	To certify or confirm.

EVIDENCE	Facts that prove or tend to prove something.
THIRD PARTY DEBT ORDER	Notice of proceedings to a Third Party who holds or owes monies to a Judgment Debtor.
HEARING	A gathering within a courtroom for the purpose of conducting a legal procedure.
INJUNCTION	Court Order requiring something to be or not to be done.
IN REM (LATIN)	Designating a proceeding instituted for the disposition of property and not directed against any specific person.
IN PERSONAM (LATIN)	Against the person rather than specific things, used in certain legal proceedings.
JUDGMENT	Decision of a Court.
JUDICATURE	Judicial system of a country. Judges collectively.
JURISDICTION	The geographic area in which a Court and/or area of law administers justice.
NOTARY PUBLIC	A person empowered to notarise (certify) documents, usually pertaining to Foreign Courts of Law.
ORDER	A direction, or directive of the Court
ORIGINATING	Commencing.
PETITION	Formal application in writing to a Court.
PLAINTIFF	Person who commenced an action in a Court of Law but now referred to as Claimant
PROCESS	Documents issued during the course of legal actions.
RESPONDENT	One who answers in defence in a Court case.
SUBPOENA	An order requiring a person to attend Court and/or to produce items to the Court, now called a Witness Summons.
SERVE	To deliver a Summons or Notice of legal process to someone.
SUMMONS	Notice to appear in Court.
TORT	Private or civil wrong.
WITNESS SUMMONS	An order requiring a person to attend Court and/or produce items to the Court, previously called a Subpoena.

WRIT	Previously, the commencing document in a civil High Court case but now called a Claim Form.
SUSPECT	A person or persons considered to be potentially liable or guilty of a particular act or omission.
INTELLIGENCE	Information that has been or can be developed in the context of the investigation
INFORMATION	Facts or knowledge provided or learned
DATA	Facts and statistics used for reference or analysis
CLIENT	A person engaging the services of an investigator
THIRD PARTY	Party other than the client or investigator
RECORDS	Retained data or information
INTELLIGENCE MODEL	A current best practice model for collation, evaluation, dissemination of intelligence
FURTH	Outside or beyond. Usually used in Scottish legalese
COURT OF SESSION	The Court of Session is the Scottish supreme civil court. It is both a court of first instance and a court of appeal and sits exclusively in Parliament House in Edinburgh. The court of first instance is known as the Outer House, the court of appeal the Inner House.
SHERIFF COURT	The Sheriff Court is the other Scottish civil court; this sits locally. Although the Court of Session and Sheriff Courts have a largely co-extensive jurisdiction, with the choice of court being given in the first place to the pursuer (the claimant) , the majority of difficult or high-value cases in Scotland are brought in the Court of Session. Any final decision of a Sheriff may be appealed against. There is a right of appeal in civil cases to the Sheriff Principal, and in most cases onwards to the Court of Session.

NATIONAL OCCUPATIONAL STANDARDS

National Occupational Standards for Investigations published an approved Suite of NOS in May 2010. Only the following units are relevant to Process Serving;

INV 14 Carry out legal process serving	INV 14.1 Prepare to serve legal process
	INV 14.2 Serve and provide proof of service

DA5 Present evidence in court and at other hearings (This unit has been imported and tailored from a Skills for Justice approved suite of NOS)	DA5.1 Prepare for court or other hearings
	DA5.2 Present evidence to court or other hearings

Unit INV 14

CARRY OUT LEGAL PROCESS SERVING

Overview

This unit sets out the skills, knowledge and understanding for you to serve and provide proof of service of legal process.

This unit consists of two elements:

- Prepare to serve legal process (INV 14.1)
- Serve and provide proof of service (INV 14.2)

Unit: INV 14

Unit Title: Carry out legal process serving

Element: INV 14.1

Element Title: Prepare to serve legal process

Performance Criteria

You must be able to –

    a. understand and agree clients' instructions to serve the legal process
    b. confirm the process papers are accurate and complete
    c. clarify information or instructions about which you are unclear
    d. agree and record accurate details of costs and timescales
    e. negotiate, agree and record accurate details of providing 'conduct money' if required

Knowledge Criteria

You must know and understand –

1. current legislation, regulations, codes of practice and guidelines relating to serving legal process
2. how to serve legal process
3. the importance of checking the process papers are accurate and complete
4. how to understand and agree your clients' instructions to serve the legal process
5. how to agree, plan and schedule costs and timescale
6. how to negotiate and agree provisions of providing conduct money

Range Statement

You must be competent to deal with the following types of:-

1. process papers: notice of application, court orders, statutory demands, writs, summonses, subpoenas, petitions, injunctions

Unit: INV 14

Unit Title: Carry out legal process serving

Element: INV 14.2

Element Title: Serve and provide proof of service

Performance Criteria

You must be able to –

a. carry out the method of service in line with legal requirements and client instructions
b. corroborate the identity of persons or locations on which to serve the process prior to the legal process being activated
c. notify the client promptly where you are unable to complete the service
d. prepare and produce proofs of service correctly and in accordance with legal requirements
e. compile and submit client completion reports accurately and in the required format

Knowledge Criteria

You must know and understand –

1. current legislation, regulations, code of practice and guidelines relating to service of process and proofs of service (corroborating the serving of legal process, preparation of affidavits, swearing or affirming of affidavits)
2. how to confirm the identities of persons or locations on which to serve the process before the legal process starts
3. how and why it is important to notify the client quickly when you are unable to complete the service
4. how and why it is important to prepare proofs of service
5. how to gather information and prepare accurate client completion reports
6. why it is important and how to respect the rights of individuals

Range Statement

You must be competent to deal with the following types of:-

1. method of service: by post, in person, substituted, affixing to premises and property
2. locations: private premises and property, business premises, public places
3. unable to complete: non-location of persons, uncorroborated identities, deliberate obstructions

Unit DA5

PRESENT EVIDENCE IN COURT AND AT OTHER HEARINGS

Overview

This unit focuses preparing and presenting evidence in courts and at other hearings. You may be required to provide evidence in various capacities.

You must prepare for court or other hearings, ensuring that you identify and obtain all relevant exhibits, notes and materials in advance. You must also liaise with the relevant parties as required and take action to resolve any problems or difficulties that arise.

You must present evidence in an effective manner complying with the rules of evidence, court/hearing procedures and acceptable professional standards. You must also ensure that all relevant aspects of community and race relations, diversity and human rights are adhered to.

There are two elements:

DA5.1 Prepare for court or other hearings

DA5.2 Present evidence to court or other hearings

This unit has been imported from a Skills for Justice approved suite of standards and tailored by Skills for Security to meet requirements

Unit: DA5

Unit Title: Present evidence in court and at other hearings

Element: DA5.1

Element Title: Prepare for court or other hearings

Performance Criteria

You must be able to –

a. respond promptly to any warnings, citations or notifications received from courts or other hearings
b. provide any information requested by the court or hearing accurately and expeditiously

c. ensure the availability of exhibits within your area of responsibility taking steps to maintain their continuity and integrity at all times
d. consider your evidence in advance of the hearing and ensure that you are in possession of the appropriate notes and materials
e. liaise with appropriate agencies to confirm witness
f. liaise with relevant authorities as required
g. deal with individuals in an ethical manner, recognising their needs with respect to race, diversity and human rights

Knowledge Criteria

You must know and understand –

The knowledge which you need to perform this element is listed at the end of DA5.2

Range Statement

There is no Range Statement for this element

Unit: DA5

Unit Title: Present evidence in court and at other hearings

Element: DA5.2

Element Title: Present evidence to court or other hearings

Performance Criteria

You must be able to –

a. present yourself at the venue in a timely manner and in possession of all necessary exhibits and documents
b. ensure your appearance and behaviour confirms to acceptable professional standards at all times
c. liaise with victims, witnesses and defendants in according with current policy and legislation
d. deliver your evidence and respond to questions in a truthful, objective, clear and concise manner with due regard for the rules of evidence and the procedures of the venue
e. provide oral evidence that is consistent with any written materials provided by you as part of the case
f. respond to all directions of the court or hearing promptly and appropriately

Knowledge Criteria

You must know and understand –

The knowledge which you need to perform this element is listed at the end of this unit.

THE ENGLISH COURT SYSTEM

The Royal Courts of Justice houses an administrative group which is divided into a number of divisions each of which has its own courts. The Royal Courts of Justice building accommodates both the Court of Appeal and the High Court.

The Court of Appeal consists of two divisions:

- The civil division which hears appeals from the High Court
- The criminal division which hears appeals from the Crown Court

The High Court deals with higher level civil disputes. There are three divisions of the High Court:

- The Queen's Bench Division
- The Chancery Division
- The Family Division

Other areas of the High Court include:

The Administrative Court which is one of the most varied in terms of what it covers. The types of cases it deals with are:

- Judicial Reviews
- Statutory appeals and applications
- Applications for Habeas Corpus
- Applications under the Drug Trafficking Act 1994 and the Criminal Justice Act 1988

In addition to the Court of Appeal and the High Court, the Royal Courts of Justice Group is responsible for:

- Office of the Judge Advocate General (OJAG).
- The Office of the Chief Magistrate

Part of the work of HM Courts & Tribunals Service is the administration of the courts in England and Wales. This work provides administration and support for the Magistrates' courts, County Courts, the Crown Court, the High Court, the Court of Appeal and the Probate Service.

Magistrates' Courts

Magistrates' courts are a key part of the criminal justice system and 97% of cases are completed there. In addition magistrates' courts deal with many civil cases e.g. anti-social behaviour, public health and are responsible for the enforcement of fines and community punishments.

Where cases required a penalty greater than magistrates' sentencing powers, cases will be sent to the Crown Court.

County Courts

The county court, often referred to as the small claims court, deals with civil matters, such as:

- Claims for debt repayment, including enforcing court orders and return of goods bought on credit,
- Personal Injury
- Breach of contract concerning goods or property
- Family issues such as relationship breakdown or adoption
- Housing disputes, including mortgage and council rent arrears and re-possession.

The Crown Court

The Crown Court deals with more serious criminal cases such as murder, rape or robbery, some of which are on appeal or referred from magistrates' courts. Trials are heard by a Judge and a 12 person jury. Members of the public are selected for jury service or may have to go to court as witnesses. Crown Court cases originate from magistrates' courts.

The Crown Court also hears appeals against decisions of magistrate's courts.

The High Court

The High Court deals with higher level civil disputes within three divisions;

- the Queen's Bench Division
- the Chancery Division
- the Family Division

and deals with other jurisdictions including the Administrative Court.

The High Court sits at the Royal Courts of Justice.

The Queen's Bench Division is one of the three divisions of the High Court together with the Chancery Division and Family Division. Sir John Thomas is President of the Queen's Bench Division, and certain High Court Judges and Masters are assigned to it. Lady Justice Hallett has been appointed by the Lord Chief Justice to be the Vice-President of the Division; a High Court Judge is appointed as Judge in charge of the Jury List; another is appointed as Judge in charge of the Trial List.

Outside London, the work of the Queen's Bench Division is administered in provincial offices known as District Registries. In London, the work is administered in the Central Office at the Royal Courts of

Justice. The work in the Central Office of the Queen's Bench Division is the responsibility of the Senior Master, acting under the authority of the President of the Queen's Bench Division.

The work of the Queen's Bench Division, not including the specialist courts, consists mainly of claims for damages in respect of:

- personal injury
- negligence
- breach of contract,
- libel and slander (defamation)
- non-payment of a debt, and
- possession of land or property.

Proceedings retained to be dealt with in the Central Office of the Queen's Bench Division will almost invariably be multi-track claims.

In many types of claim - for example claims in respect of negligence by solicitors, accountants, etc. or claims for possession of land - the claimant has a choice whether to bring the claim in the Queen's Bench Division or in the Chancery Division. However, there are certain claims that may be brought only in the Queen's Bench Division, namely:

- Sheriff's interpleader proceedings, (see Rule 17 Supreme Court Rules for further information)
- Enrolment of deeds,
- Registration of foreign judgments under the Civil Jurisdictions and Judgments Act 1982,
- Applications for bail in criminal proceedings,
- Applications under the Administration of Justice Act 1920 and the Foreign Judgments (Reciprocal Enforcement) Act 1933,
- Registration and satisfaction of Bills of Sale,
- Election Petitions,
- Obtaining evidence for foreign courts.

The work of the Queen's Bench Division is (with certain exceptions) governed by the Civil Procedure Rules (CPR) . The Divisional Court, the Admiralty Court, Commercial Court and Technology and Construction Court are all part of the Queen's Bench Division. However, each does specialised work requiring a distinct procedure that to some extent modifies the CPR. For that reason each publishes its own Guide or Practice Direction, to which reference should be made by parties wishing to proceed in the specialist courts.

The Chancery Division is a part of the High Court of Justice. The areas of work that it deals with are:

- business and property related disputes
- competition
- general Chancery Claims
- patents claims
- intellectual Property claims
- companies claims
- insolvency claims
- trust claims
- probate claims
- appeals to the High Court, Chancery Division from the lower court

The Division is based at the Rolls Building (off Chancery Lane/Fetter Lane).

The Head of Division, The Chancellor of the High Court, is the Right Honourable Sir Andrew Morritt CVO.

There are currently seventeen High Court Judges attached to the Chancery Division. In addition, in the Royal Courts of Justice in London, there are six judges referred to as Chancery Masters (one of whom is the Chief Master) and six judges referred to as Bankruptcy Registrars (one of whom is the Chief Registrar).

In District Registries, the work done by Masters in London is done by District Judges.

Deputies sit on a regular basis for both Judges and Masters.

The Division includes:

- Chancery Chambers (Masters)
- Bankruptcy and Companies Court
- Patents Court

Chancery sittings outside the Royal Courts of Justice

Central London County Court

With effect from Wednesday 6 April 2011 creditors and debtors' petitions below the value of £50,000 and £100,000 respectively will be dealt with as a County Court matter. For this purpose the Central London County Court will sit at the Thomas More Building, Royal Courts of Justice, where petitions will continue to be issued and heard.

There are cases where, notwithstanding these monetary limits, the proceedings will continue to be presented in the High Court:-

- where the bankruptcy petition is being presented against a member of a partnership being wound up by the High Court in London;

- where the debtor is not resident in England and Wales and has not carried on business or resided in England and Wales in the 6 months before the presentation of the petition; and

- where the petitioner is unable to determine the debtor's place of residence and place of business.

Any person wishing to take notes in court must obtain the permission of the judge beforehand.

You can do this by:

1. Informing the court clerk or a member of Resource security staff in the courtroom before proceedings start. They will arrange to submit your request to the judge.

2. Submitting your request in writing or via email to the Court Office before the relevant court hearing commences.

You should make your request as far in advance as possible and ensure you state the name and reference number of the case and give your reasons for wanting to take notes.

The judge will decide whether you are permitted to do so and you will be informed by a member of court staff or Resource.

High Court Family Division

Information with regard to issuing and fees for applications should be directed to the relevant sections at the Principal Registry of the Family Division.

Clerk of the Rules

The Clerk of the Rules provides administrative support to the President of the Family Division and all of the High Court Judges within the Family Division.

The Family Division of the High Court has Jurisdiction to deal with all matrimonial matters, the Children Act 1989 and the Child Abduction and Custody Act 1985. It also deals with matters relating to Part IV Family Law Act 1996 (Family Homes and Domestic Violence), Adoption Section Inheritance Act 1975 applications and Probate and Court of Protection work.

Listing Office

Responsible for:

- listing High Court cases
- preparation and distribution of the Daily Cause List
- fixing cases through counsel's clerks, solicitors and litigants in person, and by order of the court via the:
- Application to Clerk of the Rules for listing of a case form

Administrative Office

Responsible for:

- service of the court orders drawn by the Associates (these are posted out or, following arrangement with the relevant associate can be collected at the counter)
- written correspondence relating to High Court cases
- telephone queries
- serving the public counter (swearing affidavits and answering general queries)
- producing notices of hearing for High Court Cases
- collating files for hearings in High Court
- lodging of bundles and preparing papers for hearings.

Family Associates and In-Court Support

Responsible for the smooth running of the family courts and the drafting and perfecting of orders.

Urgent medical and abduction cases frequently bypass the list office and go straight to the High Court Applications Court. With these unlisted cases or 'Without Notice Applications' the associate is the first point of contact.

CIVIL PROCEDURE RULES

The Civil Procedure Rules (CPR) are the rules of civil procedure used by the Court of Appeal, High Court of Justice, and County Courts in civil cases in England and Wales. They apply to all cases commenced after 26 April 1999, and largely replace the Rules of the Supreme Court and the County Court Rules.

The CPR were designed to improve access to justice by making legal proceedings cheaper, quicker, and easier to understand for non-lawyers. Unlike the previous rules of civil procedure, the CPR commence with a statement of their "Overriding Objective", both to aid in the application of specific provisions and to guide behaviour where no specific rule applies.

In 1994, the Lord Chancellor instructed the Master of the Rolls, Lord Woolf, to report on options to consolidate the existing rules of civil procedure.

On 26 July 1996, Lord Woolf published his Access to Justice Report 1996 in which he "...identified a number of principles which the civil justice system should meet in order to ensure access to justice. The system should:

   a. be just in the results it delivers;
   b. be fair in the way it treats litigants;
   c. offer appropriate procedures at a reasonable cost;
   d. deal with cases with reasonable speed;
   e. be understandable to those who use it;
   f. be responsive to the needs of those who use it;
   g. provide as much certainty as the nature of particular cases allows; and
   h. be effective: adequately resourced and organised."

Lord Woolf listed two of the requirements of case management as: "...fixing timetables for the parties to take particular steps in the case; and limiting disclosure and expert evidence".

The second thread of the report was to control the cost of litigation, both in time and money, by focusing on key issues rather than every possible issue and limiting the amount of work that has to be done on the case.

The report was accompanied by draft rules of practice designed to implement Lord Woolf's proposals. These rules granted wide management powers to the court proposed that cases be allocated to one of three tracks depending on their nature, limiting or requiring specific actions; and introduced the concept of proportionality to the costs regime.

Civil Procedure Act 1997 (c. 12) was enacted on 27 February 1997. It conferred the power to make civil procedure rules. It also established the Civil Justice Council, a body composed of members of the judiciary, members of the legal professions and civil servants and charged with reviewing the civil justice system.

The Civil Procedure Rules 1998 (SI 1998/3132) were made on 10 December 1998 and came into force on 26 April 1999. The draft rules of practice formed their core.

Implemented as a result of reforms suggested by Lord Woolf and his committee, one of the revelations of the rules is the "Overriding Objective" embodied in Part 1 of the Rules, which states:

1.1 (1) These Rules are a new procedural code with the overriding objective of enabling the court to deal with cases justly.

(2) Dealing with a case justly includes, so far as is practicable –

(a) ensuring that the parties are on an equal footing;

(b) saving expense;

(c) dealing with the case in ways which are proportionate –

(i) to the amount of money involved;

(ii) to the importance of the case;

(iii) to the complexity of the issues; and

(iv) to the financial position of each party;

(d) ensuring that it is dealt with expeditiously and fairly; and

(e) allotting to it an appropriate share of the court's resources, while taking into account the need to allot resources to other cases.

1.2 The court must seek to give effect to the overriding objective when it –

(a) exercises any power given to it by the Rules; or

(b) interprets any rule.

The rules are written not just for lawyers but are intended to be intelligible for a litigant in person.

THE CIVIL PROCEDURE AMENDMENT RULES 2008 AS AMENDED BY VARIOUS UPDATES UNTIL 2011

Part 6 Service of Documents

I Scope Of This Part and Interpretation

Part 6 Rules about Service apply generally

6.1 The rules in this Part apply to the service of documents, except where -

    (a) *any other enactment, a rule in another Part, or a practice direction makes a different provision; or

    (b) the Court Orders otherwise.

Interpretation

6.2 In this Part -

    (a) 'bank holiday' means a bank holiday under the Banking and Financial Dealings Act 1971[1] in the part of the United Kingdom where service is to take place;

    (b) 'business day' means any day except Saturday, Sunday, a bank holiday, Good Friday or Christmas Day;

    (c) 'claim' includes petition and any application made before action or to commence proceedings and 'claim form', 'claimant' and 'defendant' are to be construed accordingly; and

    (d) 'solicitor' includes any other person who, for the purposes of the Legal Services Act 2007, is an authorised person in relation to an activity which constitutes the conduct of litigation (within the meaning of that Act).

II Service of the Claim Form in the Jurisdiction

Methods of Service - General

6.3 (1) A document may be served by any of the following methods -

    (a) personal service in accordance with rule 6.5;

    (b) first class post, document exchange or other service which provides for delivery on the next business day, in accordance with Practice Direction 6A;

    (c) leaving it at a place specified in rule 6.7, 6.8, 6.9 or 6.10;

    (d) fax or other means of electronic communication in accordance with Practice Direction 6A; or

(e) any method authorised by the court under rule 6.15.

(2) A company may be served –

(a) by any method permitted under this Part; or

(b) by any of the methods of service permitted under the Companies Act 2006.

(3) A limited liability partnership may be served –

(a) by any method permitted under this Part; or

(b) by any of the methods of service permitted under the Companies Act 2006 as applied with modification by regulations made under the Limited Liability Partnerships Act 2004.

N.B. (Rule 6.8 provides for the Court to permit service by an alternative method)

Who Is To Serve The Claim Form

6.4.1 (1) The Court will serve a document which it has issued or prepared except where –

(a) a rule or practice direction provides that the claimant must serve it;

(b) the claimant notifies the court that the claimant wishes to serve it; or

(c) the court orders or directs otherwise.

(2) Where the court is to serve the claim form, it is for the court to decide which method of service is to be used.

(3) Where the court is to serve the claim form, the claimant must, in addition to filing a copy for the court, provide a copy for each defendant to be served.

(4) Where the court has sent –

(a) a notification of outcome of postal service to the claimant in accordance with rule 6.18; or

(b) a notification of non-service by a bailiff in accordance with rule 6.19,

the court will not try to serve the claim form again.

Personal Service

6.5 (1) Where required by another Part, any other enactment, a practice direction or a court order, a claim form must be served personally.

(2) In other cases, a claim form may be served personally except –

(a) where rule 6.7 applies; or

(b) in any proceedings against the Crown.

N.B. Part 54 contains provisions about judicial review claims and Part 66 contains provisions about Crown proceedings.

(3) A claim form is served personally on –

(a) an individual by leaving it with that individual;

(b) a company or other corporation by leaving it with a person holding a senior position within the company or corporation; or

(c) a partnership (where partners are being sued in the name of their firm) by leaving it with –

(i) a partner; or

(ii) a person who, at the time of service, has the control or management of the partnership business at its principal place of business.

N.B. Practice Direction 6A sets out the meaning of 'senior position'.

ADVICE: IF THE PERSON BEING SERVED REFUSES TO ACCEPT THE DOCUMENTS, IT IS SUFFICIENT TO PLACE THE DOCUMENTS AT THEIR FEET AFTER HAVING INFORMED THEM OF ITS NATURE. IT'S NO LONGER NECESSARY TO TOUCH THE DOCUMENTS TO THE RECIPIENTS PERSON.

Where To Serve The Claim Form – General Provisions

6.6 (1) The claim form must be served within the jurisdiction except where rule 6.7(2) or 6.11 applies or as provided by Section IV of this Part.

(2) The claimant must include in the claim form an address at which the defendant may be served. That address must include a full postcode, unless the court orders otherwise.

N.B. Paragraph 2.4 of Practice Direction 16 contains provisions about postcodes

(3) Paragraph (2) does not apply where an order made by the court under rule 6.15 (service by an alternative method or at an alternative place) specifies the place or method of service of the claim form.

Service of the Claim Form on a Solicitor within the Jurisdiction or in any EEA State

6.7 (1) Subject to rule 6.5(1), where –

(a) the defendant has given in writing the business address within the jurisdiction of a solicitor as an address at which the defendant may be served with the claim form; or

(b) a solicitor acting for the defendant has notified the claimant in writing that the solicitor is instructed by the defendant to accept service of the claim form on behalf of the defendant at a business address within the jurisdiction,

the claim form must be served at the business address of that solicitor.

N.B. Solicitor' has the extended meaning set out in rule 6.2(d) .

(2) Subject to rule 6.5(1) and the provisions of Section IV of this Part, where –

(a) the defendant has given in writing the business address within any EEA state of a solicitor as an address at which the defendant may be served with the claim form; or

(b) a solicitor acting for the defendant has notified the claimant in writing that the solicitor is instructed by the defendant to accept service of the claim form on behalf of the defendant at a business address within any EEA state,

the claim form must be served at the business address of that solicitor.

Service of the Claim Form where the Defendant gives an address at which the Defendant may be served

6.8 Subject to rules 6.5(1) and 6.7 –

(a) the defendant may be served with the claim form at an address within the jurisdiction which the defendant has given for the purpose of being served with the proceedings; or

(b) in any claim by a tenant against a landlord, the claim form may be served at an address given by the landlord under section 48 of the Landlord and Tenant Act 1987.

Service of the claim form where the defendant does not give an address at which the defendant may be served

6.9 (1) This rule applies where –

(a) rule 6.5(1) (personal service) ;

(b) rule 6.7 (service of claim form on solicitor) ; and

(c) rule 6.8 (defendant gives address at which the defendant may be served) ,

do not apply and the claimant does not wish to effect personal service under rule 6.5(2) .

(2) Subject to paragraphs (3) to (6) , the claim form must be served on the defendant at the place shown in the following table.

Nature of defendant to be served	Place of service
1. Individual	Usual or last known residence.
2. Individual being sued in the name of a business	Usual or last known residence of the individual; or principal or last known place of business.

Nature of defendant to be served	Place of service
3. Individual being sued in the business name of a partnership	Usual or last known residence of the individual; or
	principal or last known place of business of the partnership.
4. Limited liability partnership	Principal office of the partnership; or
	any place of business of the partnership within the jurisdiction which has a real connection with the claim.
5. Corporation (other than a company) incorporated in England and Wales	Principal office of the corporation; or
	any place within the jurisdiction where the corporation carries on its activities and which has a real connection with the claim.
6. Company registered in England and Wales	Principal office of the company; or
	any place of business of the company within the jurisdiction which has a real connection with the claim.
7. Any other company or corporation	Any place within the jurisdiction where the corporation carries on its activities; or
	any place of business of the company within the jurisdiction.

(3) Where a claimant has reason to believe that the address of the defendant referred to in entries 1, 2 or 3 in the table in paragraph (2) is an address at which the defendant no longer resides or carries on business, the claimant must take reasonable steps to ascertain the address of the defendant's current residence or place of business ('current address').

(4) Where, having taken the reasonable steps required by paragraph (3), the claimant-

    (a) ascertains the defendant's current address, the claim form must be served at that address; or

(b) is unable to ascertain the defendant's current address, the claimant must consider whether there is –

    (i) an alternative place where; or

    (ii) an alternative method by which,

service may be effected.

(5) If, under paragraph (4) (b), there is such a place where or a method by which service may be effected, the claimant must make an application under rule 6.15.

(6) Where paragraph (3) applies, the claimant may serve on the defendant's usual or last known address in accordance with the table in paragraph (2) where the claimant –

    (a) cannot ascertain the defendant's current residence or place of business; and

    (b) cannot ascertain an alternative place or an alternative method under paragraph (4) (b)

Service of the claim form in proceedings against the crown

6.10 In proceedings against the Crown –

    (a) service on the Attorney General must be effected on the Treasury Solicitor; and

    (b) service on a government department must be effected on the solicitor acting for that department.

N.B. Practice Direction 66 gives the list published under section 17 of the Crown Proceedings Act 1976 of the solicitors acting in civil proceedings (as defined in that Act) for the different government departments on whom service is to be effected, and of their addresses.

Service of the claim form by contractually agreed method

6.11.1 (1) Where –

    (a) a contract contains a term providing that, in the event of a claim being started in relation to the contract, the claim form may be served by a method or at a place specified in the contract; and

    (b) a claim solely in respect of that contract is started,

the claim form may, subject to paragraph (2), be served on the defendant by the method or at the place specified in the contract.

(2) Where in accordance with the contract the claim form is to be served out of the jurisdiction, it may be served –

    (a) if permission to serve it out of the jurisdiction has been granted under rule 6.36; or

    (b) without permission under rule 6.32 or 6.33.

Service of the claim form relating to a contract on an agent of a principal who is out of the jurisdiction

6.12 (1) The court may, on application, permit a claim form relating to a contract to be served on the defendant's agent where –

(a) the defendant is out of the jurisdiction;

(b) the contract to which the claim relates was entered into within the jurisdiction with or through the defendant's agent; and

(c) at the time of the application either the agent's authority has not been terminated or the agent is still in business relations with the defendant.

(2) An application under this rule –

(a) must be supported by evidence setting out –

(i) details of the contract and that it was entered into within the jurisdiction or through an agent who is within the jurisdiction;

(ii) that the principal for whom the agent is acting was, at the time the contract was entered into and is at the time of the application, out of the jurisdiction; and

(iii) why service out of the jurisdiction cannot be effected; and

(c) may be made without notice.

(3) An order under this rule must state the period within which the defendant must respond to the particulars of claim.

(4) Where the court makes an order under this rule –

(a) a copy of the application notice and the order must be served with the claim form on the agent; and

(b) unless the court orders otherwise, the claimant must send to the defendant a copy of the application notice, the order and the claim form.

(5) This rule does not exclude the court's power under rule 6.15 (service by an alternative method or at an alternative place).

Service Of The Claim Form On Children And Protected Parties

6.13 (1) Where the defendant is a child who is not also a protected party, the claim form must be served on –

(a) one of the child's parents or guardians; or

(b) if there is no parent or guardian, an adult with whom the child resides or in whose care the child is.

(2) Where the defendant is a protected party, the claim form must be served on –

(a) one of the following persons with authority in relation to the protected party as –

(i) the attorney under a registered enduring power of attorney;

(ii) the donee of a lasting power of attorney; or

(iii) the deputy appointed by the Court of Protection; or

(b) if there is no such person, an adult with whom the protected party resides or in whose care the protected party is.

(3) Any reference in this Section to a defendant or a party to be served includes the person to be served with the claim form on behalf of a child or protected party under paragraph (1) or (2).

(4) The court may make an order permitting a claim form to be served on a child or protected party, or on a person other than the person specified in paragraph (1) or (2).

(5) An application for an order under paragraph (4) may be made without notice.

(6) The court may order that, although a claim form has been sent or given to someone other than the person specified in paragraph (1) or (2), it is to be treated as if it had been properly served.

(7) This rule does not apply where the court has made an order under rule 21.2(3) allowing a child to conduct proceedings without a litigation friend.

N.B. Part 21 contains rules about the appointment of a litigation friend and 'child' and 'protected party' have the same meaning as in rule 21.1.

Deemed Service

6.14 A claim form served in accordance with this Part is deemed to be served on the second business day after completion of the relevant step under rule 7.5(1).

Service of the claim form by an alternative method or at an alternative place

6.15 (1) Where it appears to the court that there is a good reason to authorise service by a method or at a place not otherwise permitted by this Part, the court may make an order permitting service by an alternative method or at an alternative place.

(2) On an application under this rule, the court may order that steps already taken to bring the claim form to the attention of the defendant by an alternative method or at an alternative place is good service.

(3) An application for an order under this rule –

(a) must be supported by evidence; and

(b) may be made without notice.

(4) An order under this rule must specify –

(a) the method or place of service;

(b) the date on which the claim form is deemed served; and

(c) the period for –

(i) filing an acknowledgment of service;

(ii) filing an admission; or

(iii) filing a defence.

Power Of Court To Dispense With Service Of The Claim Form

6.16 (1) The court may dispense with service of a claim form in exceptional circumstances.

(2) An application for an order to dispense with service may be made at any time and-

(a) must be supported by evidence; and

(b) may be made without notice.

Notice And Certificate Of Service Relating To The Claim Form

6.17 (1) Where the court serves a claim form, the court will send to the claimant a notice which will include the date on which the claim form is deemed served under rule 6.14.

(2) Where the claimant serves the claim form, the claimant –

(a) must file a certificate of service within 21 days of service of the particulars of claim, unless all the defendants to the proceedings have filed acknowledgments of service within that time; and

(b) may not obtain judgment in default under Part 12 unless a certificate of service has been filed.

(3) The certificate of service must state –

(a) where rule 6.7, 6.8, 6.9 or 6.10 applies, the category of address at which the claimant believes the claim form has been served; and

(b) the details set out in the following table.

Method of service	Details to be certified
1. Personal service	Date of personal service.
2. First class post, document exchange or other service which provides for delivery on the next business day.	Date of posting, or
	leaving with, delivering to or collection by the relevant service provider.
3. Delivery of document to or leaving it at a permitted place.	Date when the document was delivered to or left at the permitted place.
4. Fax.	Date of completion of the transmission.
5. Other electronic method.	Date of sending the e-mail or other electronic transmission.
6. Alternative method or place.	As required by the court.

Notification Of Outcome Of Postal Service By The Court

6.18 (1) Where –

(a) the court serves the claim form by post; and

(b) the claim form is returned to the court,

the court will send notification to the claimant that the claim form has been returned.

(2) The claim form will be deemed to be served unless the address for the defendant on the claim form is not the relevant address for the purpose of rules 6.7 to 6.10.

III Service of Documents other than the Claim Form in the United Kingdom

Methods of service

6.20 (1) A document may be served by any of the following methods –

(a) personal service, in accordance with rule 6.22;

(b) first class post, document exchange or other service which provides for delivery on the next business day, in accordance with Practice Direction 6A;

(c) leaving it at a place specified in rule 6.23;

(d) fax or other means of electronic communication in accordance with Practice Direction 6A; or

(e) any method authorised by the court under rule 6.27.

(2) A company may be served –

(a) by any method permitted under this Part; or

(b) by any of the methods of service permitted under the Companies Act 2006.

(3) A limited liability partnership may be served –

(a) by any method permitted under this Part; or

(b) by any of the methods of service permitted under the Companies Act 2006 as applied with modification by regulations made under the Limited Liability Partnerships Act 2000.

Who is to serve

6.21 (1) A party to proceedings will serve a document which that party has prepared except where;

(a) a rule or practice direction provides that the court will serve the document; or

(b) the court orders otherwise.

(2) The court will serve a document which it has prepared except where –

    (a) a rule or practice direction provides that a party must serve the document;

    (b) the party on whose behalf the document is to be served notifies the court that the party wishes to serve it; or

    (c) the court orders otherwise.

(3) Where the court is to serve a document, it is for the court to decide which method of service is to be used.

(4) Where the court is to serve a document prepared by a party, that party must provide a copy for the court and for each party to be served.

Personal service

6.22   (1) Where required by another Part, any other enactment, a practice direction or a court order, a document must be served personally.

(2) In other cases, a document may be served personally except –

    (a) where the party to be served has given an address for service under rule 6.23(2) (a) ; or

    (b) in any proceedings by or against the Crown.

(3) A document may be served personally as if the document were a claim form in accordance with rule 6.5(3) .

Address for service

6.23   (1) A party to proceedings must give an address at which that party may be served with documents relating to those proceedings. The address must include a full postcode unless the court orders otherwise.

N.B. Paragraph 2.4 of Practice Direction 16 contains provisions about postcodes.

(2) A party's address for service must be –

    (a) the business address either within the United Kingdom or any other EEA state of a solicitor acting for the party to be served; or

    (b) where there is no solicitor acting for the party to be served, an address within the United Kingdom at which the party resides or carries on business.

(3) Where there is no solicitor acting for the party to be served and the party does not have an address within the United Kingdom at which that party resides or carries on business, the party must give an address for service within the United Kingdom.

Service on children and protected parties

6.25 (1) An application for an order appointing a litigation friend where a child or protected party has no litigation friend must be served in accordance with rule 21.8(1) and (2).

(2) Any other document which would otherwise be served on a child or a protected party must be served on the litigation friend conducting the proceedings on behalf of the child or protected party.

(3) The court may make an order permitting a document to be served on the child or protected party or on some person other than the person specified in rule 21.8 or paragraph (2).

(4) An application for an order under paragraph (3) may be made without notice.

(5) The court may order that, although a document has been sent or given to someone other than the person specified in rule 21.8 or paragraph (2), the document is to be treated as if it had been properly served.

(6) This rule does not apply where the court has made an order under rule 21.2(3) allowing a child to conduct proceedings without a litigation friend.

Deemed Service

6.26 A document, other than a claim form, served in accordance with these Rules or any relevant practice direction is deemed to be served on the day shown in the following table –

Method of service	Deemed date of service
1. First class post (or other service which provides for delivery on the next business day)	The second day after it was posted, left with, delivered to or collected by the relevant service provider provided that day is a business day; or
	if not, the next business day after that day.
2. Document exchange	The second day after it was left with, delivered to or collected by the relevant service provider provided that day is a business day; or
	if not, the next business day after that day.

Method of service	Deemed date of service
3. Delivering the document to or leaving it at a permitted address	If it is delivered to or left at the permitted address on a business day before 4.30p.m., on that day; or
	in any other case, on the next business day after that day.
4. Fax	If the transmission of the fax is completed on a business day before 4.30p.m., on that day; or
	in any other case, on the next business day after the day on which it was transmitted.
5. Other electronic method	If the e-mail or other electronic transmission is sent on a business day before 4.30p.m., on that day; or
	in any other case, on the next business day after the day on which it was sent.
6. Personal service	If the document is served personally before 4.30p.m. on a business day, on that day; or
	in any other case, on the next business day after that day.

N.B. Paragraphs 10.1 to 10.7 of Practice Direction 6A contain examples of how the date of deemed service is calculated.

Service by an alternative method or at an alternative place

6.27   Rule 6.15 applies to any document in the proceedings as it applies to a claim form and reference to the defendant in that rule is modified accordingly.

Power to dispense with service

6.28   (1) The court may dispense with service of any document which is to be served in the proceedings.

(2) An application for an order to dispense with service must be supported by evidence and may be made without notice.

Certificate of service

6.29   Where a rule, practice direction or court order requires a certificate of service, the certificate must state the details required by the following table –

Method of Service	Details to be certified
1. Personal service	Date and time of personal service.
2. First class post, document exchange or other service which provides for delivery on the next business day	Date of posting, or leaving with, delivering to or collection by the relevant service provider.
3. Delivery of document to or leaving it at a permitted place	Date and time of when the document was delivered to or left at the permitted place.
4. Fax	Date and time of completion of the transmission.
5. Other electronic method	Date and time of sending the e-mail or other electronic transmission.
6. Alternative method or place permitted by the court	As required by the court.

Service of claim form or other document on a State

6.44

(1) This rule applies where a party wishes to serve the claim form or other document on a State.

(2) In this rule, 'State' has the meaning given by section 14 of the State Immunity Act 1978.

(3) The party must file in the Central Office of the Royal Courts of Justice –

(a) a request for service to be arranged by the Foreign and Commonwealth Office;

(b) a copy of the claim form or other document; and

(c) any translation required under rule 6.45.

(4) The Senior Master will send the documents filed under this rule to the Foreign and Commonwealth Office with a request that it arranges for them to be served.

(5) An official certificate by the Foreign and Commonwealth Office stating that a claim form or other document has been duly served on a specified date in accordance with a request made under this rule is evidence of that fact.

(6) A document purporting to be such a certificate is to be treated as such a certificate, unless it is proved not to be.

(7) Where –

(a) section 12(6) of the State Immunity Act 1978 applies; and

(b) the State has agreed to a method of service other than through the Foreign and Commonwealth Office,

The claim form or other document may be served either by the method agreed or in accordance with this rule.

N.B. Section 12(6) of the State Immunity Act 1978 provides that section 12(1) enables the service of a claim form or other document in a manner to which the State has agreed.

Translation of claim form or other document

6.45

(1) Except where paragraph (4) or (5) applies, every copy of the claim form or other document filed under rule 6.43 (service through foreign governments, judicial authorities etc.) or 6.44 (service of claim form or other document on a State) must be accompanied by a translation of the claim form or other document.

(2) The translation must be –

(a) in the official language of the country in which it is to be served; or

(b) if there is more than one official language of that country, in any official language which is APPROPRIATE to the place in the country where the claim form or other document is to be served.

(3) Every translation filed under this rule must be accompanied by a statement by the person making it that it is a correct translation, and the statement must include that person's name, address and qualifications for making the translation.

(4) A party is not required to file a translation of a claim form or other document filed under rule 6.43 (service through foreign governments, judicial authorities etc.) where the claim form or other document is to be served –

(a) in a country of which English is an official language; or

(b) on a British citizen (within the meaning of the British Nationality Act 1981),

Unless a Civil Procedure Convention or Treaty requires a translation.

(5) A party is not required to file a translation of a claim form or other document filed under rule 6.44 (service of claim form or other document on a State) where English is an official language of the State in which the claim form or other document is to be served.

N.B. The Service Regulation contains provisions about the translation of documents.

After service

6.52

(1) Where service of a document has been effected by a process server, the process server must –

(a) send to the Senior Master a copy of the document, and

(i) proof of service; or

(ii) a statement why the document could not be served; and

(b) if the Senior Master directs, specify the costs incurred in serving or attempting to serve the document.

(2) The Senior Master will send to the person who requested service –

(a) a certificate, sealed with the seal of the Senior Courts for use out of the jurisdiction, stating –

(i) when and how the document was served or the reason why it has not been served; and

(ii) where appropriate, an amount certified by a costs judge to be the costs of serving or attempting to serve the document; and

(b) a copy of the document.

PRACTICE DIRECTION 6A - SERVICE WITHIN THE UNITED KINGDOM

This practice direction supplements CPR Part 6

Scope of this Practice Direction

1.1

This Practice Direction supplements –

(1) Section II (service of the claim form in the jurisdiction) of Part 6;

(2) Section III (service of documents other than the claim form in the United Kingdom) of Part 6; and

(3) rule 6.40 in relation to the method of service on a party in Scotland or Northern Ireland.

Practice Direction 6B contains provisions relevant to service on a party in Scotland or Northern Ireland, including provisions about service out of the jurisdiction where permission is and is not required and the period for responding to an application notice.

When service may be by document exchange

2.1

Service by document exchange (DX) may take place only where –

(1) the address at which the party is to be served includes a numbered box at a DX, or

(2) the writing paper of the party who is to be served or of the solicitor acting for that party sets out a DX box number, and

(3) the party or the solicitor acting for that party has not indicated in writing that they are unwilling to accept service by DX.

How service is effected by post, an alternative service provider or DX

3.1

Service by post, DX or other service which provides for delivery on the next business day is effected by –

(1) placing the document in a post box;

(2) leaving the document with or delivering the document to the relevant service provider; or

(3) having the document collected by the relevant service provider.

Service by fax or other electronic means

4.1

Subject to the provisions of rule 6.23(5) and (6), where a document is to be served by fax or other electronic means –

(1) the party who is to be served or the solicitor acting for that party must previously have indicated in writing to the party serving –

(a) that the party to be served or the solicitor is willing to accept service by fax or other electronic means; and

(b) the fax number, e-mail address or other electronic identification to which it must be sent; and

(2) the following are to be taken as sufficient written indications for the purposes of paragraph 4.1(1) –

(a) a fax number set out on the writing paper of the solicitor acting for the party to be served;

(b) an e-mail address set out on the writing paper of the solicitor acting for the party to be served but only where it is stated that the e-mail address may be used for service; or

(c) a fax number, e-mail address or electronic identification set out on a statement of case or a response to a claim filed with the court.

4.2

Where a party intends to serve a document by electronic means (other than by fax) that party must first ask the party who is to be served whether there are any limitations to the recipient's agreement to accept service by such means (for example, the format in which documents are to be sent and the maximum size of attachments that may be received).

4.3

Where a document is served by electronic means, the party serving the document need not in addition send or deliver a hard copy.

Service on members of the Regular Forces and United States Air Force

5.1

The provisions that apply to service on members of the regular forces (within the meaning of the Armed Forces Act 2006) and members of the United States Air Force are annexed to this practice direction.

Personal service on a company or other corporation

6.1 Personal service on a registered company or corporation in accordance with rule 6.5(3) is effected by leaving a document with a person holding a senior position.

6.2

Each of the following persons is a person holding a senior position –

(1) in respect of a registered company or corporation, a director, the treasurer, the secretary of the company or corporation, the chief executive, a manager or other officer of the company or corporation; and

(2) in respect of a corporation which is not a registered company, in addition to any of the persons set out in sub-paragraph (1) , the mayor, the chairman, the president, a town clerk or similar officer of the corporation.

Certificate of service where claimant serves the claim form

7.1

Where, pursuant to rule 6.17(2) , the claimant files a certificate of service, the claimant is not required to and should not file –

(1) a further copy of the claim form with the certificate of service; and

(2) a further copy of –

(a) the particulars of claim (where not included in the claim form) ; or

(b) any document attached to the particulars of claim,

with the certificate of service where that document has already been filed with the court.

Rule 7.4 requires the claimant to file a copy of the particulars of claim (where served separately from the claim form) within 7 days of service on the defendant.

Application for an order for service by an alternative method or at an alternative place

9.1

Where an application for an order under rule 6.15 is made before the document is served, the application must be supported by evidence stating –

(1) the reason why an order is sought;

(2) what alternative method or place is proposed, and

(3) why the applicant believes that the document is likely to reach the person to be served by the method or at the place proposed.

9.2

Where the application for an order is made after the applicant has taken steps to bring the document to the attention of the person to be served by an alternative method or at an alternative place, the application must be supported by evidence stating –

(1) the reason why the order is sought;

(2) what alternative method or alternative place was used;

(3) when the alternative method or place was used; and

(4) why the applicant believes that the document is likely to have reached the person to be served by the alternative method or at the alternative place.

9.3

Examples –

(1) an application to serve by posting or delivering to an address of a person who knows the other party must be supported by evidence that if posted or delivered to that address, the document is likely to be brought to the attention of the other party;

(2) an application to serve by sending a SMS text message or leaving a voicemail message at a particular telephone number saying where the document is must be accompanied by evidence that the person serving the document has taken, or will take, appropriate steps to ensure that the party being served is using that telephone number and is likely to receive the message; and

(3) an application to serve by e-mail to a company (where paragraph 4.1 does not apply) must be supported by evidence that the e-mail address to which the document will be sent is one which is likely to come to the attention of a person holding a senior position in that company.

Deemed service of a document other than a claim form

10.1

Rule 6.26 contains provisions about deemed service of a document other than a claim form. Examples of how deemed service is calculated are set out below.

10.2 *Example 1*

Where the document is posted (by first class post) on a Monday (a business day), the day of deemed service is the following Wednesday (a business day).

10.3 *Example 2*

Where the document is left in a numbered box at the DX on a Friday (a business day), the day of deemed service is the following Monday (a business day).

10.4 *Example 3*

Where the document is sent by fax on a Saturday and the transmission of that fax is completed by 4.30p.m. on that day, the day of deemed service is the following Monday (a business day).

10.5 *Example 4*

Where the document is served personally before 4.30p.m. on a Sunday, the day of deemed service is the next day (Monday, a business day).

10.6 *Example 5*

Where the document is delivered to a permitted address after 4.30p.m. on the Thursday (a business day) before Good Friday, the day of deemed service is the following Tuesday (a business day) as the Monday is a bank holiday.

10.7 *Example 6*

Where the document is posted (by first class post) on a bank holiday Monday, the day of deemed service is the following Wednesday (a business day).

ANNEX - SERVICE ON MEMBERS OF THE REGULAR FORCES

1. The following information is for litigants and legal representatives who wish to serve legal documents in civil proceedings in the courts of England and Wales on parties to the proceedings who are (or who, at the material time, were) members of the regular forces (as defined in the Armed Forces Act 2006).

2. The proceedings may take place in the county court or the High Court, and the documents to be served may be claim forms, interim application notices and pre-action application notices. Proceedings for divorce or maintenance and proceedings in the Family Courts generally are subject to special rules as to service which are explained in a practice direction issued by the Senior District Judge of the Principal Registry on 26 June 1979.

3. In this Annex, the person wishing to effect service is referred to as the 'claimant' and the member of the regular forces to be served is referred to as 'the member'; the expression 'overseas' means outside the United Kingdom.

Enquiries as to address

4. As a first step, the claimant's legal representative will need to find out where the member is serving, if this is not already known. For this purpose the claimant's legal representative should write to the appropriate officer of the Ministry of Defence as specified in paragraph 10 below.

5. The letter of enquiry should in every case show that the writer is a legal representative and that the enquiry is made solely with a view to the service of legal documents in civil proceedings.

6. In all cases the letter must give the full name, service number, rank or rate, and Ship, Arm or Trade, Regiment or Corps and Unit or as much of this information as is available. Failure to quote the service number and the rank or rate may result either in failure to identify the member or in considerable delay.

7. The letter must contain an undertaking by the legal representative that, if the address is given, it will be used solely for the purpose of issuing and serving documents in the proceedings and that so far as is possible the legal representative will disclose the address only to the court and not to the claimant or to any other person or body. A legal representative in the service of a public authority or private company must undertake that the address will be used solely for the purpose of issuing and serving documents in the proceedings and that the address will not be disclosed so far as is possible to any other part of the legal representative's employing organisation or to any other person but only to the court. Normally on receipt of the required information and undertaking the appropriate office will give the service address.

8. If the legal representative does not give the undertaking, the only information that will be given is whether the member is at that time serving in England or Wales, Scotland, Northern Ireland or overseas.

9. It should be noted that a member's address which ends with a British Forces Post Office address and reference (BFPO) will nearly always indicate that the member is serving overseas.

10. The letter of enquiry should be addressed as follows –

    (a) Royal Navy and Royal Marine Officers, Ratings and Other Ranks

Director Naval Personnel
Fleet Headquarters
MP 3.1
Leach Building
Whale Island
Portsmouth
Hampshire
PO2 8BY

Army Officers and other Ranks –

Army Personnel Centre
Disclosures 1
MP 520
Kentigern House
65 Brown Street
Glasgow
G2 8EX

Royal Air Force Officers and Other Ranks –

Manning 22E
RAF Disclosures
Room 221B
Trenchard Hall
RAF Cranwell
Sleaford
Lincolnshire
NG34 8HB

Assistance in serving documents on members

11. Once the claimant's legal representative has ascertained the member's address, the legal representative may use that address as the address for service by post, in cases where this method of service is allowed by the Civil Procedure Rules. There are, however, some situations in which service of the proceedings, whether in the High Court or in the County Court, must be effected personally; in these cases an appointment will have to be sought, through the Commanding Officer of the Unit, Establishment or Ship concerned, for the purpose of effecting service. The procedure for obtaining an appointment is described below, and it applies whether personal service is to be effected by the claimant's legal representative or the legal representative's agent or by a court bailiff, or, in the case of proceedings served overseas (with the leave of the court) through the British Consul or the foreign judicial authority.

12. The procedure for obtaining an appointment to effect personal service is by application to the Commanding Officer of the Unit, Establishment or Ship in which the member is serving. The Commanding Officer may grant permission for the document server to enter the Unit, Establishment or Ship but if this is not appropriate the Commanding Officer may offer arrangements for the member to attend at a place in the vicinity of the Unit, Establishment or Ship in order that the member may be served. If suitable arrangements cannot be made the legal representative will have evidence that personal service is impracticable, which may be useful in an application for service by an alternative method or at an alternative place.

General

13. Subject to the procedure outlined in paragraphs 11 and 12, there are no special arrangements to assist in the service of legal documents when a member is outside the United Kingdom. The appropriate office will, however, give an approximate date when the member is likely to return to the United Kingdom.

14. It sometimes happens that a member has left the regular forces by the time an enquiry as to address is made. If the claimant's legal representative confirms that the proceedings result from an occurrence when the member was in the regular forces and the legal representative gives the undertaking referred to in paragraph 7, the last known private address after discharge will normally be provided. In no other case, however, will the Ministry of Defence disclose the private address of a member of the regular forces.

Service on Members of United States Air Force

15. In addition to the information contained in the memorandum of 26 July 1979, and after some doubts having been expressed as to the correct procedure to be followed by persons having civil claims against members of the United States Air Force in England and Wales, the Lord Chancellor's Office (as it was then) issued the following notes for guidance with the approval of the appropriate United States authorities.

16. Instructions have been issued by the United States authorities to the commanding officers of all their units in England and Wales that every facility is to be given for the service of documents in civil proceedings on members of the United States Air Force. The proper course to be followed by a creditor or other person having a claim against a member of the United States Air Force is for that person to communicate with the commanding officer or, where the unit concerned has a legal officer, with the legal officer of the defendant's unit requesting the provision of facilities for the service of documents on the defendant. It is not possible for the United States authorities to act as arbitrators when a civil claim is made against a member of their forces. It is, therefore, essential that the claim should either be admitted by the defendant or judgment should be obtained on it, whether in the High Court or a county court. If a claim has been admitted or judgment has been obtained and the claimant has failed to obtain satisfaction within a reasonable period, the claimant's proper course is then to write to: Office of the Staff Judge Advocate, Headquarters, Third Air Force, R.A.F. Mildenhall, Suffolk, enclosing a copy of the defendant's written admission of the claim or, as the case may be, a copy of the judgment. Steps will then be taken by the Staff Judge Advocate to ensure that the matter is brought to the defendant's attention with a view to prompt satisfaction of the claim.

***

SECTION 2 – SERVICE OF CLAIM FORMS

PART 7 - HOW TO START PROCEEDINGS – THE CLAIM FORM

Service of a claim form

7.5

(1) Where the claim form is served within the jurisdiction, the claimant must complete the step required by the following table in relation to the particular method of service chosen, before 12.00 midnight on the calendar day four months after the date of issue of the claim form.

Method of service	Step required
First class post, document exchange or other service which provides for delivery on the next business day	Posting, leaving with, delivering to or collection by the relevant service provider
Delivery of the document to or leaving it at the relevant place	Delivering to or leaving the document at the relevant place
Personal service under rule 6.5	Completing the relevant step required by rule 6.5(3)
Fax	Completing the transmission of the fax
Other electronic method	Sending the e-mail or other electronic transmission

(2) Where the claim form is to be served out of the jurisdiction, the claim form must be served in accordance with Section IV of Part 6 within 6 months of the date of issue.

Extension of time for serving a claim form

7.6

(1) The claimant may apply for an order extending the period for compliance with rule 7.5.

(2) The general rule is that an application to extend the time for compliance with rule 7.5 must be made

(a) within the period specified by rule 7.5; or

(b) where an order has been made under this rule, within the period for service specified by that order.

(3) If the claimant applies for an order to extend the time for compliance after the end of the period specified by rule 7.5 or by an order made under this rule, the court may make such an order only if –

(a) the court has failed to serve the claim form; or

(b) the claimant has taken all reasonable steps to comply with rule 7.5 but has been unable to do so; and

(c) in either case, the claimant has acted promptly in making the application.

(4) An application for an order extending the time for compliance with rule 7.5 –

(a) must be supported by evidence; and

(b) may be made without notice.

Application by defendant for service of claim form

7.7

(1) Where a claim form has been issued against a defendant, but has not yet been served on him, the defendant may serve a notice on the claimant requiring him to serve the claim form or discontinue the claim within a period specified in the notice.

(2) The period specified in a notice served under paragraph (1) must be at least 14 days after service of the notice.

(3) If the claimant fails to comply with the notice, the court may, on the application of the defendant –

(a) dismiss the claim; or

(b) make any other order it thinks just.

Part 2 Application and interpretation of the rules
Time for effecting service

A claim form may be served at any time of the day or night. CCR Order 7 Rule 3, the rule against service of proceedings on Sundays and Bank Holidays has been revoked. This applies to all legal process. Service abroad on a Sunday is a matter which would be governed by the local law.

Civil Procedure Rules Part 2, with regard to the service of process reads -

Time

2.8

(1) This rule shows how to calculate any period of time for doing any act which is specified –

(a) by these Rules;

(b) by a practice direction; or

(c) by a judgment or order of the court.

(2) A period of time expressed as a number of days shall be computed as clear days.

(3) In this rule 'clear days' means that in computing the number of days –

(a) the day on which the period begins; and

(b) if the end of the period is defined by reference to an event, the day on which that event occurs

are not included.

Examples

(i) Notice of an application must be served at least 3 days before the hearing.

An application is to be heard on Friday 20 October. The last date for service is Monday 16 October.

(ii) The court is to fix a date for a hearing.

The hearing must be at least 28 days after the date of notice. If the court gives notice of the date of the hearing on 1 October, the earliest date for the hearing is 30 October.

(iii) Particulars of claim must be served within 14 days of service of the claim form.

The claim form is served on 2 October. The last day for service of the particulars of claim is 16 October.

(4) Where the specified period –

(a) is 5 days or less; and

(b) includes –

(i) a Saturday or Sunday; or

(ii) a Bank Holiday, Christmas Day or Good Friday,

that day does not count.

Example

Notice of an application must be served at least 3 days before the hearing.

An application is to be heard on Monday 20 October.

The last date for service is Tuesday 14 October.

>(5) Subject to the provisions of Practice Direction 5C, when the period specified –
>
>>(a) by these Rules or a practice direction; or
>>
>>(b) by any judgment or court order,
>
>for doing any act at the court office ends on a day on which the office is closed, that act shall be in time if done on the next day on which the court office is open.

Dates for compliance to be calendar dates and to include time of day

2.9 (1) Where the Court gives a Judgment, Order or Direction which imposes a time limit for doing any act, the last date for compliance must, wherever practicable -

>(a) be expressed as a calendar date; and
>
>(b) include the time of day by which the act must be done.

(2) Where the date by which an act must be done is inserted in any document, the date must, wherever practicable, be expressed as a calendar date.

Meaning of 'month' in judgments, etc.

2.10 Where 'month' occurs in any judgment, Order, direction or other document, it means a calendar month.

Time limits may be varied by parties

2.11 Unless these Rules or a practice direction provides otherwise or the Court Orders otherwise, the time specified by a rule or by the Court for a person to do any act may be varied by the written agreement of the parties.

Rules 3.8 (sanction to have effect unless defaulting party obtains relief) , 28.4 (variation of case management timetable - fast track) ; 29.5 (variation of case management timetable - multi-track) and RSC 0.59 r.2C (appeals to the Court of Appeal) in Schedule 1, provide for time limits that cannot be varied by agreement between the parties

Specialist proceedings

The above rules are of general application in the County Court, High Court and the Court of Appeal. However, the CPR also make separate provision for some specialist proceedings.

These specialist proceedings are:

(i) Contentious Probate Proceedings

(ii) Proceedings under the Companies Act 1985 and the Companies Act 1989

(iii) Technology and Construction Court Business

(iv) Patents Court Business and Proceedings

(v) Admiralty Proceedings

(vi) Arbitration Proceedings

(vii) Commercial and Mercantile Actions

The rules governing these specialist proceedings are set out at Part 49 of the CPR.

Place of service

There are certain places where service of a claim form would be held invalid. Service of a claim form in a Royal Palace, which is also a residence of the Sovereign, has been held to have been invalid.

It has been declared a breach of privilege to effect service within "the precincts of Parliament" on a day when the House is sitting, even if at the time of service the House is not in session.

Service on consecrated ground i.e. a church, is not usual but no mention is made in the practice.

It is not usual for service to be effected in Court but there have been several cases on this point, one where service was upheld. It may well be safer to effect service outside the Court if at all possible. Where service is effected the precise place should be shown in the Affidavit, Certificate or Statement of Service, i.e. "at or outside No.10 Blank Street" or "at the corner of White Place and Blank Street".

Where a defendant is in prison an application should be made to the Governor of the prison for an appointment. Should the prison not be known an application may be made to H.M. Prison Service Headquarters, Cleland House, Page Street, London SW1P 4LN giving the place and the date of conviction and the sentence.

Companies Act 2006 (c.46) Service addresses
1139 Service of documents on company

(1) A document may be served on a company registered under this Act by leaving it at, or sending it by post to, the company's registered office.

(2) A document may be served on an overseas company whose particulars are registered under section 1046—

(a) by leaving it at, or sending it by post to, the registered address of any person resident in the United Kingdom who is authorised to accept service of documents on the company's behalf, or

(b) if there is no such person, or if any such person refuses service or service cannot for any other reason be effected, by leaving it at or sending by post to any place of business of the company in the United Kingdom.

(3) For the purposes of this section a person's "registered address" means any address for the time being shown as a current address in relation to that person in the part of the register available for public inspection.

(4) Where a company registered in Scotland or Northern Ireland carries on business in England and Wales, the process of any court in England and Wales may be served on the company by leaving it at, or sending it by post to, the company's principal place of business in England and Wales, addressed to the manager or other head officer in England and Wales of the company.

Where process is served on a company under this subsection, the person issuing out the process must send a copy of it by post to the company's registered office.

(5) Further provision as to service and other matters is made in the company communications provisions (see section 1143).

1140 Service of documents on directors, secretaries and others

(1) A document may be served on a person to whom this section applies by leaving it at, or sending *it by post to, the person's registered address.*

(2) This section applies to—

(a) a director or secretary of a company;

(b) in the case of an overseas company whose particulars are registered under section 1046, a person holding any such position as may be specified for the purposes of this section by regulations under that section;

(c) a person appointed in relation to a company as—

(i) a judicial factor (in Scotland),

(ii) [an interim manager] appointed under section 18 of the Charities Act 1993 (c. 10), or

(iii) a manager appointed under section 47 of the Companies (Audit, Investigations and Community Enterprise) Act 2004 (c. 27).

(3) This section applies whatever the purpose of the document in question.

It is not restricted to service for purposes arising out of or in connection with the appointment or position mentioned in subsection (2) or in connection with the company concerned.

(4) For the purposes of this section a person's "registered address" means any address for the time being shown as a current address in relation to that person in the part of the register available for public inspection.

(5) If notice of a change of that address is given to the registrar, a person may validly serve a document at the address previously registered until the end of the period of 14 days beginning with the date on which notice of the change is registered.

(6) Service may not be effected by virtue of this section at an address—

(a) if notice has been registered of the termination of the appointment in relation to which the address was registered and the address is not a registered address of the person concerned in relation to any other appointment;

(b) in the case of a person holding any such position as is mentioned in subsection (2) (b) , if the overseas company has ceased to have any connection with the United Kingdom by virtue of which it is required to register particulars under section 1046.

(7) Further provision as to service and other matters is made in the company communications provisions (see section 1143) .

(8) Nothing in this section shall be read as affecting any enactment or rule of law under which permission is required for service out of the jurisdiction.

1141 Service addresses

In the Companies Acts a "service address", in relation to a person, means an address at which documents may be effectively served on that person.

The Secretary of State may by regulations specify conditions with which a service address must comply

Regulations under this section are subject to negative resolution procedure.

Documents To Be Served

Where documents are served at the same time as the Claim Form they must be included in the Affidavit, Statement or Certificate of Service. An additional paragraph can be added to the affidavit of service and might read: **"At the same time and place of service I served the said defendant with the Statement of Claim herein."**

In the case of the Statement or Certificate of Service such documents can be listed.

Part 55 – Possession Claims
Service of claims against trespassers

55.6 Where, in a possession claim against trespassers, the claim has been issued against 'persons unknown', the claim form, particulars of claim and any witness statements must be served on those persons by –

(a) (i) attaching copies of the claim form, particulars of claim and any witness statements to the main door or some other part of the land so that they are clearly visible; and

(ii) if practicable, inserting copies of those documents in a sealed transparent envelope addressed to 'the occupiers' through the letter box; or

(b) placing stakes in the land in places where they are clearly visible and attaching to each stake copies of the claim form, particulars of claim and any witness statements in a sealed transparent envelope addressed to 'the occupiers'.

Possession claims relating to mortgaged residential property
Interim Possession Orders (IPO)

Service and enforcement of the IPO

55.26

(1) An IPO must be served within 48 hours after it is sealed.

(2) The claimant must serve the IPO on the defendant together with copies of

(a) the claim form; and

(b) the written evidence in support, in accordance with rule 55.6(a).

(3) CCR Order 26, rule 17 does not apply to the enforcement of an IPO.

(4) If an IPO is not served within the time limit specified by this rule, the claimant may apply to the court for directions for the claim for possession to continue under Section I of this Part.

Practice Direction 55a – Possession Claims
This Practice Direction supplements Part 55

55.6 – Service In Claims Against Trespassers

4.1 If the claim form is to be served by the court and in accordance with rule 55.6(b) the claimant must provide sufficient stakes and transparent envelopes.

Taking Possession Of Mortgaged Property

Where an agent is required to take over the premises from a Bailiff or Sheriff's officer the following notes on the question of Security of the property should be helpful.

Securing the property:

1. Secure the house against unlawful entry, or re-entry by dispossessed owner.

2. Ensure no damage by water overflowing or leaking by turning off the supply and draining down the system, using specialist help if needed. There may be occasions where this could be detrimental and the advice of a skilled plumber would then be required.

3. Avoid risk of explosion by turning off the gas at the main, checking for pilot lights. In doubtful cases, the Gas Board recommendations should be followed.

4. Avoid risk of fire by switching off electricity. Once again some concern for items such as freezers or fish tanks may be necessary.

To protect the contents against loss or damage and to safeguard the Society against any claims for loss:

1. Prepare a complete list of any contents left in the property.

2. Make an individual report on any particular items of special value or interest.

Part 61 - Admiralty
Claims in rem

61.3

(1) This rule applies to claims in rem.

(2) A claim in rem is started by the issue of an in rem claim form as set out in Practice Direction 61.

(3) Subject to rule 61.4, the particulars of claim must –

(a) be contained in or served with the claim form; or

(b) be served on the defendant by the claimant within 75 days after service of the claim form.

(4) An acknowledgment of service must be filed within 14 days after service of the claim form.

(5) The claim form must be served –

(a) in accordance with Practice Direction 61; and

(b) within 12 months after the date of issue and rules 7.5 and 7.6 are modified accordingly.

(6) If a claim form has been issued (whether served or not), any person who wishes to defend the claim may file an acknowledgment of service.

PRACTICE DIRECTION 61 – ADMIRALTY CLAIMS

This Practice Direction Supplements CPR Part 61

61.3 – Claims in rem

3.1 A claim form in rem must be in Form ADM1.

3.2 The claimant in a claim in rem may be named or may be described, but if not named in the claim form must identify himself by name if requested to do so by any other party.

3.3 The defendant must be described in the claim form.

3.4 The acknowledgment of service must be in Form ADM2. The person who acknowledges service must identify himself by name.

3.5 The period for acknowledging service under rule 61.3(4) applies irrespective of whether the claim form contains particulars of claim.

3.6 A claim form in rem may be served in the following ways:

>(1) on the property against which the claim is brought by fixing a copy of the claim form –
>
>>(a) on the outside of the property in a position which may reasonably be expected to be seen; or
>>
>>(b) where the property is freight, either –
>>
>>>(i) on the cargo in respect of which the freight was earned; or
>>>
>>>(ii) on the ship on which the cargo was carried;
>
>(2) if the property to be served is in the custody of a person who will not permit access to it, by leaving a copy of the claim form with that person;
>
>(3) where the property has been sold by the Marshal, by filing the claim form at the court;
>
>(4) where there is a notice against arrest, on the person named in the notice as being authorised to accept service;
>
>(5) on any solicitor authorised to accept service;
>
>(6) in accordance with any agreement providing for service of proceedings; or
>
>(7) in any other manner as the court may direct under rule 6.15 provided that the property against which the claim is brought or part of it is within the jurisdiction of the court.

3.7 In claims where the property –

>(1) is to be arrested; or
>
>(2) is already under arrest in current proceedings, the Marshal will serve the in rem claim form if the claimant requests the court to do so.

3.8 In all other cases in rem claim forms must be served by the claimant.

3.9 Where the defendants are described and not named on the claim form (for example as 'the Owners of the Ship X') , any acknowledgment of service in addition to stating that description must also state the full names of the persons acknowledging service and the nature of their ownership.

3.10 After the acknowledgment of service has been filed, the claim will follow the procedure applicable to a claim proceeding in the Commercial list except that the claimant is allowed 75 days to serve the particulars of claim.

3.11 A defendant who files an acknowledgment of service to an in rem claim does not lose any right he may have to dispute the jurisdiction of the court (see rule 10.1(3) (b) and Part 11) .

3.12 Any person who pays the prescribed fee may, during office hours, search for, inspect and take a copy of any claim form in rem whether or not it has been served.

PRACTICE DIRECTION 66 – CROWN PROCEEDINGS

This Practice Direction supplements CPR Part 66

Service of Documents

2.1 In civil proceedings by or against the Crown, documents required to be served on the Crown must be served in accordance with rule 6.10 or 6.23(7).

The list published under section 17 of the Crown Proceedings Act 1947 of the solicitors acting for the different government departments on whom service is to be effected, and of their addresses is annexed to this Practice Direction.

CROWN PROCEEDINGS ACT 1947

List of Authorised Government Departments and the names and addresses for service of the person who is, or is acting for the purposes of the Act as, Solicitor for such Departments, published by the Minister for the Civil Service in pursuance of Section 17 of the Crown Proceedings Act 1947.

This list supersedes the list published on 19 February 2009

AUTHORISED GOVERNMENT DEPARTMENTS	SOLICITOR AND ADDRESSES FOR SERVICE
Advisory, Conciliation and Arbitration Service)	The Treasury Solicitor
Board of Trade)	One Kemble Street
Cabinet Office)	London
Central Office of Information)	WC2B 4TS
Commissioners for the Reduction of National Debt (see Note (3)))	(see Notes (1) and (2))
Crown Prosecution Service)	
Department for Business, Innovation and Skills)	
Department for Children, Schools and Families)	
Department for Culture, Media and Sport)	
Department for Communities and Local Government)	
Department of Energy and Climate Change)	
Department for International Development)	
Department for Transport)	

Food Standards Agency)

Foreign and Commonwealth Office)

Government Actuary's Department)

Government Equalities Office)

Health and Safety Executive)

Office for Standards in Education, Children's

Services and Skills)

Her Majesty's Chief Inspector of   Schools in Wales)

Her Majesty's Treasury)

Home Office)

Ministry of Defence)

Ministry of Justice (see Note (4)))

National Savings and Investments)

National School of Government)

Northern Ireland Office)

Ordnance Survey)

Privy Council Office)

Public Works Loan Board (see Note (3)))

Royal Mint)

Serious Fraud Office)

The National Archives)

Wales Office (Office of the Secretary of State for Wales)

(see Note (5)))

Child Maintenance and Enforcement Commission Department of Health Department for Work and Pensions UK Statistics Authority	The Solicitor to the Department for Work and Pensions and the Department of Health The Adelphi 1-11 John Adam Street London WC2N 6HT
Crown Estate Commissioners	Legal Director The Crown Estate 16 New Burlington Place London W1S 2HX
Department for Environment, Food and Rural Affairs (see Note (5)) Forestry Commissioners	The Solicitor to the Department for Environment, Food and Rural Affairs Nobel House 17 Smith Square London SW1P 3JR
Export Credits Guarantee Department	The General Counsel, Export Credits Guarantee Department, P.O. Box 2200, 2 Exchange Tower, Harbour Exchange Square, London E14 9GS
Gas and Electricity Markets Authority	Senior Legal Director Office of Gas and Electricity Markets 9 Millbank London SW1P 3GE
Her Majesty's Revenue and Customs	General Counsel and Solicitor to Her Majesty's Revenue and Customs HM Revenue and Customs South West Wing Bush House, Strand London, WC2B 4RD
Office of Fair Trading	General Counsel Fleetbank House 2-6 Salisbury Square London EC4Y 8JX
Office of Rail Regulation	Director of Legal Services ORR One Kemble Street London WC2B 4AN
Postal Services Commission	The Chief Legal Adviser Postal Services Commission Hercules House 6 Hercules Road London SE1 7DB
Revenue and Customs Prosecutions Office (RCPO)	The Director Revenue and Customs Prosecutions Office New King's Beam House 22 Upper Ground London SE1 9BT

Water Services Regulation Authority	Director of Legal Services and Board Secretary

(OFWAT)	Water Services Regulation Authority (OFWAT) Centre City Tower 7 Hill Street Birmingham B5 4UA
Welsh Assembly Government	The Director of Legal Services to the Welsh Assembly Government Cathays Park Cardiff CF10 3NQ

Notes

(1) Section 17(3) and section 18 of the Crown Proceedings Act 1947 provide as follows:

17(3) Civil proceedings against the Crown shall be instituted against the appropriate authorised Government department, or, if none of the authorised Government departments is appropriate or the person instituting the proceedings has any reasonable doubt whether any and if so which of those departments is appropriate, against the Attorney General.

18 All documents required to be served on the Crown for the purpose of or in connection with any civil proceedings by or against the Crown shall, if those proceedings are by or against an authorised Government department, be served on the solicitor, if any, for that department, or the person, if any, acting for the purposes of this Act as solicitor for that department, or if there is no such solicitor and no person so acting, or if the proceedings are brought by or against the Attorney General, on the Solicitor for the affairs of His Majesty's Treasury. Proceedings brought against the Attorney General should be served on the Treasury Solicitor.

(2) The above-mentioned provisions do not apply to Scotland, where in accordance with the Crown Suits (Scotland) Act 1857, as amended by the Scotland Act 1998, civil proceedings against the Crown (other than the Scottish Administration) or any Government Department (other than the Scottish Executive) may be directed against the Advocate General for Scotland. The Advocate General's address for service is the Office of the Solicitor to the Advocate General for Scotland, Victoria Quay, Edinburgh EH6 6QQ. Civil proceedings against the Scottish Administration may be directed against the Scottish Ministers at St. Andrew's House, Edinburgh EH1 3DG, or against the Lord Advocate for and on behalf of the Scottish Executive. The Lord Advocate's address for service is 25 Chambers Street, Edinburgh, EH1 1LA.

(3) The functions of the Commissioners for the Reduction of National Debt and the Public Works Loan Board are carried out within the UK Debt Management Office.

(4) The reference to the Ministry of Justice includes a reference to the Lord Chancellor's Department.

(5) The Solicitor and address for service for the purposes of or in connection with civil proceedings brought by or against the Crown which relate to those matters for which the Secretary of State is responsible in Wales and for which the Secretary of State for Environment, Food and Rural Affairs is responsible is the Solicitor to the Department for Environment, Food and Rural Affairs, Nobel House, 17 Smith Square, London, SW1P 3JR. The Treasury Solicitor is the Solicitor acting for the Wales Office (Office of the Secretary of State for Wales) in all other civil proceedings affecting that Office.

CABINET OFFICE, WHITEHALL, LONDON, SW1

(Signed) SIR GUS O'DONNELL
23 September 2009

PART 71 - ORDERS TO OBTAIN INFORMATION FROM JUDGMENT DEBTORS
SERVICE OF ORDER

71.3

(1) An order to attend court must, unless the court otherwise orders, be served personally on the person ordered to attend court not less than 14 days before the hearing.

(2) If the order is to be served by the judgment creditor, he must inform the court not less than 7 days before the date of the hearing if he has been unable to serve it.

Travelling expenses

71.4

(1) A person ordered to attend court may, within 7 days of being served with the order, ask the judgment creditor to pay him a sum reasonably sufficient to cover his travelling expenses to and from court.

(2) The judgment creditor must pay such a sum if requested.

Judgment creditor's affidavit

71.5

(1) The judgment creditor must file an affidavit(GL) or affidavits –

    (a) by the person who served the order (unless it was served by the court) giving details of how and when it was served;

    (b) stating either that –

        (i) the person ordered to attend court has not requested payment of his travelling expenses; or

        (ii) the judgment creditor has paid a sum in accordance with such a request; and

    (c) stating how much of the judgment debt remains unpaid.

(2) The judgment creditor must either –

    (a) file the affidavit(GL) or affidavits not less than 2 days before the hearing; or

    (b) produce it or them at the hearing.

Adjournment of the hearing

71.7

If the hearing is adjourned, the court will give directions as to the manner in which notice of the new hearing is to be served on the judgment debtor.

PART 72 - THIRD PARTY DEBT ORDER
Service of interim order

72.5

(1) Copies of an interim third party debt order, the application notice and any documents filed in support of it must be served –

    (a) on the third party, not less than 21 days before the date fixed for the hearing; and

    (b) on the judgment debtor not less than –

        (i) 7 days after a copy has been served on the third party; and

        (ii) 7 days before the date fixed for the hearing.

(2) If the judgment creditor serves the order, he must either –

    (a) file a certificate of service not less than 2 days before the hearing; or

    (b) produce a certificate of service at the hearing.

PART 73 - Charging Orders, Stop Orders And Stop Notices
Scope of this Part and interpretation

Service of interim order

73.5

(1) Copies of the interim charging order, the application notice and any documents filed in support of it must, not less than 21 days before the hearing, be served on the following persons –

    (a) the judgment debtor;

    (b) such other creditors as the court directs;

    (c) if the order relates to an interest under a trust, on such of the trustees as the court directs;

    (d) if the interest charged is in securities other than securities held in court, then –

(i) in the case of stock for which the Bank of England keeps the register, the Bank of England;

(ii) in the case of government stock to which (i) does not apply, the keeper of the register;

(iii) in the case of stock of anybody incorporated within England and Wales, that body;

(iv) in the case of stock of anybody incorporated outside England and Wales or of any state or territory outside the United Kingdom, which is registered in a register kept in England and Wales, the keeper of that register;

(v) in the case of units of any unit trust in respect of which a register of the unit holders is kept in England and Wales, the keeper of that register; and

(e) if the interest charged is in funds in court, the Accountant General at the Court Funds Office.

(2) If the judgment creditor serves the order, he must either –

(a) file a certificate of service not less than 2 days before the hearing; or

(b) produce a certificate of service at the hearing.

***

SECTION 3 – WITNESSES AND DEPOSITIONS

PART 34

Time for serving a witness summons

34.5

(1) The general rule is that a witness summons is binding if it is served at least 7 days before the date on which the witness is required to attend before the court or tribunal.

(2) The court may direct that a witness summons shall be binding although it will be served less than 7 days before the date on which the witness is required to attend before the court or tribunal.

(3) A witness summons which is –

(a) served in accordance with this rule; and

(b) requires the witness to attend court to give evidence, is binding until the conclusion of the hearing at which the attendance of the witness is required.

Who is to serve a witness summons

34.6

(1) A witness summons is to be served by the court unless the party on whose behalf it is issued indicates in writing, when he asks the court to issue the summons, that he wishes to serve it himself.

(2) Where the court is to serve the witness summons, the party on whose behalf it is issued must deposit, in the court office, the money to be paid or offered to the witness under rule 34.7.

Right of witness to travelling expenses and compensation for loss of time

34.7

At the time of service of a witness summons the witness must be offered or paid –

(a) a sum reasonably sufficient to cover his expenses in travelling to and from the court; and

(b) such sum by way of compensation for loss of time as may be specified in Practice Direction 34A.

Practice Direction 34A – Depositions and Court Attendance by Witnesses

This Practice Direction supplements CPR Part 34

Travelling expenses and compensation for loss of time

3.1

When a witness is served with a witness summons he must be offered a sum to cover his travelling expenses to and from the court and compensation for his loss of time5.

3.4

Where the party issuing the witness summons wishes to serve it himself, he must:

(1) notify the court in writing that he wishes to do so, and

(2) at the time of service offer the witness the sums mentioned in paragraph 3.2 above.

Proof of Service:

An Affidavit, Statement or Certificate of Service may be required.

***

SECTION 4 – INSOLVENCY PROCEEDINGS

The Insolvency Act 1986 is an Act of the Parliament of the United Kingdom that provides the legal platform for all matters relating to personal and corporate insolvency in the UK. The Insolvency Act 1986 together with a number of Practice Directions govern the procedure with regard to Bankruptcy proceedings, both personal and corporate. The latest Practice Direction came out 23rd February 2012 and replaces all previous Practice Directions, Practice Statements and Practice Notes relating to insolvency proceedings. For this reason, we reproduce it here in its entirety.

MODERNISATION OF INSOLVENCY RULES

In 2009 and 2010 The Insolvency Service put into force a series of amendments to modernise the Insolvency Rules 1986:-

> 1. In April 2009 amendments were made to the Rules (and also to sections 95 and 98 of the Insolvency Act 1986) to deliver a more flexible and better targeted regime for the advertising and/or publicity of insolvency events; and

> 2. In April 2010 a wide range of amendments were made to the Rules (complemented by various changes to the Insolvency Act 1986) aimed at modernising insolvency processes. Amongst many other things, these measures have opened up the possibility of electronic communication and use of websites as a means of communication within those processes.

In April 2011 The Insolvency Service announced that Ministerial approval had been given to continue work on the final phase of the modernisation which is to produce a new set of Insolvency Rules to restructure and entirely replace the 1986 Rules, which have been amended more than 20 times since they came into force.

The Insolvency Service are now working to produce a full consultation draft of the new Rules for the purpose of inviting feedback on the structure, content and detailed drafting. It is anticipated that the draft for consultation will be published during the first half of 2012 and comments from stakeholders will be very welcome at that stage in order to assist in developing and finalising the new Rules. The new Rules will not come into force before October 2013.

The link below under the heading "New Insolvency Rules for 2013" relates to this current work. The links further down the page relate to the earlier 2009 and 2010 amendments.

Any enquiries regarding the above should be directed towards Jane Tranter, Policy Unit, Zone B, Third Floor, 21 Bloomsbury Street, London WC1B 3QW; e-mail jane.tranter@insolvency.gsi.gov.uk

New insolvency rules for 2013

- Stakeholder letter - April 2011

THE INSOLVENCY SERVICE

Anne Willcocks
Director of Insolvency Policy and Practitioner Regulation
Area 3.7
21 Bloomsbury Street
London
WC1B 3QW

Tel: 020 7637 1110
Fax: 020 7291 6746
DX address : 120675
DX exchange: BLOOMSBURY 6
www.insolvency.gov.uk

Dear Stakeholder

New Insolvency Rules

Towards the end of last year we invited views on whether or not to continue our work on a full re-write of the 1986 rules, as the final phase of work to modernise the Insolvency Rules. We asked for opinions also on an alternative option of making only necessary amendments to the existing rules.

A range of views were subsequently expressed by stakeholders, both in terms of their preferred option and in relation to several questions of detail posed, such as whether or not we should continue to prescribe forms. I am very grateful to those who submitted responses.

I am now writing to inform you that, having considered those responses, Ministers have decided that work on a full new set of rules should continue, although those rules will not now come into force before October 2013. This will take into account some concerns expressed about the introduction of the new rules so soon after the changes introduced in April 2010.

We plan to publish a full working draft of the new rules in the near future for the purpose of inviting feedback on the structure, content and detailed drafting. That will be the final open invitation stakeholders will have to help shape these new rules so I really would welcome as much feedback as you are able to provide.

You might also be aware of the work we are undertaking to review the administration expense rules, particularly in light of the impact of Mr Justice Briggs' decision at the end of last year about the costs of complying with a Financial Support Direction issued by the Pensions Regulator. Again we are grateful for the helpful suggestions and information that stakeholders have provided. If Ministers are persuaded that legislative changes are required, I would expect those changes to be implemented well before the new rules.

Should you have any queries please contact my colleague Tom Phillips on 020 7637 6421 or at tom.phillips@insolvency.gsi.gov.uk.

Yours faithfully

Anne Willcocks
Director of Insolvency Policy and Practitioner Regulation

New Insolvency Rules for 2012

Insolvency Service Policy Unit has delivered the first two phases of the project to modernize the Insolvency Rules, thanks in no small part to the valuable contributions and feedback received from a wide range of insolvency stakeholders and from the Insolvency Rules Committee.

We are now preparing a new set of Insolvency Rules for implementation in 2012 and from August 2010 we will commence the roll out, on The Insolvency Service website, of individual draft Parts of those new Rules in a form that also demonstrates the overall proposed structure for the new Insolvency Rules. The intention is to provide users with an early opportunity to review and comment on individual draft Parts as these are prepared. It is hoped that this piecemeal provision of draft Parts will afford users the opportunity to consider and provide feedback on the content. The overall structure proposed for the new Rules may be subject to change as drafting proceeds but we would welcome observations on this too.

The substantive changes in content to modernize the Rules have already been delivered in April 2009 (new insolvency advertising regime & DRO Rules) and in April 2010 (wider range of modernization changes, including e-delivery provisions etc) . The final phase of Rules modernization will deliver a new set of Insolvency Rules which will restructure the existing Insolvency Rules 1986 (as amended more than 20 times) and drive consistency across all insolvency procedures. We are planning to make only a very limited number of further changes to the substance of the provisions within the new Insolvency Rules, principally in response to feedback that we receive from our engagement with insolvency users.

On 23rd July 2010, twenty six external stakeholders from a cross section of interested insolvency users attended an Insolvency Rules Focus Group meeting at the offices of The Insolvency Service. The meeting generated an enthusiastic response from users and a lively debate on the look and feel of the new Rules template. Our thanks go to those who attended and have provided us with preliminary feedback upon the proposals for the new Rules.

Insolvency Service Policy Unit will continue to engage closely with stakeholders as the project moves forward and we look forward to receiving further feedback from insolvency users. Our timetable towards implementation in 2012 is challenging and would require all user comment on the draft Parts to be received by January 2011.

Any enquiries regarding the above should be directed towards Neil Ogilvie, Policy Unit, Zone B, Third Floor, 21 Bloomsbury Street, London WC1B 3QW; e-mail Neil.Ogilvie@insolvency.gsi.gov.uk

Any enquiries regarding the Scottish Rules should be directed towards Steven Chown, Policy Unit, Zone B, Third Floor, 21 Bloomsbury Street, London WC1B 3QW;
e-mail Steven.Chown@insolvency.gsi.gov.uk

Rules Modernisation Update with Stakeholder Commentary – March 2010

Insolvency Service Policy Unit has successfully delivered the second phase of modernisation of the Insolvency Rules.

Following on from the new insolvency advertising regime delivered in April 2009, the following instruments have been made and laid in Parliament, and will come into force from 6th April 2010:

- The Legislative Reform (Insolvency) (Miscellaneous Provisions) Order 2010 (2010 No.18)
- The Insolvency (Amendment) Rules 2010 (2010 No.686) ;
- The Insolvency (Amendment) (No 2) Rules 2010 (2010 No.734) ;

- The Insolvency (Scotland) Amendment Rules 2010 (2010 No. 688) ;

The Legislative Reform (Insolvency) (Miscellaneous Provisions) Order 2010 was required to make changes within the Insolvency Act to permit the extensive modernisation changes planned for the Insolvency Rules.

Each of these instruments can now be viewed on the OPSI and Insolvency Service websites.

The changes implemented by the project to modernise the Insolvency Rules will provide estimated annual savings of £48 million in the cost of administering insolvencies, including the advertising changes in April 2009. These savings are expected to be passed on to creditors in the form of improved returns and the new e-delivery provisions will also provide for a significant reduction in the insolvency carbon footprint. The amendment Rules, by their nature, amend the Insolvency Rules 1986.

The changes will deliver benefits for stakeholders, including:

Insolvency Practitioners/Lawyers

Insolvency practitioners will be able to send insolvency notices and reports electronically (with the consent of the recipient) and by website. This will result in significant cost savings.

Insolvency practitioners will be able to offer remote attendance at creditors and company meetings, removing the need and cost of securing a physical venue for the meeting in many cases.

Pre-appointment administration costs will be recoverable as an expense with the express agreement of the creditors.

A streamlined process for "disclaiming" will enable liquidators and trustees in bankruptcy to deal with onerous property more quickly and efficiently.

Annual meetings in voluntary liquidations have been abolished and replaced with annual reports, to match those which are already produced in administrations. This will stop costs being wasted on arranging meetings that were rarely attended and ensure that all creditors receive regular information.

Creditors

There will be better returns from insolvency procedures as insolvency practitioners are able to save money by taking advantage of electronic means of communication and simplified administrative processes. These savings are estimated to amount to around £30m a year.

Creditors will be able to receive information from insolvency office-holders in a modern, more convenient, way and have the opportunity of attending meetings of creditors remotely. This will make it easier for creditors to get involved with insolvency processes.

Creditors will benefit from greater transparency in respect of insolvency practitioners' fees, information on which will be provided to them in regular reports.

Creditors will have new rights to request fuller information and explanations of anything contained in the office-holder's report, plus clearer rights to challenge any excessive fees and expenses.

Documents in corporate insolvencies will be more accessible as they will be filed at Companies House instead of the court.

Debtors and Others

Individual debtors facing bankruptcy who are at risk of violence may apply to court for an order to limit disclosure of their home address.

Debtors wanting to declare themselves bankrupt will not have to go to the trouble of finding someone to swear the documents in front of, as all requirements for affidavits have been abolished and replaced with statements of truth.

A bankrupt who can repay all the debts and expenses of their bankruptcy will have a new right to challenge their trustee's remuneration and expenses at court if they consider the amounts charged to be excessive.

To make it easier for a bankrupt to obtain an "annulment" of the bankruptcy order in circumstances where they propose to pay the bankruptcy debts and expenses using third party monies or by means of a subsequent remortgage of property.

Public notices of insolvency events in the London Gazette and other media will follow a standardised format to ensure that users such as credit reference agencies will have access to the information they need in a more consistent way. "

The next phase of the Rules Modernisation is the work on simplifying the drafting of the Insolvency Rules by rewriting and reordering them for easier use, incorporating a review and probable removal of most of the prescribed forms within the Rules. We also want to pick up any issues flowing from the practical implementation of the April 2010 Modernisation changes. This final phase to the project involves the preparation of a new set of Insolvency Rules, a draft of which will be published for comment in due course.

15 Affidavits

15.1 Throughout the Rules, references to affidavits have been removed. They have been replaced with a requirement for a statement of truth. In some cases this statement will be incorporated into the document to be verified and in others the reference to an affidavit is replaced by a reference to a witness statement supported by a statement of truth. There is a new definition in Rule 13.13 (expressions used generally) explaining that "statement of truth" has the same meaning as in the CPR.

15.2 Consequential changes have been made to references to "swear", "sworn", "oath" and "exhibited". In Parts 2 (administration procedure) and 4 (companies winding up) the discretionary requirement that a claim of debt must be verified by affidavit has been removed. In Part 6, the provision requiring a petition in respect of a moneylending transaction to be supported by an affidavit has been removed.

15.3 The position for statutory declarations (eg Declaration of Solvency under section 89 of the Act) has not been changed.

16 Ex parte

16.1 Throughout the Rules, references to ex parte have been removed. They have been replaced with the phrase "without notice to any other party".

17 Leave of the court

17.1 Throughout the Rules, references to obtaining "leave" of the court have been replaced with references to obtaining "permission" of the court.

18   Deponents

18.1   Throughout the Rules, references to deponents have been removed. Other than in Part 3 (administrative receivership), they have been replaced with the phrase "person making the statement". In Part 3, they have been replaced with the term "nominated person" which is defined in that Part.

31   Electronic delivery

31.1.   One of the key facets of the modernisation reforms is to facilitate the delivery of documents electronically. With this in mind the amending Rules make a number of provisions facilitating the sending of documents by electronic means. The general principle found in Rules 12A.7 and 12A.10 is that documents may be delivered by electronic means provided that the recipient has consented and provides an electronic address. The provisions do not apply to petitions or applications to court, evidence in support of such applications or petitions or orders of the court; nor do certain other provisions apply to the filing of notices or other documents with the court, the submission of documents to the registrar of companies or to the service of a statutory demand. Uniformity is facilitated by the provision of the LRO.

32   Service of court documents

32.1.   CPR Part 6 is to apply, except for the serving of a winding up petition, a bankruptcy petition and any document relating to such an application or petition or the serving of an administration, winding up, or bankruptcy order, But the provisions of CPR Part 6 relating to service outside the jurisdiction apply, with such modifications as the court may direct, in every case (including bankruptcy petitions etc) so there is no bespoke Rule in the Insolvency Rules. These Rules are now contained in Chapter 3 of the new Part 12A.

The Insolvency Service's Website

The Insolvency Service maintains a public register which shows current information in the following areas: Individual Voluntary Arrangements (IVAs), Bankruptcy Orders and Bankruptcy Restriction Orders/ Undertakings (BROs/BRUs).

There are several ways to access this information. For a link direct to the register please go to: www.insolvencydirect.bis.gov.uk/eiir/

London Gazette

Available in paper or electronic form: The London Gazette is the Official Newspaper of Record in recording and disseminating official, regulatory and legal information. As detailed above where an insolvency office-holder is required to advertise insolvency events it will be in this publication.

In its electronic format it is free to search and view individual notices via their website. For individual insolvency notices please go to: www.london-gazette.co.uk/issues/recent/10/personal-insolvency

For company insolvency notices please go to: www.london-gazette.co.uk/issues/recent/10/corp-insolvency

The London Gazette also provides the information in large electronic formats mainly aimed at the commercial user. A fee is required for these services. For more information on the services provided by The London Gazette related to insolvency please go to: www.london-gazette.co.uk/insolvency

PRACTICE DIRECTION – INSOLVENCY PROCEEDINGS

Contents of this Practice Direction

Title	Number
PART I – GENERAL PROVISIONS	
1. Definitions	Para. 1.1
2. Coming into force	Para. 2.1
3. Distribution of business	Para. 3.1
4. Court documents	Para. 4.1
5. Evidence	Para. 5.1
6. Service of court documents in insolvency proceedings	Para. 6.1
7. Jurisdiction	Para. 7.1
8. Drawing up of orders	Para. 8.1
9. Urgent applications	Para. 9.1
PART II – COMPANY INSOLVENCY	
10. Administrations	Para. 10.1
11. Winding-up petitions	Para. 11.1
Gazetting of the petition	Para. 11.5
Errors in petitions	Para. 11.6
Rescission of a winding up order	Para. 11.7
Validation orders	Para. 11.8
12. Applications	Para. 12.1
PART III – PERSONAL INSOLVENCY	
13. Statutory demands	
Deemed date of service	Para. 13.1
Service abroad of statutory demands	Para. 13.2
Substituted service of statutory demands	Para. 13.3
Setting aside a statutory demand	Para. 13.4
14. Bankruptcy petitions	
Listing of petitions	Para. 14.1
Content of petitions	Para. 14.2

Contents of this Practice Direction

Title	Number
Searches	Para. 14.3
Deposit	Para. 14.4
Certificates of continuing debt and of notice of adjournment	Para. 14.5
Extension of hearing date of petition	Para. 14.6
Substituted service of bankruptcy petitions	Para. 14.7
Validation orders	Para. 14.8
15. Applications	Para. 15.1
16. Orders without attendance	Para. 16.1
17. Bankruptcy restrictions undertakings	Para. 17.1
18. Persons at risk of violence	Para. 18.1
PART IV – APPEALS	
19. Appeals	
Filing Appeals	Para. 19.5
PART V – APPLICATIONS RELATING TO THE REMUNERATION OF APPOINTEES	
20. Remuneration of Appointees	
Introduction	Para. 20.1
The objective and guiding principles	Para. 20.2
Hearing of remuneration applications	Para. 20.3
Relevant criteria and procedure	Para. 20.4

PART I – GENERAL PROVISIONS

1. Definitions

1.1

In this Practice Direction –

(1) 'The Act' means the Insolvency Act 1986 and includes the Act as applied to limited liability partnerships by the Limited Liability Partnerships Regulations 2001 or to any other person or body by virtue of the Act or any other legislation;

(2) 'The Insolvency Rules' means the rules for the time being in force and made under s.411 and s.412 of the Act in relation to insolvency proceedings, and, save where otherwise provided, any reference to a rule is to a rule in the Insolvency Rules;

(3) 'CPR' means the Civil Procedure Rules and 'CPR' followed by a Part or rule identified by number means the Part or rule with that number in those Rules;

(4) 'EC Regulation on Insolvency Proceedings' means Council Regulation (EC) No 1346/2000 of 29 May 2000 on Insolvency Proceedings;

(5) 'Service Regulation' means Council Regulation (EC) No. 1393/2007 of 13 November 2007 on the service in the Member States of judicial and extrajudicial documents in civil and commercial matters (service of documents) ;

(6) 'Insolvency proceedings' means –

    (a) any proceedings under the Act, the Insolvency Rules, the Administration of Insolvent Estates of Deceased Persons Order 1986 (S.I. 1986 No.1999) , the Insolvent Partnerships Order 1994 (S.I. 1994 No. 2421) or the Limited Liability Partnerships Regulations 2001;

    (b) any proceedings under the EC Regulation on Insolvency Proceedings or the Cross-Border Insolvency Regulations 2006 (S.I. 2006/1030) ;

(7) References to a 'company' include a limited liability partnership and references to a 'contributory' include a member of a limited liability partnership;

(8) References to a 'Registrar' are to a Registrar in Bankruptcy of the High Court and (save in cases where it is clear from the context that a particular provision applies only to the Royal Courts of Justice) include a District Judge in a District Registry of the High Court and in any county court having insolvency jurisdiction;

(9) 'Court' means any court having insolvency jurisdiction;

(10) 'Royal Courts of Justice' means the Royal Courts of Justice, Strand, London WC2A 2LL or such other place in London where the Registrars sit;

(11) In Part Five of this Practice Direction –

    (a) 'appointee' means–
        (i) a provisional liquidator appointed under section 135 of the Act;
        (ii) a special manager appointed under section 177 or section 370 of the Act;
        (iii) a liquidator appointed by the members of a company or partnership or by the creditors of a company or partnership or by the Secretary of State pursuant to section 137 of the Act, or by the court pursuant to section 140 of the Act;
        (iv) an administrator of a company appointed to manage the property, business and affairs of that company under the Act or other enactment and to which the provisions of the Act are applicable;
        (v) a trustee in bankruptcy (other than the Official Receiver) appointed under the Act;
        (vi) a nominee or supervisor of a voluntary arrangement under Part I or Part VIII of the Act;
        (vii) a licensed insolvency practitioner appointed by the court pursuant to section 273 of the Act;
        (viii) an interim receiver appointed by the court pursuant to section 286 of the Act;

    (b) 'assessor' means a person appointed in accordance with CPR 35.15;

(c) 'remuneration application' means any application to fix, approve or challenge the remuneration or expenses of an appointee or the basis of remuneration;

(d) 'remuneration' includes expenses (where the Act or the Insolvency Rules give the court jurisdiction in relation thereto) and, in the case of an administrator, any pre-appointment administration costs or remuneration.

2. Coming into force

2.1 This Practice Direction shall come into force on 23 February 2012 and shall replace all previous Practice Directions, Practice Statements and Practice Notes relating to insolvency proceedings.

3. Distribution of business

3.1 As a general rule all petitions and applications (except those listed in paragraphs 3.2 and 3.3 below) should be listed for initial hearing before a Registrar in accordance with rule 7.6A(2) and (3).

3.2 The following applications relating to insolvent companies should always be listed before a Judge –

(1) applications for committal for contempt;

(2) applications for an administration order;

(3) applications for an injunction;

(4) applications for the appointment of a provisional liquidator;

(5) interim applications and applications for directions or case management after any proceedings have been referred or adjourned to the Judge (except where liberty to apply to the Registrar has been given).

3.3 The following applications relating to insolvent individuals should always be listed before a Judge:

(1) applications for committal for contempt;

(2) applications for an injunction;

(3) interim applications and applications for directions or case management after any proceedings have been referred or adjourned to the Judge (except where liberty to apply to the Registrar has been given).

3.4 When deciding whether to hear proceedings or to refer or adjourn them to the Judge, the Registrar should have regard to the following factors –

(1) the complexity of the proceedings;

(2) whether the proceedings raise new or controversial points of law;

(3) the likely date and length of the hearing;

(4) public interest in the proceedings.

4. Court documents

4.1 All insolvency proceedings should be commenced and applications in proceedings should be made using the forms prescribed by the Act, the Insolvency Rules or other legislation under which the same is or are brought or made and/or should contain the information prescribed by the Act, the Insolvency Rules or other legislation.

4.2 Every court document in insolvency proceedings under Parts I to VII of the Act shall be headed –

IN THE HIGH COURT OF JUSTICE
CHANCERY DIVISION

[DISTRICT REGISTRY] or in the Royal Courts of Justice [COMPANIES COURT]

or

IN THE [   ] COUNTY COURT

followed by

IN THE MATTER OF [name of company]

AND IN THE MATTER OF THE INSOLVENCY ACT 1986

4.3 Every court document in insolvency proceedings under Parts IX to XI of the Act shall be headed –

IN THE [HIGH COURT OF JUSTICE] or [[   ] COUNTY COURT] IN BANKRUPTCY

IN THE MATTER OF [name of bankrupt]

or

RE: [name of bankrupt].

Every application should also be headed–

AND IN THE MATTER OF THE INSOLVENCY ACT 1986

4.4 Every court document in proceedings to which the Act applies by virtue of other legislation should also be headed –

IN THE MATTER OF [THE FINANCIAL SERVICES AND MARKETS ACT 2000 or as the case may be]

AND IN THE MATTER OF THE INSOLVENCY ACT 1986

5. Evidence

5.1 Subject to the provisions of rule 7.9 or any other provisions or directions as to the form in which evidence should be given, written evidence in insolvency proceedings must be given by witness statement.

6. Service of court documents in insolvency proceedings

6.1 Except where the Insolvency Rules otherwise provide, CPR Part 6 applies to the service of court documents both within and out of the jurisdiction as modified by this Practice Direction or as the court may otherwise direct.

6.2 Except where the Insolvency Rules otherwise provide or as may be required under the Service Regulation, service of documents in insolvency proceedings will be the responsibility of the parties and will not be undertaken by the court.

6.3 A document which, pursuant to rule 12A.16(3) (b) , is treated as a claim form, is deemed to have been served on the date specified in CPR Part 6.14, and any other document is deemed to have been served on the date specified in CPR Part 6.26, unless the court otherwise directs.

6.4 Except as provided below, service out of the jurisdiction of an application which is to be treated as a claim form under rule 12A.16(3) requires the permission of the court.

6.5 An application which is to be treated as a claim form under rule 12A.16(3) may be served out of the jurisdiction without the permission of the court if –

(1) the application is by an office-holder appointed in insolvency proceedings in respect of a company with its centre of main interests within the jurisdiction exercising a statutory power under the Act, and the person to be served is to be served within the EU; or
(2) it is a copy of an application, being served on a member State liquidator.

6.6 An application for permission to serve out of the jurisdiction must be supported by a witness statement setting out –

(1) the nature of the claim or application and the relief sought;
(2) that the applicant believes that the claim has a reasonable prospect of success; and
(3) the address of the person to be served or, if not known, in what place or country that person is, or is likely, to be found.

6.7 CPR 6.36 and 6.37(1) and (2) do not apply in insolvency proceedings.

7. Jurisdiction

7.1 Where CPR 2.4 provides for the court to perform any act, that act may be performed by a Registrar.

8. Drawing up of orders

8.1 The court will draw up all orders except orders on the application of the Official Receiver or for which the Treasury Solicitor is responsible or where the court otherwise directs.

9. Urgent applications

9.1 In the Royal Courts of Justice the Registrars (and in other courts exercising insolvency jurisdiction the District Judges) operate urgent applications lists for urgent and time-critical applications and may be available to hear urgent applications at other times. Parties asking for an application to be dealt with in the urgent applications lists or urgently at any other time must complete the certificate below –

Heading of action   No:

I estimate that this matter is likely to occupy the court for……………mins/hours.

I certify that it is urgent for the following reasons:

…………………………
[name of representative]

…………………………
[telephone number]

Counsel/Solicitor for the…………………………

WARNING. If, in the opinion of the Registrar/District Judge, the application is not urgent then such sanction will be applied as is thought appropriate in all the circumstances.

PART II – COMPANY INSOLVENCY
10. Administrations

10.1 In the absence of special circumstances, an application for the extension of an administration should be made not less than one month before the end of the administration. The evidence in support of any later application must explain why the application is being made late. The court will consider whether any part of the costs should be disallowed where an application is made less than one month before the end of the administration.

11. Winding-up petitions

11.1 Before presenting a winding-up petition the creditor must conduct a search to ensure that no petition is already pending. Save in exceptional circumstances a second winding up petition should not be presented whilst a prior petition is pending. A petitioner who presents his own petition while another petition is pending does so at risk as to costs.

11.2 Every creditor's winding-up petition must (in the case of a company) contain the following –

(1) the full name and address of the petitioner;

(2) the name and number of the company in respect of which a winding up order is sought;

(3) the date of incorporation of the company and the Companies Act or Acts under which it was incorporated;

(4) the address of the company's registered office;

(5) a statement of the nominal capital of the company, the manner in which its shares are divided up and the amount of the capital paid up or credited as paid up;

(6) brief details of the principal objects for which the company was established followed, where appropriate, by the words 'and other objects stated in the memorandum of association of the company';

(7) details of the basis on which it is contended that the company is insolvent including, where a debt is relied on, sufficient particulars of the debt (the amount, nature and approximate date(s) on which it was incurred) to enable the company and the court to identify the debt;

(8) a statement that the company is insolvent and unable to pay its debts

(9) a statement that for the reasons set out in the evidence verifying the petition the EC Regulation on Insolvency Proceedings either applies or does not and if the former whether the proceedings will be main, territorial or secondary proceedings;

(10) the statement that, 'In the circumstances it is just and equitable that the company be wound up under the provisions of the Insolvency Act 1986';

(11) a prayer that the company be wound up, for such other order as the court thinks fit and any other specific relief sought.

Similar information (so far as is appropriate) should be given where the petition is presented against a partnership.

11.3   The statement of truth verifying the petition in accordance with rule 4.12 should be made no more than ten business days before the date of issue of the petition.

11.4   Where the company to be wound up has been struck off the register, the petition should state that fact and include as part of the relief sought an order that it be restored to the register. Save where the petition has been presented by a Minister of the Crown or a government department, evidence of service on the Treasury Solicitor or the Solicitor for the affairs of the Duchy of Lancaster (as appropriate) should be filed exhibiting the bona vacantia waiver letter.

Gazetting of the petition

11.5

(11.5.1)   Rule 4.11 must be complied with (unless waived by the court) : it is designed to ensure that the class remedy of winding up by the court is made available to all creditors, and is not used as a means of putting improper pressure on the company to pay the petitioner's debt or costs. Failure to comply with the rule, without good reason accepted by the court, may lead to the summary dismissal of the petition on the return date (rule 4.11(6)) or to the court depriving the petitioner of the costs of the hearing. If the court, in its discretion, grants an adjournment, this will usually be on terms that notice of the petition is gazetted or otherwise given in accordance with the rule in due time for the adjourned hearing. No further adjournment for the purpose of gazetting will normally be granted.

(11.5.2) Copies of every notice gazetted in connection with a winding up petition, or where this is not practicable a description of the form and content of the notice, must be lodged with the court as soon as possible after publication and in any event not later than five business days before the hearing of the petition. This direction applies even if the notice is defective in any way (e.g. is published on a date not in accordance with the Insolvency Rules, or omits or misprints some important words) or if the petitioner decides not to pursue the petition (e.g. on receiving payment)

Errors in petitions

11.6

(11.6.1) Applications for permission to amend errors in petitions which are discovered after a winding up order has been made should be made to the member of court staff in charge of the winding up list in the Royal Courts of Justice or to a District Judge in any other court.

(11.6.2) Where the error is an error in the name of the company, the member of court staff in charge of the winding up list in the Royal Courts of Justice or a District Judge in any other court may make any necessary amendments to ensure that the winding up order is drawn up with the correct name of the company inserted. If there is any doubt, e.g. where there might be another company in existence which could be confused with the company to be wound up, the member of court staff in charge of the winding up list will refer the application to a Registrar at the Royal Courts of Justice and a District Judge may refer it to a Judge.

(11.6.3) Where it is discovered that the company has been struck off the Register of Companies prior to the winding up order being made, the matter must be restored to the list as soon as possible to enable an order for the restoration of the name to be made as well as the order to wind up.

Rescission of a winding up order

11.7

(11.7.1) An application to rescind a winding up order must be made by application.

(11.7.2) The application should normally be made within five business days after the date on which the order was made (rule 7.47(4)) failing which it should include an application to extend time. Notice of any such application must be given to the petitioning creditor, any supporting or opposing creditor and the Official Receiver.

(11.7.3) Applications will only be entertained if made (a) by a creditor, or (b) by a contributory, or (c) by the company jointly with a creditor or with a contributory. The application must be supported by a witness statement which should include details of assets and liabilities and (where appropriate) reasons for any failure to apply within five business days.

(11.7.4) In the case of an unsuccessful application the costs of the petitioning creditor, any supporting creditors and of the Official Receiver will normally be ordered to be paid by the creditor or the contributory making or joining in the application. The reason for this is that if the costs of an unsuccessful application are made payable by the company, they fall unfairly on the general body of creditors.

Validation orders

11.8

(11.8.1) A company against which a winding up petition has been presented may apply to the court after presentation of the petition for relief from the effects of section 127(1) of the Act by seeking an order that a disposition or dispositions of its property, including payments out of its bank account (whether such account is in credit or overdrawn), shall not be void in the event of a winding up order being made on the hearing of the petition (a validation order).

(11.8.2) An application for a validation order should generally be made to the Registrar. An application should be made to the Judge only if: (a) it is urgent and no Registrar is available to hear it; or (b) it is complex or raises new or controversial points of law; or (c) it is estimated to last longer than 30 minutes.

(11.8.3) Save in exceptional circumstances, notice of the making of the application should be given to: (a) the petitioning creditor; (b) any person entitled to receive a copy of the petition pursuant to rule 4.10; (c) any creditor who has given notice to the petitioner of his intention to appear on the hearing of the petition pursuant to rule 4.16; and (d) any creditor who has been substituted as petitioner pursuant to rule 4.19.

(11.8.4) The application should be supported by a witness statement which, save in exceptional circumstances, should be made by a director or officer of the company who is intimately acquainted with the company's affairs and financial circumstances. If appropriate, supporting evidence in the form of a witness statement from the company's accountant should also be produced.

(11.8.5) The extent and contents of the evidence will vary according to the circumstances and the nature of the relief sought, but in the majority of cases it should include, as a minimum, the following information –

(1) when and to whom notice has been given in accordance with paragraph 11.8.3 above;

(2) the company's registered office;

(3) the company's nominal and paid up capital;

(4) brief details of the circumstances leading to presentation of the petition;

(5) how the company became aware of presentation of the petition;

(6) whether the petition debt is admitted or disputed and, if the latter, brief details of the basis on which the debt is disputed;

(7) full details of the company's financial position including details of its assets (including details of any security and the amount(s) secured) and liabilities, which should be supported, as far as possible, by documentary evidence, e.g. the latest filed accounts, any draft audited accounts, management accounts or estimated statement of affairs;

(8) a cash flow forecast and profit and loss projection for the period for which the order is sought;

(9) details of the dispositions or payments in respect of which an order is sought;

(10) the reasons relied on in support of the need for such dispositions or payments to be made;

(11) any other information relevant to the exercise of the court's discretion;

(12) details of any consents obtained from the persons mentioned in paragraph 11.8.3 above (supported by documentary evidence where appropriate) ;

(13) details of any relevant bank account, including its number and the address and sort code of the bank at which such account is held.

(11.8.6) Where an application is made urgently to enable payments to be made which are essential to continued trading (e.g. wages) and it is not possible to assemble all the evidence listed above, the court may consider granting limited relief for a short period, but there should be sufficient evidence to satisfy the court that the interests of creditors are unlikely to be prejudiced.

(11.8.7) Where the application involves a disposition of property the court will need details of the property (including its title number if the property is land) and to be satisfied that any proposed disposal will be at a proper value. Accordingly, an independent valuation should be obtained and exhibited to the evidence.

(11.8.8) The court will need to be satisfied by credible evidence either that the company is solvent and able to pay its debts as they fall due or that a particular transaction or series of transactions in respect of which the order is sought will be beneficial to or will not prejudice the interests of all the unsecured creditors as a class (Denney v John Hudson & Co Ltd [1992] BCLC 901; Re Fairway Graphics Ltd [1991] BCLC 468) .

(11.8.9) A draft of the order sought should be attached to the application.

(11.8.10) Similar considerations to those set out above are likely to apply to applications seeking ratification of a transaction or payment after the making of a winding-up order.

12. Applications

12.1 In accordance with rule 13.2(2) , in the Royal Courts of Justice the member of court staff in charge of the winding up list has been authorised to deal with applications –

(1) to extend or abridge time prescribed by the Insolvency Rules in connection with winding up (rule 4.3) ;

(2) for permission to withdraw a winding up petition (rule 4.15) ;

(3) for the substitution of a petitioner (rule 4.19) ;

(4) by the Official Receiver for limited disclosure of a statement of affairs (rule 4.35) ;

(5) by the Official Receiver for relief from duties imposed upon him by the Insolvency Rules (rule 4.47) ;

(6) by the Official Receiver for permission to give notice of a meeting by advertisement only (rule 4.59) ;

(7) to transfer proceedings from the High Court (Royal Courts of Justice) to a county court after the making of a winding-up order (rule 7.11) .

12.2 In District Registries or a county court such applications must be made to a District Judge.

PART III – PERSONAL INSOLVENCY

13. Statutory demands
Deemed date of service

13.1

(13.1.1) A statutory demand is deemed to be served on the date applicable to the method of service set out in CPR Part 6.26 unless the statutory demand is advertised in which case it is deemed served on the date of the appearance of the advertisement pursuant to rule 6.3.

Service abroad of statutory demands

13.2

(13.2.1) A statutory demand is not a document issued by the court. Permission to serve out of the jurisdiction is not, therefore, required.

(13.2.2) Rule 6.3(2) ('Requirements as to service') applies to service of the statutory demand whether within or out of the jurisdiction.

(13.2.3) A creditor wishing to serve a statutory demand out of the jurisdiction in a foreign country with which a civil procedure convention has been made (including the Hague Convention) may and, if the assistance of a British Consul is desired, must adopt the procedure prescribed by CPR Part 6.42 and 6.43. In the case of any doubt whether the country is a 'convention country', enquiries should be made of the Queen's Bench Masters' Secretary Department, Room E216, Royal Courts of Justice.

(13.2.4) In all other cases, service of the demand must be effected by private arrangement in accordance with rule 6.3(2) and local foreign law.

(13.2.5) When a statutory demand is to be served out of the jurisdiction, the time limits of 21 days and 18 days respectively referred to in the demand must be amended as provided in the next paragraph. For this purpose reference should be made to the table set out in the practice direction supplementing Section IV of CPR Part 6.

(13.2.6) A creditor should amend the statutory demand as follows –

(1) for any reference to 18 days there must be substituted the appropriate number of days set out in the table plus 4 days;

(2) for any reference to 21 days there must be substituted the appropriate number of days in the table plus 7 days.

(13.2.7) Attention is drawn to the fact that in all forms of the statutory demand the figure 18 and the figure 21 occur in more than one place.

Substituted service of statutory demands

13.3

(13.3.1) The creditor is under an obligation to do all that is reasonable to bring the statutory demand to the debtor's attention and, if practicable, to cause personal service to be effected (rule 6.3(2)).

(13.3.2) In the circumstances set out in rule 6.3(3) the demand may instead be advertised. As there is no statutory form of advertisement, the court will accept an advertisement in the following form –

STATUTORY DEMAND
(Debt for liquidated sum payable immediately following a judgment or order of the court)

To (Block letters)
of

TAKE NOTICE that a statutory demand has been issued by:

Name of Creditor:
Address:

The creditor demands payment of £   the amount now due on a judgment or order of the (High Court of Justice   Division) (…………County Court) dated the [day] of [month] 20[ ].
The statutory demand is an important document and it is deemed to have been served on you on the date of the first appearance of this advertisement. You must deal with this demand within 21 days of the service upon you or you could be made bankrupt and your property and goods taken away from you. If you are in any doubt as to your position, you should seek advice immediately from a solicitor or your nearest Citizens' Advice Bureau. The statutory demand can be obtained or is available for inspection and collection from:

Name:
Address:
(Solicitor for) the Creditor
Tel. No.   Reference:

You have only 21 days from the date of the first appearance of this advertisement before the creditor may present a bankruptcy petition. You have only 18 days from the date of the first appearance of this advertisement within which to apply to the court to set aside the demand.

(13.3.3) Where personal service is not effected or the demand is not advertised in the limited circumstances permitted by rule 6.3(3) , substituted service is permitted, but the creditor must have taken all those steps which would justify the court making an order for substituted service of a petition. The steps to be taken to obtain an order for substituted service of a petition are set out below. Failure to comply with these requirements may result in the court declining to issue the petition (rule 6.11(9)) or dismissing it.

(13.3.4) In most cases, evidence of the following steps will suffice to justify acceptance for presentation of a petition where the statutory demand has been served by substituted service (or to justify making an order for substituted service of a petition) –

(1) One personal call at the residence and place of business of the debtor where both are known or at either of such places as is known. Where it is known that the debtor has more than one residential or business address, personal calls should be made at all the addresses.

(2) Should the creditor fail to effect personal service, a first class prepaid letter should be written to the debtor referring to the call(s) , the purpose of the same and the failure to meet the debtor, adding that a further call will be made for the same purpose on the [day] of [month] 20[ ] at [ ] hours at [place]. At least two business days' notice should be given of the appointment and copies of the letter sent to all known addresses of the debtor. The appointment letter should also state that:

(a) in the event of the time and place not being convenient, the debtor should propose some other time and place reasonably convenient for the purpose;

(b) (In the case of a statutory demand) if the debtor fails to keep the appointment the creditor proposes to serve the debtor by [advertisement] [post] [insertion through a letter box] or as the case may be, and that, in the event of a bankruptcy petition being presented, the court will be asked to treat such service as service of the demand on the debtor;

(c) (In the case of a petition) if the debtor fails to keep the appointment, application will be made to the Court for an order for substituted service either by advertisement, or in such other manner as the court may think fit.

(3) When attending any appointment made by letter, inquiry should be made as to whether the debtor has received all letters left for him. If the debtor is away, inquiry should also be made as to whether or not letters are being forwarded to an address within the jurisdiction (England and Wales) or elsewhere.

(4) If the debtor is represented by a solicitor, an attempt should be made to arrange an appointment for personal service through such solicitor. The Insolvency Rules enable a solicitor to accept service of a statutory demand on behalf of his client but there is no similar provision in respect of service of a bankruptcy petition.

(5) The certificate of service of a statutory demand filed pursuant to rule 6.11 should deal with all the above matters including all relevant facts as to the debtor's whereabouts and whether the appointment letter(s) have been returned. It should also set out the reasons for the belief that the debtor resides at the relevant address or works at the relevant place of business and whether, so far as is known, the debtor is represented by a solicitor.

Setting aside a statutory demand

13.4

(13.4.1) The application (Form 6.4) and witness statement in support (Form 6.5) exhibiting a copy of the statutory demand must be filed in court within 18 days of service of the statutory demand on the debtor. Where service is effected by advertisement the period of 18 days is calculated from the date of the first appearance of the advertisement. Three copies of each document must be lodged with the application to enable the court to serve notice of the hearing date on the applicant, the creditor and the person named in Part B of the statutory demand.

(13.4.2) Where copies of the documents are not lodged with the application, any order of the Registrar fixing a venue is conditional upon copies of the documents being lodged on the next business day after the Registrar's order otherwise the application will be deemed to have been dismissed.

(13.4.3) Where the debt claimed in the statutory demand is based on a judgment, order, liability order, costs certificate, tax assessment or decision of a tribunal, the court will not at this stage inquire into the validity of the debt nor, as a general rule, will it adjourn the application to await the result of an application to set aside the judgment, order decision, costs certificate or any appeal.

(13.4.4) Where the debtor (a) claims to have a counterclaim, set-off or cross demand (whether or not he could have raised it in the action in which the judgment or order was obtained) which equals or exceeds the amount of the debt or debts specified in the statutory demand or (b) disputes the debt (not being a debt subject to a judgment, order, liability order, costs certificate or tax assessment) the court will normally set aside the statutory demand if, in its opinion, on the evidence there is a genuine triable issue.

(13.4.5) A debtor who wishes to apply to set aside a statutory demand after the expiration of 18 days from the date of service of the statutory demand must apply for an extension of time within which to apply. If the applicant wishes to apply for an injunction to restrain presentation of a petition the application must be made to the Judge. Paragraphs 1 and 2 of Form 6.5 (witness statement in support of application to set aside statutory demand) should be used in support of the application for an extension of time with the following additional paragraphs–
"(3) To the best of my knowledge and belief the creditor(s) named in the demand has/have not presented a petition against me.
(4) The reasons for my failure to apply to set aside the demand within 18 days after service are as follows: ..."
If application is made to restrain presentation of a bankruptcy petition the following additional paragraph should be added:
"(5) Unless restrained by injunction the creditor(s) may present a bankruptcy petition against me".

14. Bankruptcy petitions
Listing of petitions

14.1

(14.1.1) All petitions presented will be listed under the name of the debtor unless the court directs otherwise.

Content of petitions

14.2

(14.2.1) The attention of practitioners is drawn to the following points –

(1) A creditor's petition does not require dating, signing or witnessing but must be verified in accordance with rule 6.12.

(2) In the heading it is only necessary to recite the debtor's name e.g. Re John William Smith or Re J W Smith (Male). Any alias or trading name will appear in the body of the petition.

(14.2.2)　　Where the petition is based solely on a statutory demand, only the debt claimed in the demand may be included in the petition.

(14.2.3)　　The attention of practitioners is also drawn to rules 6.7 and 6.8, and in particular to rule 6.8(1) where the 'aggregate sum' is made up of a number of debts.

(14.2.4)　　The date of service of the statutory demand should be recited as follows –

(1) In the case of personal service, the date of service as set out in the certificate of service should be recited and whether service is effected before/after 1700 hours on Monday to Friday or at any time on a Saturday or a Sunday.

(2) In the case of substituted service (other than by advertisement), the date alleged in the certificate of service should be recited.

(3) In the strictly limited case of service by advertisement under rule 6.3, the date to be alleged is the date of the advertisement's appearance or, as the case may be, its first appearance (see rules 6.3(3) and 6.11(8)) .

Searches

14.3

(14.3.1)　　The petitioning creditor shall, before presenting a petition, conduct a search for petitions presented against the debtor in the previous 18 months (a) in the Royal Courts of Justice, (b) in the Central London County Court and (c) in any county court which he believes is or was within that period the debtor's own county court within the meaning of rule 6.9A(3) and shall include the following certificate at the end of the petition –

"I/we certify that I/we have conducted a search for petitions presented against the debtor in the period of 18 months ending today and that [no prior petitions have been presented in the said period which are still pending] [a prior petition (No [   ]) has been presented and is pending in the [Court] and we are issuing this petition at risk as to costs].

Signed………　　Dated………".

Deposit

14.4

(14.4.1)　　The deposit will be taken by the court and forwarded to the Official Receiver. In the Royal Courts of Justice the petition fee and deposit should be paid in the Fee Room, which will record the receipt and will impress two entries on the original petition, one in respect of the court fee and the other in respect of the deposit. In a District Registry or a county court, the petition fee and deposit should be handed to the duly authorised officer of the court's staff who will record its receipt.

(14.4.2)　　In all cases cheque(s) for the whole amount should be made payable to 'HM Courts and Tribunals Service' or 'HMCTS'.

Certificates of continuing debt and of notice of adjournment

14.5

(14.5.1) On the hearing of a petition where a bankruptcy order is sought, in order to satisfy the court that the debt on which the petition is founded has not been paid or secured or compounded for the court will normally accept as sufficient a certificate signed by the person representing the petitioning creditor in the following form –

"I certify that I have/my firm has made enquiries of the petitioning creditor(s) within the last business day prior to the hearing/adjourned hearing and to the best of my knowledge and belief the debt on which the petition is founded is still due and owing and has not been paid or secured or compounded for save as to...

Signed.........   Dated.........".

(14.5.2) For convenience, in the Royal Courts of Justice this certificate is incorporated in the attendance sheet for the parties to complete when they come to court and which is filed after the hearing. A fresh certificate will be required on each adjourned hearing.

(14.5.3) On any adjourned hearing of a petition where a bankruptcy order is sought, in order to satisfy the court that the petitioner has complied with rule 6.29, the petitioner will be required to file evidence of the date on which, manner in which and address to which notice of the making of the order of adjournment and of the venue for the adjourned hearing has been sent to –

(1) the debtor, and

(2) any creditor who has given notice under rule 6.23 but was not present at the hearing when the order for adjournment was made or was present at the hearing but the date of the adjourned hearing was not fixed at that hearing. For convenience, in the Royal Courts of Justice this certificate is incorporated in the attendance sheet for the parties to complete when they come to court and which is filed after the hearing and is as follows –

"I certify that the petitioner has complied with rule 6.29 by sending notice of adjournment to the debtor [supporting/opposing creditor(s)] on [date] at [address]".

A fresh certificate will be required on each adjourned hearing.

Extension of hearing date of petition

14.6

(14.6.1) Late applications for extension of hearing dates under rule 6.28, and failure to attend on the listed hearing of a petition, will be dealt with as follows–

(1) If an application is submitted less than two clear working days before the hearing date (for example, later than Monday for Thursday, or Wednesday for Monday) the costs of the application will not be allowed under rule 6.28(3).

(2) If the petition has not been served and no extension has been granted by the time fixed for the hearing of the petition, and if no one attends for the hearing, the petition may be dismissed or re-listed for hearing about 21 days later. The court will notify the petitioning creditor's solicitors (or the petitioning creditor in person), and any known supporting or opposing creditors or their

solicitors, of the new date and times. Written evidence should then be filed on behalf of the petitioning creditor explaining fully the reasons for the failure to apply for an extension or to appear at the hearing, and (if appropriate) giving reasons why the petition should not be dismissed.

(3) On the re-listed hearing the court may dismiss the petition if not satisfied it should be adjourned or a further extension granted.

(14.6.2) All applications for an extension should include a statement of the date fixed for the hearing of the petition.

(14.6.3) The petitioning creditor should contact the court (by solicitors or in person) on or before the hearing date to ascertain whether the application has reached the file and been dealt with. It should not be assumed that an extension will be granted.

Substituted service of bankruptcy petitions

14.7

(14.7.1) In most cases evidence that the steps set out in paragraph 13.3.4 have been taken will suffice to justify an order for substituted service of a bankruptcy petition.

Validation orders

14.8

(14.8.1) A person against whom a bankruptcy petition has been presented ('the debtor') may apply to the court after presentation of the petition for relief from the effects of section 284(1) - (3) of the Act by seeking an order that any disposition of his assets or payment made out of his funds, including any bank account (whether it is in credit or overdrawn) shall not be void in the event of a bankruptcy order being made on the petition (a 'validation order').

(14.8.2) Save in exceptional circumstances, notice of the making of the application should be given to (a) the petitioning creditor(s) or other petitioner, (b) any creditor who has given notice to the petitioner of his intention to appear on the hearing of the petition pursuant to r 6.23 1986, (c) any creditor who has been substituted as petitioner pursuant to r 6.30 Insolvency Rules 1986 and (d) any creditor who has carriage of the petition pursuant to r 6.31 Insolvency Rules 1986.

(14.8.3) The application should be supported by a witness statement which, save in exceptional circumstances, should be made by the debtor. If appropriate, supporting evidence in the form of a witness statement from the debtor's accountant should also be produced.

(14.8.4) The extent and contents of the evidence will vary according to the circumstances and the nature of the relief sought, but in a case where the debtor is trading or carrying on business it should include, as a minimum, the following information –

(1) when and to whom notice has been given in accordance with paragraph 14.8.2 above;

(2) brief details of the circumstances leading to presentation of the petition;

(3) how the debtor became aware of the presentation of the petition;

(4) whether the petition debt is admitted or disputed and, if the latter, brief details of the basis on which the debt is disputed;

(5) full details of the debtor's financial position including details of his assets (including details of any security and the amount(s) secured) and liabilities, which should be supported, as far as possible, by documentary evidence, e.g. accounts, draft accounts, management accounts or estimated statement of affairs;

(6) a cash flow forecast and profit and loss projection for the period for which the order is sought;

(7) details of the dispositions or payments in respect of which an order is sought;

(8) the reasons relied on in support of the need for such dispositions or payments to be made;

(9) any other information relevant to the exercise of the court's discretion;

(10) details of any consents obtained from the persons mentioned in paragraph 14.8.2 above (supported by documentary evidence where appropriate) ;

(11) details of any relevant bank account, including its number and the address and sort code of the bank at which such account is held.

(14.8.5) Where an application is made urgently to enable payments to be made which are essential to continued trading (e.g. wages) and it is not possible to assemble all the evidence listed above, the court may consider granting limited relief for a short period, but there must be sufficient evidence to satisfy the court that the interests of creditors are unlikely to be prejudiced.

(14.8.6) Where the debtor is not trading or carrying on business and the application relates only to a proposed sale, mortgage or re-mortgage of the debtor's home evidence of the following will generally suffice –

(1) when and to whom notice has been given in accordance with 14.8.2 above;

(2) whether the petition debt is admitted or disputed and, if the latter, brief details of the basis on which the debt is disputed;

(3) details of the property to be sold, mortgaged or re-mortgaged (including its title number) ;

(4) the value of the property and the proposed sale price, or details of the mortgage or re-mortgage;

(5) details of any existing mortgages or charges on the property and redemption figures;

(6) the costs of sale (e.g. solicitors' or agents' costs) ;

(7) how and by whom any net proceeds of sale (or sums coming into the debtor's hands as a result of any mortgage or re-mortgage) are to be held pending the final hearing of the petition;

(8) any other information relevant to the exercise of the court's discretion;

(9) details of any consents obtained from the persons mentioned in 14.8.2 above (supported by documentary evidence where appropriate) .

(14.8.7) Whether or not the debtor is trading or carrying on business, where the application involves a disposition of property the court will need to be satisfied that any proposed disposal will be at a proper value. Accordingly an independent valuation should be obtained and exhibited to the evidence.

(14.8.8) The court will need to be satisfied by credible evidence that the debtor is solvent and able to pay his debts as they fall due or that a particular transaction or series of transactions in respect of which the order is sought will be beneficial to or will not prejudice the interests of all the unsecured creditors as a class (Denney v John Hudson & Co Ltd [1992] BCLC 901, [1992] BCC 503, CA; Re Fairway Graphics Ltd [1991] BCLC 468).

(14.8.9) A draft of the order sought should be attached to the application.

(14.8.10) Similar considerations to those set out above are likely to apply to applications seeking ratification of a transaction or payment after the making of a bankruptcy order.

15. Applications

15.1 In accordance with rule 13.2(2), in the Royal Courts of Justice the member of court staff in charge of the winding up list has been authorised to deal with applications –

(1) by petitioning creditors to extend the time for hearing petitions (rule 6.28);

(2) by the Official Receiver–
(a) to transfer proceedings from the High Court to a county court (rule 7.13);
(b) to amend the title of the proceedings (rules 6.35 and 6.47).

15.2 In District Registries or a county court such applications must be made to the District Judge.

16. Orders without attendance

16.1 In suitable cases the court will normally be prepared to make orders under Part VIII of the Act (Individual Voluntary Arrangements), without the attendance of the parties, provided there is no bankruptcy order in existence and (so far as is known) no pending petition. The orders are–

(1) A 14 day interim order adjourning the application for 14 days for consideration of the nominee's report, where the papers are in order, and the nominee's signed consent to act includes a waiver of notice of the application or the consent by the nominee to the making of an interim order without attendance.

(2) A standard order on consideration of the nominee's report, extending the interim order to a date seven weeks after the date of the proposed meeting, directing the meeting to be summoned and adjourning to a date about three weeks after the meeting. Such an order may be made without attendance if the nominee's report has been delivered to the court and complies with section 256(1) of the Act and rule 5.11(2) and (3) and proposes a date for the meeting not less than 14 days from that on which the nominee's report is filed in court under rule 5.11 nor more than 28 days from that on which that report is considered by the court under rule 5.13.

(3) A 'concertina' order, combining orders as under (1) and (2) above. Such an order may be made without attendance if the initial application for an interim order is accompanied by a report of the nominee and the conditions set out in (1) and (2) above are satisfied.

(4) A final order on consideration of the chairman's report. Such an order may be made without attendance if the chairman's report has been filed and complies with rule 5.27(1) . The order will record the effect of the chairman's report and may discharge the interim order.

16.2 Provided that the conditions under sub-paragraphs (2) and (4) above are satisfied and that the appropriate report has been lodged with the court in due time the parties need not attend or be represented on the adjourned hearing for consideration of the nominee's report or of the chairman's report (as the case may be) unless they are notified by the court that attendance is required. Sealed copies of the order made (in all four cases as above) will be posted by the court to the applicant or his solicitor and to the nominee.

16.3 In suitable cases the court may also make consent orders without attendance by the parties. The written consent of the parties will be required. Examples of such orders are as follows –

(1) on applications to set aside a statutory demand, orders –

(a) dismissing the application, with or without an order for costs as may be agreed (permission will be given to present a petition on or after the seventh day after the date of the order, unless a different date is agreed) ;

(b) setting aside the demand, with or without an order for costs as may be agreed; or

(2) On petitions where there is a negative list of supporting or opposing creditors in Form 6.21, or a statement signed by or on behalf of the petitioning creditor that no notices have been received from supporting or opposing creditors, orders –

(a) dismissing the petition, with or without an order for costs as may be agreed; or

(b) if the petition has not been served, giving permission to withdraw the petition (with no order for costs) .

(3) On other applications, orders–

(a) for sale of property, possession of property, disposal of proceeds of sale;

(b) giving interim directions;

(c) dismissing the application, with or without an order for costs as may be agreed;

(d) giving permission to withdraw the application, with or without an order for costs as may be agreed.

16.4 If, as may often be the case with orders under subparagraphs 3(a) or (b) above, an adjournment is required, whether generally with liberty to restore or to a fixed date, the order by consent may include an order for the adjournment. If adjournment to a date is requested, a time estimate should be given and the court will fix the first available date and time on or after the date requested.

16.5 The above lists should not be regarded as exhaustive, nor should it be assumed that an order will be made without attendance as requested.

16.6 Applications for consent orders without attendance should be lodged at least two clear working days (and preferably longer) before any hearing date.

16.7 Whenever a document is lodged or a letter sent, the correct case number should be quoted. A note should also be given of the date and time of the next hearing (if any).

17. Bankruptcy restrictions undertakings

17.1 Where a bankrupt has given a bankruptcy restrictions undertaking, the Secretary of State or official receiver must file a copy in court and send a copy to the bankrupt as soon as reasonably practicable (rule 6.250). In addition the Secretary of State must notify the court immediately that the bankrupt has given such an undertaking in order that any hearing date can be vacated.

18. Persons at risk of violence

18.1 Where an application is made pursuant to rule 5.67, 5.68, 5A 18, or 6.235B or otherwise to limit disclosure of information as to a person's current address by reason of the possibility of violence, the relevant application should be accompanied by a witness statement which includes the following –

(1) The grounds upon which it is contended that disclosure of the current address as defined by the Insolvency Rules might reasonably be expected to lead to violence against the debtor or a person who normally resides with him or her as a member of his or her family or where appropriate any other person.

(2) Where the application is made in respect of the address of the debtor, the debtor's proposals with regard to information which may safely be given to potential creditors in order that they can recognise that the debtor is a person who may be indebted to them, in particular the address at which the debtor previously resided or carried on business and the nature of such business.

(3) The terms of the order sought by the applicant by reference to the court's particular powers as set out in the rule under which the application is made and, unless impracticable, a draft of the order sought.

(4) Where the application is made by the debtor in respect of whom a nominee or supervisor has been appointed or against whom a bankruptcy order has been made, evidence of the consent of the nominee/supervisor, or, in the case of bankruptcy, the trustee in bankruptcy, if one has been appointed, and the official receiver if a trustee in bankruptcy has not been appointed. Where such consent is not available the statement must indicate whether such consent has been refused.

The application shall in any event make such person a respondent to the application.

18.2 The application shall be referred to the Registrar who will consider it without a hearing in the first instance but without prejudice to the right of the court to list it for hearing if –

(1) the court is minded to refuse the application;

(2) the consent of any respondent is not attached;

(3) the court is of the view that there is another reason why listing is appropriate.

PART IV – APPEALS

19. Appeals

19.1 An appeal from a decision of a county court (whether made by a District Judge, a Recorder or a Circuit Judge) or of a Registrar in insolvency proceedings lies to a Judge of the High Court.

19.2 An appeal from a decision of a Judge of the High Court, whether at first instance or on appeal, lies to the Court of Appeal.

19.3 A first appeal, whether under 19.1 or 19.2 above, is subject to the permission requirements of CPR Part 52, rule 3.

19.4 An appeal from a decision of a Judge of the High Court which was made on a first appeal requires the permission of the Court of Appeal.

Filing Appeals

19.5

(19.5.1) An appeal from a decision of a Registrar must be filed at the Royal Courts of Justice in London.

(19.5.2) An appeal from a decision of a District Judge sitting in a district registry of the High Court may be filed –

(1) at the Royal Courts of Justice in London; or

(2) in that district registry.

19.6 The court centres at which appeals from decisions of county courts on any particular Circuit must be filed, managed and heard (unless the appeal court otherwise orders) are as follows –

Midland Circuit: Birmingham
North Eastern Circuit: Leeds or Newcastle upon Tyne
Northern Circuit: Manchester or Liverpool
Wales Circuit: Cardiff, Caernarfon or Mold
Western Circuit: Bristol
South Eastern Circuit: Royal Courts of Justice.

19.7 Where the lower court is a county court –

(1) an appeal or application for permission to appeal from a decision of a District Judge will be heard or considered by a High Court Judge or by any person authorised under section 9 of the Senior Courts Act 1981 to act as a judge of the High Court in the Chancery Division;

(2) an appeal or application for permission to appeal from a decision of a Recorder or a Circuit Judge will be heard or considered by a High Court Judge or by a person authorised under paragraphs (1), (2) or (4) of the table in section 9(1) of the Senior Courts Act 1981 to act as a judge of the High Court in the Chancery Division;

(3) other applications in any appeal or application for permission to appeal may be heard or considered and directions may be given by a High Court Judge or by any person authorised under section 9 of the Senior Courts Act 1981 to act as a judge of the High Court in the Chancery Division.

19.8 In the case of appeals from decisions of Registrars or District Judges in the High Court, appeals, applications for permission to appeal and other applications may be heard or considered and directions may be given by a High Court Judge or by any person authorised under section 9 of the Senior Courts Act 1981 to act as a judge of the High Court in the Chancery Division.

(19.9.1) CPR Part 52 and sections I and IV of Practice Direction 52 and its Forms shall, as appropriate, apply to appeals in insolvency proceedings, save as provided below.

(19.9.2) Paragraphs 8.2 to 8.8, 8.13, 8.14 and 8A.1 of Practice Direction 52 shall not apply, and paragraph 8.9 shall apply with the exclusion of the last sentence.

PART V – APPLICATIONS RELATING TO THE REMUNERATION OF APPOINTEES

20. Remuneration of Appointees
Introduction

20.1

(20.1.1) This Part of the Practice Direction applies to any remuneration application made under the Act or the Insolvency Rules.

The objective and guiding principles

20.2

(20.2.1) The objective of this Part of the Practice Direction is to ensure that the remuneration of an appointee which is fixed and approved by the court is fair, reasonable and commensurate with the nature and extent of the work properly undertaken by the appointee in any given case and is fixed and approved by a process which is consistent and predictable.

(20.2.2) Set out below are the guiding principles by reference to which remuneration applications are to be considered both by applicants, in the preparation and presentation of their application, and by the court determining such applications.

(20.2.3) The guiding principles are as follows –

(1) 'Justification'

It is for the appointee who seeks to be remunerated at a particular level and / or in a particular manner to justify his claim and in order to do so the appointee should be prepared to provide full particulars of the basis for and the nature of his claim for remuneration.

(2) 'The benefit of the doubt'

The corollary of guiding principle (1) is that on any remuneration application, if after considering the evidence before it and after having regard to the guiding principles (in particular guiding principle (3)), the matters contained in paragraph 20.4.2 (in particular paragraph 20.4.2 (10)) and the matters referred to in paragraph 20.4.3 (as appropriate) there remains any element of doubt as to the appropriateness, fairness or reasonableness of the remuneration sought or to be fixed (whether arising from a lack of particularity as to the basis for and the nature of the appointee's claim to remuneration or otherwise) such element of doubt should be resolved by the court against the appointee.

(3) 'Professional integrity'

The court should (where this is the case) give weight to the fact that the appointee is a member of a regulated profession and as such is subject to rules and guidance as to professional conduct and the fact that (where this is the case) the appointee is an officer of the court.

(4) 'The value of the service rendered'

The remuneration of an appointee should reflect the value of the service rendered by the appointee, not simply reimburse the appointee in respect of time expended and cost incurred.

(5) 'Fair and reasonable'

The amount of the appointee's remuneration should represent fair and reasonable remuneration for the work properly undertaken or to be undertaken.

(6) 'Proportionality'

(a) 'Proportionality of information'

In considering the nature and extent of the information which should be provided by an appointee in respect of a remuneration application the court, the appointee and any other parties to the application shall have regard to what is proportionate by reference to the amount of remuneration to be fixed, the nature, complexity and extent of the work to be completed (where the application relates to future remuneration) or that has been completed by the appointee and the value and nature of the assets and liabilities with which the appointee will have to deal or has had to deal.

(b) 'Proportionality of remuneration'

The amount of remuneration to be fixed by the court should be proportionate to the nature, complexity and extent of the work to be completed (where the application relates to future remuneration) or that has been completed by the appointee and the value and nature of the assets and/or potential assets and the liabilities and/or potential liabilities with which the appointee will have to deal or has had to deal, the nature and degree of the responsibility to which the appointee has been subject in any given case, the nature and extent of the risk (if any) assumed by the appointee and the efficiency (in respect of both time and cost) with which the appointee has completed the work undertaken.

(7) 'Professional guidance'
In respect of an application for the fixing and approval of the remuneration of an appointee, the appointee may have regard to the relevant and current statements of practice promulgated by any relevant regulatory and professional bodies in relation to the fixing of the remuneration of an appointee. In considering a remuneration application, the court may also have regard to such statements of practice and the extent of compliance with such statements of practice by the appointee.

(8) 'Timing of application'
   The court will take into account whether any application should have been made earlier and if so the reasons for any delay in making it.

Hearing of remuneration applications

20.3

(20.3.1)   On the hearing of the application the court shall consider the evidence then available to it and may either summarily determine the application or adjourn it giving such directions as it thinks appropriate.

(20.3.2)   Whilst the application will normally be determined summarily by a Registrar sitting alone, where it is sufficiently complex, the court may direct that –

(1) an assessor or a Costs Judge prepare a report to the court in respect of the remuneration which is sought to be fixed and approved; and/or

(2) the application be heard by the Registrar sitting with or without an assessor or a Costs Judge or by a Judge sitting with or without an assessor or a Costs Judge.

Relevant criteria and procedure

20.4

(20.4.1)   When considering a remuneration application the court shall have regard to the objective, the guiding principles and all relevant circumstances including the matters referred to in paragraph 20.4.2 and where appropriate paragraph 20.4.3, each of which should be addressed in the evidence placed before the court.

(20.4.2)
   On any remuneration application, the appointee should –

   (1) Provide a narrative description and explanation of –

   (a) the background to, the relevant circumstances of and the reasons for the appointment;

   (b) the work undertaken or to be undertaken in respect of the appointment; the description should be divided, insofar as possible, into individual tasks or categories of task (general descriptions of work, tasks, or categories of task should (insofar as possible) be avoided) ;

   (c) the reasons why it is or was considered reasonable and/or necessary and/or beneficial for such work to be done, giving details of why particular tasks or categories of task were undertaken and why such tasks or categories of task are to be undertaken or have been undertaken by particular individuals and in a particular manner;

   (d) the amount of time to be spent or that has been spent in respect of work to be completed or that has been completed and why it is considered to be fair, reasonable and proportionate;

(e) what is likely to be and has been achieved, the benefits that are likely to and have accrued as a consequence of the work that is to be or has been completed, the manner in which the work required in respect of the appointment is progressing and what, in the opinion of the appointee, remains to be achieved.

(2) Provide details sufficient for the court to determine the application by reference to the criteria which are required to be taken into account by reference to the Insolvency Rules and any other applicable enactments or rules relevant to the fixing of the remuneration.

(3) Provide a statement of the total number of hours of work undertaken or to be undertaken in respect of which the remuneration is sought, together with a breakdown of such hours by individual member of staff and individual tasks or categories of tasks to be performed or that have been performed. Where appropriate, a proportionate level of detail should also be given of –

(a) the tasks or categories of tasks to be undertaken as a proportion of the total amount of work to be undertaken in respect of which the remuneration is sought and the tasks or categories of tasks that have been undertaken as a proportion of the total amount of work that has been undertaken in respect of which the remuneration is sought; and

(b) the tasks or categories of task to be completed by individual members of staff or grade of personnel including the appointee as a proportion of the total amount of work to be completed by all members of staff including the appointee in respect of which the remuneration is sought, or the tasks or categories of task that have been completed by individual members of staff or grade of personnel as a proportion of the total amount of work that has been completed by all members of staff including the appointee in respect of which the remuneration is sought.

(4) Provide a statement of the total amount to be charged for the work to be undertaken or that has been undertaken in respect of which the remuneration is sought which should include–

(a) a breakdown of such amounts by individual member of staff and individual task or categories of task performed or to be performed;

(b) details of the time expended or to be expended and the remuneration charged or to be charged in respect of each individual task or category of task as a proportion (respectively) of the total time expended or to be expended and the total remuneration charged or to be charged.

In respect of an application pursuant to which some or all of the amount of the appointee's remuneration is to be fixed on a basis other than time properly spent, the appointee shall provide (for the purposes of comparison) the same details as are required by this paragraph (4), but on the basis of what would have been charged had he been seeking remuneration on the basis of the time properly spent by him and his staff.

(5) Provide details of each individual to be engaged or who has been engaged in work in respect of the appointment and in respect of which the remuneration is sought, including details of their relevant experience, training, qualifications and the level of their seniority.

(6) Provide an explanation of –

(a) the steps, if any, to be taken or that have been taken by the appointee to avoid duplication of effort and cost in respect of the work to be completed or that has been completed in respect of which the remuneration is sought;

(b) the steps to be taken or that have been taken to ensure that the work to be completed or that has been completed is to be or was undertaken by individuals of appropriate experience and seniority relative to the nature of the work to be or that has been undertaken.

(7) Provide details of the individual rates charged by the appointee and members of his staff in respect of the work to be completed or that has been completed and in respect of which the remuneration is sought. Such details should include –

(a) a general explanation of the policy adopted in relation to the fixing or calculation of such rates and the recording of time spent;

(b) where, exceptionally, the appointee seeks remuneration in respect of time spent by secretaries, cashiers or other administrative staff whose work would otherwise be regarded as an overhead cost forming a component part of the rates charged by the appointee and members of his staff, a detailed explanation as to why such costs should be allowed should be provided.

(8) Where the remuneration application is in respect of a period of time during which the charge-out rates of the appointee and/or members of his staff engaged in work in respect of the appointment have increased, provide an explanation of the nature, extent and reason for such increase and the date when such increase took effect. This paragraph (8) does not apply to applications to which paragraph 20.4.3 applies.

(9) Provide details of any remuneration previously fixed or approved in relation to the appointment (whether by the court or otherwise) including in particular the amounts that were previously sought to be fixed or approved and the amounts that were in fact fixed or approved and the basis upon which such amounts were fixed or approved.

(10) In order that the court may be able to consider the views of any persons who the appointee considers have an interest in the assets that are under his control, provide details of–

(a) what (if any) consultation has taken place between the appointee and those persons and if no such consultation has taken place an explanation as to the reason why;

(b) the number and value of the interests of the persons consulted including details of the proportion (by number and by value) of the interests of such persons by reference to the entirety of those persons having an interest in the assets under the control of the appointee.

(11) Provide such other relevant information as the appointee considers, in the circumstances, ought to be provided to the court.

(20.4.3) This paragraph applies to applications where some or all of the remuneration of the appointee is to be fixed and approved on a basis other than time properly spent. On such applications in addition to the matters referred to in paragraph 20.4.2 (as applicable) the appointee shall –

(1) Provide a full description of the reasons for remuneration being sought by reference to the basis contended for.

(2) Where the remuneration is sought to be fixed by reference to a percentage of the value of the assets which are realised or distributed, provide a full explanation of the basis upon which any

percentage rates to be applied to the values of the assets realised and/or distributed have been chosen.

(3) Provide a statement that to the best of the appointee's belief the percentage rates or other bases by reference to which some or all of the remuneration is to be fixed are similar to the percentage rates or other bases that are applied or have been applied in respect of other appointments of a similar nature.

(4) Provide a comparison of the amount to be charged by reference to the basis contended for and the amount that would otherwise have been charged by reference to the other available bases of remuneration, including the scale of fees in Schedule 6 to the Insolvency Rules.

(20.4.4) If and insofar as any of the matters referred to in paragraph 20.4.2 or 20.4.3 (as appropriate) are not addressed in the evidence, an explanation for why this is the case should be included in such evidence.

(20.4.5) For the avoidance of doubt and where appropriate and proportionate, paragraphs 20.4.2 to 20.4.4 (inclusive) are applicable to applications for the apportionment of remuneration as between a new appointee and a former appointee in circumstances where some or all of the former appointee's remuneration was based upon a set amount under the Insolvency Rules and the former appointee has ceased (for whatever reason) to hold office before the time has elapsed or the work has been completed in respect of which the set amount of remuneration was fixed.

(20.4.6) The evidence placed before the court by the appointee in respect of any remuneration application should include the following documents –

(1) a copy of the most recent receipts and payments account;

(2) copies of any reports by the appointee to the persons having an interest in the assets under his control relevant to the period for which the remuneration sought to be fixed and approved relates;

(3) any schedules or such other documents providing the information referred to in paragraphs 20.4.2 and 20.4.3 where these are likely to be of assistance to the court in considering the application;

(4) evidence of any consultation with those persons having an interest in the assets under the control of appointee in relation to the remuneration of the appointee.

(20.4.7) On any remuneration application the court may make an order allowing payments of remuneration to be made on account subject to final approval whether by the court or otherwise.

(20.4.8) Unless otherwise ordered by the court (or as may otherwise be provided for in any enactment or rules of procedure) the costs of and occasioned by an application for the fixing and/or approval of the remuneration of an appointee, including those of any assessor, shall be paid out of the assets under the control of the appointee.

SCHEDULE 3
PART 12A OF THE INSOLVENCY RULES 1986 RULE 4

"**Part 12A - Provisions of General Effect**

Chapter 1 - The Giving of Notice and the Supply of Documents – General 12A.1 Application

(1) Subject to paragraphs (2) and (3), this Chapter applies where a notice or other document is required to be given, delivered or sent under the Act or the Rules by any person, including an office-holder.

(2) (2) This Chapter does not apply to the service of—

    (a) any petition or application to the court;

    (b) any evidence in support of that petition or application; or

    (c) any order of the court.

(3) This Chapter does not apply to the submission of documents to the registrar of companies.

12A.2 Personal delivery of documents

Personal delivery of a notice or other document is permissible in any case.

12A.3 Postal delivery of documents

Unless in any particular case some other form of delivery is required by the Act, the Rules or an order of the court, a notice or other document may be sent by post in accordance with the rules for postal service in CPR Part 6 and sending by such means has effect as specified in those rules.

12A.4 Non-receipt of notice of meeting

Where in accordance with the Act or the Rules, a meeting of creditors or other persons is summoned by notice, the meeting is presumed to have been duly summoned and held, notwithstanding that not all those to whom the notice is to be given have received it.

12A.5 Notice etc to solicitors

Where under the Act or the Rules a notice or other document is required or authorised to be given, delivered or sent to a person, it may be given, delivered or sent instead to a solicitor authorised to accept delivery on that person's behalf.

Chapter 2

The Giving of Notice and the Supply of Documents by or to Office-holders etc 12A.6 Application

    (1) Subject to paragraphs (2) to (4), this Chapter applies where a notice or other document is required to be given, delivered or sent under the Act or the Rules.

    (2) This Chapter does not apply to the submission of documents to the registrar of companies.

(3) Rules 12A.10 to 12A.13 do not apply to—

    (a) the filing of any notice or other document with the court; or

    (b) the service of a statutory demand.

12A.7 The form of notices and other documents

Subject to any order of the court, any notice or other document required to be given, delivered or sent must be in writing and where electronic delivery is permitted a notice or other document in electronic form is treated as being in writing if a copy of it is capable of being produced in a legible form.

12A.8 Proof of sending etc

(1) Where in any insolvency proceedings a notice or other document is required to be given, delivered or sent by the office-holder, the giving, delivering or sending of it may be proved by means of a certificate that the notice or other document was duly given, delivered or sent.

(2) In the case of the official receiver the certificate may be given by—

    (a) the official receiver; or

    (b) a member of the official receiver's staff.

(3) In the case of a responsible insolvency practitioner the certificate may be given by—

    (a) the practitioner;

    (b) the practitioner's solicitor;

    (c) a partner or an employee of either of them.

(4) In the case of a notice or other document to be given, delivered or sent by a person other than the official receiver or a responsible insolvency practitioner, the giving, delivering or sending of it may be proved by means of a certificate by that person—

    (a) that the notice or document was given, delivered or sent by that person, or

    (b) that another person (named in the certificate) was instructed to give, deliver or send it.

(5) A certificate under this Rule may be endorsed on a copy or specimen of the notice or document to which it relates.

12A.9 Authentication

(1) A document or information given, delivered or sent in hard copy form is sufficiently authenticated if it is signed by the person sending or supplying it.

(2) A document or information given, delivered or sent in electronic form is sufficiently authenticated—

    (a) if the identity of the sender is confirmed in a manner specified by the recipient, or

(b) where no such manner has been specified by the recipient, if the communication contains or is accompanied by a statement of the identity of the sender and the recipient has no reason to doubt the truth of that statement.

12A.10 Electronic delivery in insolvency proceedings—general

(1) Unless in any particular case some other form of delivery is required by the Act or the Rules or an order of the court and subject to paragraph (3), a notice or other document may be given, delivered or sent by electronic means provided that the intended recipient of the notice or other document has—

(a) consented (whether in the specific case or generally) to electronic delivery (and has not revoked that consent); and

(b) provided an electronic address for delivery.

(2) In the absence of evidence to the contrary, a notice or other document is presumed to have been delivered where—

(a) the sender can produce a copy of the electronic message which—

(i) contained the notice or other document, or to which the notice or other document was attached, and

(ii) shows the time and date the message was sent; and

(b) that electronic message contains the address supplied under paragraph (1)(b).

(3) A message sent electronically is deemed to have been delivered to the recipient no later than 9.00am on the next business day after it was sent.

12A.11 Electronic delivery by office-holders

(1) Where an office-holder gives, sends or delivers a notice or other document to any person by electronic means, the notice or document must contain or be accompanied by a statement that the recipient may request a hard copy of the notice or document and specifying a telephone number, e-mail address and postal address which may be used to request a hard copy.

(2) Where a hard copy of the notice or other document is requested, it must be sent within 5 business days of receipt of the request by the office-holder.

(3) An office-holder must not require a person making a request under paragraph (2) to pay a fee for the supply of the document.

12A.12 Use of websites by office-holder

(1) This Rule applies for the purposes of sections 246B and 379B.

(2) An office-holder required to give, deliver or send a document to any person may (other than in a case where personal service is required) satisfy that requirement by sending that person a notice—

(a) stating that the document is available for viewing and downloading on a website;

(b) specifying the address of that website together with any password necessary to view and download the document from that site; and

(c) containing a statement that the person to whom the notice is given, delivered or sent may request a hard copy of the document and specifying a telephone number, e-mail address and postal address which may be used to request a hard copy.

(3) Where a notice to which this Rule applies is sent, the document to which it relates must—

(a) be available on the website for a period of not less than 3 months after the date on which the notice is sent; and

(b) must be in such a format as to enable it to be downloaded from the website within a reasonable time of an electronic request being made for it to be downloaded.

(4) Where a hard copy of the document is requested it must be sent within 5 business days of the receipt of the request by the office-holder.

(5) An office-holder must not require a person making a request under paragraph (4) to pay a fee for the supply of the document.

(6) Where a document is given, delivered or sent to a person by means of a website in accordance with this Rule, it is deemed to have been delivered—

(a) when the document was first made available on the website, or

(b) if later, when the notice under paragraph (2) was delivered to that person.

12A.13 Special provision on account of expense as to website use

(1) Where the court is satisfied that the expense of sending notices in accordance with Rule 12A.12 would, on account of the number of persons entitled to receive them, be disproportionate to the benefit of sending notices in accordance with that Rule, it may order that the requirement to give, deliver or send a relevant document to any person may (other than in a case where personal service is required) be satisfied by the office-holder sending each of those persons a notice—

(a) stating that all relevant documents will be made available for viewing and downloading on a website;

(b) specifying the address of that website together with any password necessary to view and download a relevant document from that site; and

(c) containing a statement that the person to whom the notice is given, delivered or sent may at any time request that hard copies of all, or specific, relevant documents are sent to that person, and specifying a telephone number, e-mail address and postal address which may be used to make that request.

(2) A document to which this Rule relates must—

(a) be available on the website for a period of not less than 12 months from the date when it was first made available on the website or, if later, from the date upon which the notice was sent, and

(b) must be in such a format as to enable it to be downloaded from the website within a reasonable time of an electronic request being made for it to be downloaded.

(3) Where hard copies of relevant documents have been requested, they must be sent by the office-holder—

(a) within 5 business days of the receipt by the office-holder of the request to be sent hard copies, in the case of relevant documents first appearing on the website before the request was received, or

(b) within 5 business days from the date a relevant document first appears on the website, in all other cases.

(4) An office-holder must not require a person making a request under paragraph (3) to pay a fee for the supply of the document.

(5) Where a relevant document is given, delivered or sent to a person by means of a website in accordance with this Rule, it is deemed to have been delivered—

(a) when the relevant document was first made available on the website, or

(b) if later, when the notice under paragraph (1) was delivered to that person.

(6) In this Rule a relevant document means any document which the office-holder is first required to give, deliver or send to any person after the court has made an order under paragraph (1).

12A.14 Electronic delivery of insolvency proceedings to courts

(1) Except where paragraph (2) applies or the requirements of paragraph (3) are met, no petition, application, notice or other document may be delivered or made to a court by electronic means.

(2) This paragraph applies where electronic delivery of documents to a court is permitted by another Rule.

(3) The requirements of this paragraph are—

(a) the court provides an electronic working scheme for the proceedings to which the document relates; and

(b) the electronic communication is—

(i) delivered and authenticated in a form which complies with the requirements of the scheme;

(ii) sent to the electronic address provided by the court for electronic delivery of those proceedings; and

(iii) accompanied by any payment due to the court in respect of those proceedings made in a manner which complies with the requirements of the scheme.

(4) In this Rule "an electronic working scheme" means a scheme permitting insolvency proceedings to be delivered electronically to the court set out in a practice direction.

(5) Under paragraph (3) an electronic communication is to be treated as delivered to the court at the time it is recorded by the court as having been received.

12A.15 Notice etc to joint office-holders

Where there are joint office-holders in insolvency proceedings, delivery of a document to one of them is to be treated as delivery to all of them.

Chapter 3
Service of Court Documents 12A.16 Application

(1) Subject to paragraph (2), this Chapter applies in relation to the service of—

    (a) petitions,

    (b) applications,

    (c) documents relating to petitions or applications, and

    (d) court orders,

which are required to be served by any provision of the Act or the Rules ("court documents").

(2) Rules 12A.17 to 12A.19 do not apply to the service of—

    (a) a winding-up petition,

    (b) a bankruptcy petition,

    (c) any document relating to such a petition, or

    (d) an administration, winding-up or bankruptcy order.

(3) For the purpose of the application by this Chapter of CPR Part 6 to the service of documents in insolvency proceedings—

    (a) an application commencing insolvency proceedings (including a winding-up petition, a bankruptcy petition or an administration application), or

    (b) an application within insolvency proceedings against a respondent, is to be treated as a claim form.

12A.17 Application of CPR Part 6 to service of court documents within the jurisdiction

Except where different provision is made in these Rules, CPR Part 6 applies in relation to the service of court documents within the jurisdiction with such modifications as the court may direct.

12A.18 Service of orders staying proceedings

(1) This Rule applies where the court makes an order staying any action, execution or other legal process against—

    (a) the property of a company; or

(b) the property or person of an individual debtor or bankrupt.

(2) Service within the jurisdiction of such an order as is mentioned in paragraph (1) may be effected by sending a sealed copy of the order to the address for service of the claimant or other party having the carriage of the proceedings to be stayed.

12A.19 Service on joint office-holders

Where there are joint office-holders in insolvency proceedings, service on one of them is to be treated as service on all of them.

12A.20 Application of CPR Part 6 to service of court documents outside the jurisdiction

CPR Part 6 applies to the service of court documents outside the jurisdiction with such modifications as the court may direct.

Amendment of Rule 13.13. (Definition of certain expressions used generally)

14. In Rule 13.13.–

(a) for paragraph (1) substitute–

"(1) "Business day" means any day other than a Saturday, a Sunday, Christmas Day, Good Friday or a day which is a bank holiday in any part of Great Britain under or by virtue of the Banking and Financial Dealings Act 1971(a) except in Rules 1.7., 4.10., 4.11., 4.16., 4.20., 5.10. and 6.23. where "business day" shall include any day which is a bank holiday in Scotland but not in England and Wales."; and

(b) for paragraph (6) substitute–

"(6) "Practice direction" means a direction as to the practice and procedure of any court within the scope of the CPR.

(7) "Prescribed order of priority" means the order of priority of payments laid down by Chapter 20 of Part 4 of the Rules, or Chapter 23 of Part 6.".

The Insolvent Partnerships Order 1994

The Lord Chancellor, in exercise of the powers conferred on him by section 420(1) and (2) of the Insolvency Act 1986(1) and section 21(2) of the Company Directors Disqualification Act 1986(2) and of all other powers enabling him in that behalf, with the concurrence of the Secretary of State, hereby makes the following Order:—

(1) 1986 c. 45.

(2) 1986 c. 46; the amendments to section 21(2) made by the Companies Act 1989 (c.40) are not relevant for the purposes of this Order.

Citation, commencement and extent

1.—(1) This Order may be cited as the Insolvent Partnerships Order 1994 and shall come into force on 1st December 1994.

(2) This Order—

    (a) in the case of insolvency proceedings in relation to companies and partnerships, relates to companies and partnerships which the courts in England and Wales have jurisdiction to wind up; and

    (b) in the case of insolvency proceedings in relation to individuals, extends to England and Wales only.

(3) In paragraph (2) the term "insolvency proceedings" has the meaning ascribed to it by article 2 below.

Interpretation: definitions

2.— (1) In this Order, except in so far as the context otherwise requires—

"the Act" means the Insolvency Act 1986;

"agricultural charge" has the same meaning as in the Agricultural Credits Act 1928(1) ;

"agricultural receiver" means a receiver appointed under an agricultural charge;

"corporate member" means an insolvent member which is a company;

"the court", in relation to an insolvent partnership, means the court which has jurisdiction to wind up the partnership;

"individual member" means an insolvent member who is an individual;

"insolvency order" means—

    (a) in the case of an insolvent partnership or a corporate member, a winding-up order; and

    (b) in the case of an individual member, a bankruptcy order;

"insolvency petition" means, in the case of a petition presented to the court—

    (a) against a corporate member, a petition for its winding up by the court;

    (b) against an individual member, a petition for a bankruptcy order to be made against that individual, where the petition is presented in conjunction with a petition for the winding up of the partnership by the court as an unregistered company under the Act;

"insolvency proceedings" means any proceedings under the Act, this Order or the Insolvency Rules 1986(2)

"insolvent member" means a member of an insolvent partnership, against whom an insolvency petition is being or has been presented;

"joint bankruptcy petition" means a petition by virtue of article 11 of this Order;

"joint debt" means a debt of an insolvent partnership in respect of which an order is made by virtue of Part IV or V of this Order;

"joint estate" means the partnership property of an insolvent partnership in respect of which an order is made by virtue of Part IV or V of this Order;

"joint expenses" means expenses incurred in the winding up of an insolvent partnership or in the winding up of the business of an insolvent partnership and the administration of its property;

"limited partner" has the same meaning as in the Limited Partnerships Act 1907(3) ;

"member" means a member of a partnership and any person who is liable as a partner within the meaning of section 14 of the Partnership Act 1890(4) ;

"officer", in relation to an insolvent partnership, means—

(a) a member; or

(b) a person who has management or control of the partnership business;

"partnership property" has the same meaning as in the Partnership Act 1890;

"postponed debt" means a debt the payment of which is postponed by or under any provision of the Act or of any other enactment;

"responsible insolvency practitioner" means—

(a) in winding up, the liquidator of an insolvent partnership or corporate member; and

(b) in bankruptcy, the trustee of the estate of an individual member, and in either case includes the official receiver when so acting;

"separate debt" means a debt for which a member of a partnership is liable, other than a joint debt;

"separate estate" means the property of an insolvent member against whom an insolvency order has been made;

"separate expenses" means expenses incurred in the winding up of a corporate member, or in the bankruptcy of an individual member; and

"trustee of the partnership" means a person authorised by order made by virtue of article 11 of this Order to wind up the business of an insolvent partnership and to administer its property.

(2) The definitions in paragraph (1) , other than the first definition, shall be added to those in section 436 of the Act.

(3) References in provisions of the Act applied by this Order to any provision of the Act so applied shall, unless the context otherwise requires, be construed as references to the provision as so applied.

(4) Where, in any Schedule to this Order, all or any of the provisions of two or more sections of the Act are expressed to be modified by a single paragraph of the Schedule, the modification includes the combination of the provisions of those sections into the one or more sections set out in that paragraph.

Interpretation: expressions appropriate to companies

3.— (1) This article applies for the interpretation in relation to insolvent partnerships of expressions appropriate to companies in provisions of the Act and of the Company Directors Disqualification Act 1986 applied by this Order, unless the contrary intention appears.

(2) References to companies shall be construed as references to insolvent partnerships and all references to the registrar of companies shall be omitted.

(3) References to shares of a company shall be construed—

(a) in relation to an insolvent partnership with capital, as references to rights to share in that capital; and

(b) in relation to an insolvent partnership without capital, as references to interests—

(i) conferring any right to share in the profits or liability to contribute to the losses of the partnership, or

(ii) giving rise to an obligation to contribute to the debts or expenses of the partnership in the event of a winding up.

(4) Other expressions appropriate to companies shall be construed, in relation to an insolvent partnership, as references to the corresponding persons, officers, documents or organs (as the case may be) appropriate to a partnership.

Voluntary arrangement of insolvent partnership

4.— (1) The provisions of Part I of the Act shall apply in relation to an insolvent partnership, those provisions being modified in such manner that, after modification, they are as set out in Schedule 1 to this Order.

(2) For the purposes of the provisions of the Act applied by paragraph (1), the provisions of the Act specified in paragraph (3) below, insofar as they relate to company voluntary arrangements, shall also apply in relation to insolvent partnerships.

(3) The provisions referred to in paragraph (2) are—

(a) section 233 in Part VI,

(b) Part VII, with the exception of section 250,

(c) Part XII,

(d) Part XIII,

(e) sections 411, 413, 414 and 419 in Part XV, and

(f) Parts XVI to XIX.

Voluntary arrangements of members of insolvent partnership

5.—(1) Where insolvency orders are made against an insolvent partnership and an insolvent member of that partnership in his capacity as such, Part I of the Act shall apply to corporate members and Part VIII to individual members of that partnership, with the modification that any reference to the creditors of the company or of the debtor, as the case may be, includes a reference to the creditors of the partnership.

(2) Paragraph (1) is not to be construed as preventing the application of Part I or (as the case may be) Part VIII of the Act to any person who is a member of an insolvent partnership (whether or not a winding-up order has been made against that partnership) and against whom an insolvency order has not been made under this Order or under the Act.

Administration Order in relation to insolvent partnership

6. (1) The provisions of Part II of the Act shall apply in relation to an insolvent partnership, certain of those provisions being modified in such manner that, after modification, they are as set out in Schedule 2 to this Order.

(2) For the purposes of the provisions of the Act applied by paragraph (1), the provisions of the Act specified in paragraph (3) below, insofar as they relate to administration orders, shall also apply in relation to insolvent partnerships.

(3) The provisions referred to in paragraph (2) are—

(a) section 212 in Part IV,

(b) Part VI,

(c) Part VII, with the exception of section 250,

(d) Part XIII,

(e) sections 411, 413, 414 and 419 in Part XV, and

(f) Parts XVI to XIX.

Winding up of insolvent partnership as unregistered company on petition of creditor etc. where no concurrent petition presented against member

7. (1) Subject to paragraph (2) below, the provisions of Part V of the Act shall apply in relation to the winding up of an insolvent partnership as an unregistered company on the petition of a creditor, of a responsible insolvency practitioner or of the Secretary of State, where no insolvency petition is presented by the petitioner against a member or former member of that partnership in his capacity as such.

(2) Certain of the provisions referred to in paragraph (1) are modified in their application in relation to insolvent partnerships which are being wound up by virtue of that paragraph in such manner that, after modification, they are as set out in Part I of Schedule 3 to this Order.

(3) The provisions of the Act specified in Part II of Schedule 3 to this Order shall apply as set out in that Part for the purposes of section 221(5) of the Act, as modified by Part I of that Schedule.

Winding up of insolvent partnership as unregistered company on creditor's petition where concurrent petitions presented against one or more members

8. (1) Subject to paragraph (2) below, the provisions of Part V of the Act (other than sections 223 and 224), shall apply in relation to the winding up of an insolvent partnership as an unregistered company on a creditor's petition where insolvency petitions are presented by the petitioner against the partnership and against one or more members or former members of the partnership in their capacity as such.

(2) Certain of the provisions referred to in paragraph (1) are modified in their application in relation to insolvent partnerships which are being wound up by virtue of that paragraph in such manner that, after modification, they are as set out in Part I of Schedule 4 to this Order.

(3) The provisions of the Act specified in Part II of Schedule 4 to this Order shall apply as set out in that Part for the purposes of section 221(5) of the Act, as modified by Part I of that Schedule.

(4) The provisions of the Act specified in paragraph (5) below, insofar as they relate to winding up of companies by the court in England and Wales on a creditor's petition, shall apply in relation to the winding up of a corporate member or former corporate member (in its capacity as such) of an insolvent partnership which is being wound up by virtue of paragraph (1).

(5) The provisions referred to in paragraph (4) are—

   (a) Part IV,

   (b) Part VI,

   (c) Part VII, and

   (d) Parts XII to XIX.

(6) The provisions of the Act specified in paragraph (7) below, insofar as they relate to the bankruptcy of individuals in England and Wales on a petition presented by a creditor, shall apply in relation to the bankruptcy of an individual member or former individual member (in his capacity as such) of an insolvent partnership which is being wound up by virtue of paragraph (1).

(7) The provisions referred to in paragraph (6) are—

   (a) Part IX (other than sections 269, 270, 287 and 297), and

   (b) Parts X to XIX.

(8) Certain of the provisions referred to in paragraphs (4) and (6) are modified in their application in relation to the corporate or individual members or former corporate or individual members of insolvent partnerships in such manner that, after modification, they are as set out in Part II of Schedule 4 to this Order.

(9) The provisions of the Act applied by this Article shall further be modified so that references to a corporate or individual member include any former such member against whom an insolvency petition is being or has been presented by virtue of this Article.

Part V - Winding Up of Unregistered Companies

220 Meaning of "unregistered company".

For the purposes of this Part "unregistered company" includes any association and any company, with the exception of a company registered under the Companies Act 2006 in any part of the United Kingdom.

221 Winding up of unregistered companies.

(1) Subject to the provisions of this Part, any unregistered company may be wound up under this Act; and all the provisions of this Act about winding up apply to an unregistered company with the exceptions and additions mentioned in the following subsections.

(2) If an unregistered company has a principal place of business situated in Northern Ireland, it shall not be wound up under this Part unless it has a principal place of business situated in England and Wales or Scotland, or in both England and Wales and Scotland.

(3) For the purpose of determining a court's winding-up jurisdiction, an unregistered company is deemed—

(a) to be registered in England and Wales or Scotland, according as its principal place of business is situated in England and Wales or Scotland, or

(b) if it has a principal place of business situated in both countries, to be registered in both countries;

and the principal place of business situated in that part of Great Britain in which proceedings are being instituted is, for all purposes of the winding up, deemed to be the registered office of the company.

(4) No unregistered company shall be wound up under this Act voluntarily except in accordance with the EC Regulation.

(5) The circumstances in which an unregistered company may be wound up are as follows—

(a) if the company is dissolved, or has ceased to carry on business, or is carrying on business only for the purpose of winding up its affairs;

(b) if the company is unable to pay its debts;

(c) if the court is of opinion that it is just and equitable that the company should be wound up.

(6) A petition for winding up a trustee savings bank may be presented by the Trustee Savings Banks Central Board or by a commissioner appointed under section 35 of the Trustee Savings Banks Act 1981 as well as by any person authorised under Part IV of this Act to present a petition for the winding up of a company.

On such day as the Treasury appoints by order under section 4(3) of the Trustee Savings Banks Act 1985, this subsection ceases to have effect and is hereby repealed.

(7) In Scotland, an unregistered company which the Court of Session has jurisdiction to wind up may be wound up by the court if there is subsisting a floating charge over property comprised in

the company's property and undertaking, and the court is satisfied that the security of the creditor entitled to the benefit of the floating charge is in jeopardy.

For this purpose a creditor's security is deemed to be in jeopardy if the court is satisfied that events have occurred or are about to occur which render it unreasonable in the creditor's interests that the company should retain power to dispose of the property which is subject to the floating charge.

222 Inability to pay debts: unpaid creditor for £750 or more.

(1) An unregistered company is deemed (for the purposes of section 221) unable to pay its debts if there is a creditor, by assignment or otherwise, to whom the company is indebted in a sum exceeding £750 then due and—

(a) the creditor has served on the company, by leaving at its principal place of business, or by delivering to the secretary or some director, manager or principal officer of the company, or by otherwise serving in such manner as the court may approve or direct, a written demand in the prescribed form requiring the company to pay the sum due, and

(b) the company has for 3 weeks after the service of the demand neglected to pay the sum or to secure or compound for it to the creditor's satisfaction.

(2) The money sum for the time being specified in subsection (1) is subject to increase or reduction by regulations under section 417 in Part XV; but no increase in the sum so specified affects any case in which the winding-up petition was presented before the coming into force of the increase.

223 Inability to pay debts: debt remaining unsatisfied after action brought.

An unregistered company is deemed (for the purposes of section 221) unable to pay its debts if an action or other proceeding has been instituted against any member for any debt or demand due, or claimed to be due, from the company, or from him in his character of member, and—

(a) notice in writing of the institution of the action or proceeding has been served on the company by leaving it at the company's principal place of business (or by delivering it to the secretary, or some director, manager or principal officer of the company, or by otherwise serving it in such manner as the court may approve or direct), and

(b) the company has not within 3 weeks after service of the notice paid, secured or compounded for the debt or demand, or procured the action or proceeding to be stayed or sisted, or indemnified the defendant or defender to his reasonable satisfaction against the action or proceeding, and against all costs, damages and expenses to be incurred by him because of it.

224 Inability to pay debts: other cases.

(1) An unregistered company is deemed (for purposes of section 221) unable to pay its debts—

(a) if in England and Wales execution or other process issued on a judgment, decree or order obtained in any court in favour of a creditor against the company, or any member of it as such, or any person authorised to be sued as nominal defendant on behalf of the company, is returned unsatisfied;

(b) if in Scotland the induciae of a charge for payment on an extract decree, or an extract registered bond, or an extract registered protest, have expired without payment being made;

(c) if in Northern Ireland a certificate of unenforceability has been granted in respect of any judgment, decree or order obtained as mentioned in paragraph (a) ;

(d) if it is otherwise proved to the satisfaction of the court that the company is unable to pay its debts as they fall due.

(2) An unregistered company is also deemed unable to pay its debts if it is proved to the satisfaction of the court that the value of the company's assets is less than the amount of its liabilities, taking into account its contingent and prospective liabilities.

117 High Court and County Court jurisdiction.

(1) The High Court has jurisdiction to wind up any company registered in England and Wales.

(2) Where the amount of a company's share capital paid up or credited as paid up does not exceed £120,000, then (subject to this section) the county court of the district in which the company's registered office is situated has concurrent jurisdiction with the High Court to wind up the company.

(3) The money sum for the time being specified in subsection (2) is subject to increase or reduction by order under section 416 in Part XV.

(4) The Lord Chancellor may, with the concurrence of the Lord Chief Justice, by order] in a statutory instrument exclude a county court from having winding-up jurisdiction, and for the purposes of that jurisdiction may attach its district, or any part thereof, to any other county court, and may by statutory instrument revoke or vary any such order.

In exercising the powers of this section, the Lord Chancellor shall provide that a county court is not to have winding-up jurisdiction unless it has for the time being jurisdiction for the purposes of Parts VIII to XI of this Act (individual insolvency) .

(5) Every court in England and Wales having winding-up jurisdiction has for the purposes of that jurisdiction all the powers of the High Court; and every prescribed officer of the court shall perform any duties which an officer of the High Court may discharge by order of a judge of that court or otherwise in relation to winding up.

(6) For the purposes of this section, a company's "registered office" is the place which has longest been its registered office during the 6 months immediately preceding the presentation of the petition for winding up.

(7) This section is subject to Article 3 of the EC Regulation (jurisdiction under EC Regulation) .]

(8) The Lord Chief Justice may nominate a judicial office holder (as defined in section 109(4) of the Constitutional Reform Act 2005) to exercise his functions under this section.

PRACTICE DIRECTION: DIRECTORS DISQUALIFICATION PROCEEDINGS
7. SERVICE OF THE CLAIM FORM

7.1 Service of claim forms in disqualification proceedings will be the responsibility of the claimant and will not be undertaken by the court.

7.2 The claim form shall be served by the claimant on the defendant. It may be served by sending it by first class post to his last known address; and the date of service shall, unless the contrary is shown, be deemed to be the 7th day following that on which the claim form was posted. CPR r. 6.7(1) shall be modified accordingly. Otherwise Sections I and II of CPR Part 6 apply12.

7.3 Where any claim form or order of the court or other document is required under any disqualification proceedings to be served on any person who is not in England and Wales, the court may order service on him to be effected within such time and in such manner as it thinks fit, may require such proof of service as it thinks fit, and may give such directions as to acknowledgment of service as it thinks fit. Section III of CPR Part 6 shall not apply.

7.4 The claim form served on the defendant shall be accompanied by an acknowledgement of service.

15. SERVICE OF DISQUALIFICATION ORDERS

15.1 Service of disqualification orders will be the responsibility of the claimant.

19. PROVISIONS APPLICABLE TO APPLICATIONS UNDER SECTIONS 7(2) AND 7(4) OF THE ACT

19.1 Headings: Every claim form and notice by which such an application is begun and all witness statements affidavits, notices and other documents in relation thereto must be entitled in the matter of the company or companies in question and in the matter of the Act.

19.2 Service:

(1) Service of claim forms and application notices seeking orders under section 7(2) or 7(4) of the Act will be the responsibility of the applicant and will not be undertaken by the court.

(2) Where any claim form, application notice or order of the court or other document is required in any application under section 7(2) or section 7(4) of the Act to be served on any person who is not in England and Wales, the court may order service on him to be effected within such time and in such manner as it thinks fit, may require such proof of service as it thinks fit, and may make such directions as to acknowledgment of service as it thinks fit. Section III of CPR Part 6 does not apply.

26. SERVICE

26.1 Service of application notices in disqualification proceedings will be the responsibility of the parties and will not be undertaken by the court.

26.2 Where any application notice or order of the court or other document is required in any application to be served on any person who is not in England and Wales, the court may order service on him to be effected within such time and in such manner as it thinks fit, and may also require such proof of service as it thinks fit. Section III of CPR Part 6 does not apply.

LIMITED LIABILITY PARTNERSHIPS ACT 2000
2000 CHAPTER 12

1 Limited liability partnerships.

(1) There shall be a new form of legal entity to be known as a limited liability partnership.

(2) A limited liability partnership is a body corporate (with legal personality separate from that of its members) which is formed by being incorporated under this Act; and—

(a) in the following provisions of this Act (except in the phrase "oversea limited liability partnership") , and

(b) in any other enactment (except where provision is made to the contrary or the context otherwise requires) ,

references to a limited liability partnership are to such a body corporate.

(3) A limited liability partnership has unlimited capacity.

(4) The members of a limited liability partnership have such liability to contribute to its assets in the event of its being wound up as is provided for by virtue of this Act.

(5) Accordingly, except as far as otherwise provided by this Act or any other enactment, the law relating to partnerships does not apply to a limited liability partnership.

(6) The Schedule (which makes provision about the names and registered offices of limited liability partnerships) has effect.

Incorporation
2 Incorporation document etc.

(1) For a limited liability partnership to be incorporated—

(a) two or more persons associated for carrying on a lawful business with a view to profit must have subscribed their names to an incorporation document,

(b) there must have been delivered to the registrar either the incorporation document or a copy authenticated in a manner approved by him, and

(c) there must have been so delivered a statement in a form approved by the registrar, made by either a solicitor engaged in the formation of the limited liability partnership or anyone who subscribed his name to the incorporation document, that the requirement imposed by paragraph (a) has been complied with.

(2) The incorporation document must—

(a) be in a form approved by the registrar (or as near to such a form as circumstances allow),

(b) state the name of the limited liability partnership,

(c) state whether the registered office of the limited liability partnership is to be situated in England and Wales, in Wales or in Scotland,

(d) state the address of that registered office,

(e) state the name and address of each of the persons who are to be members of the limited liability partnership on incorporation, and

(f) either specify which of those persons are to be designated members or state that every person who from time to time is a member of the limited liability partnership is a designated member.

(2A) Where a confidentiality order, made under section 723B of the Companies Act 1985 as applied to a limited liability partnerships, is in force in respect of any individual named as a member of a limited liability partnership under subsection (2) that subsection shall have effect as if the reference to the address of the individual were a reference to the address for the time being notified by him under the Limited Liability Partnerships (Particulars of Usual Residential Address) (Confidentiality Orders) Regulations 2002 to any limited liability partnership of which he is a member or if he is not such a member either the address specified in his application for a confidentiality order or the address last notified by him under such a confidentiality order as the case may be.

(2B) Where the incorporation document or a copy of such delivered under this section includes an address specified in reliance on subsection (2A) there shall be delivered with it or the copy of it a statement in a form approved by the registrar containing particulars of the usual residential address of the member whose address is so specified.]

(3) If a person makes a false statement under subsection (1) (c) which he—

(a) knows to be false, or

(b) does not believe to be true,

he commits an offence.

(4) A person guilty of an offence under subsection (3) is liable—

(a) on summary conviction, to imprisonment for a period not exceeding six months or a fine not exceeding the statutory maximum, or to both, or

(b) on conviction on indictment, to imprisonment for a period not exceeding two years or a fine, or to both.

14 Insolvency and winding up.

(1) Regulations shall make provision about the insolvency and winding up of limited liability partnerships by applying or incorporating, with such modifications as appear appropriate, Parts I to IV, VI and VII of the Insolvency Act 1986.

(2) Regulations may make other provision about the insolvency and winding up of limited liability partnerships, and provision about the insolvency and winding up of oversea limited liability partnerships, by—

(a) applying or incorporating, with such modifications as appear appropriate, any law relating to the insolvency or winding up of companies or other corporations which would not otherwise have effect in relation to them, or

(b) providing for any law relating to the insolvency or winding up of companies or other corporations which would otherwise have effect in relation to them not to apply to them or to apply to them with such modifications as appear appropriate.

(3) In this Act "oversea limited liability partnership" means a body incorporated or otherwise established outside Great Britain and having such connection with Great Britain, and such other features, as regulations may prescribe.

15 Application of company law etc.

Regulations may make provision about limited liability partnerships and oversea limited liability partnerships (not being provision about insolvency or winding up) by—

(a) applying or incorporating, with such modifications as appear appropriate, any law relating to companies or other corporations which would not otherwise have effect in relation to them,

(b) providing for any law relating to companies or other corporations which would otherwise have effect in relation to them not to apply to them or to apply to them with such modifications as appear appropriate, or

(c) applying or incorporating, with such modifications as appear appropriate, any law relating to partnerships.

2001 No. 1090
PARTNERSHIP
LIMITED LIABILITY PARTNERSHIPS
Limited Liability Partnerships Regulations 2001

PART I - CITATION, COMMENCEMENT AND INTERPRETATION

Citation and commencement

1. These Regulations may be cited as the Limited Liability Partnerships Regulations 2001 and shall come into force on 6th April 2001.

Interpretation

2. In these Regulations—

"the 1985 Act" means the Companies Act 1985;

"the 1986 Act" means the Insolvency Act 1986;

"the 2000 Act" means the Financial Services and Markets Act 2000;

"devolved", in relation to the provisions of the 1986 Act, means the provisions of the 1986 Act which are listed in Schedule 4 and, in their application to Scotland, concern wholly or partly, matters which are set out in Section C.2 of Schedule 5 to the Scotland Act 1998 as being exceptions to the reservations made in that Act in the field of insolvency;

"limited liability partnership agreement", in relation to a limited liability partnership, means any agreement express or implied between the members of the limited liability partnership or between the limited liability partnership and the members of the limited liability partnership which determines the mutual rights and duties of the members, and their rights and duties in relation to the limited liability partnership;

"the principal Act" means the Limited Liability Partnerships Act 2000; and

"shadow member", in relation to limited liability partnerships, means a person in accordance with whose directions or instructions the members of the limited liability partnership are accustomed to act (but so that a person is not deemed a shadow member by reason only that the members of the limited partnership act on advice given by him in a professional capacity).

PART III - COMPANIES ACT 1985 AND COMPANY DIRECTORS DISQUALIFICATION ACT 1986

Application of the remainder of the provisions of the 1985 Act and of the provisions of the Company Directors Disqualification Act 1986 to limited liability partnerships

4. (1) The provisions of the 1985 Act specified in the first column of Part I of Schedule 2 to these Regulations shall apply to limited liability partnerships, except where the context otherwise requires, with the following modifications—

(a) references to a company shall include references to a limited liability partnership;

(b) references to the Companies Acts shall include references to the principal Act and regulations made thereunder;

(c) references to the Insolvency Act 1986 shall include references to that Act as it applies to limited liability partnerships by virtue of Part IV of these Regulations;

(d) references in a provision of the 1985 Act to other provisions of that Act shall include references to those other provisions as they apply to limited liability partnerships by virtue of these Regulations;

PART IV - WINDING UP AND INSOLVENCY

Application of the 1986 Act to limited liability partnerships

5. (1) Subject to paragraphs (2) and (3), the following provisions of the 1986 Act, shall apply to limited liability partnerships—

(a) Parts I, II, III, IV, VI and VII of the First Group of Parts (company insolvency; companies winding up),

(b) the Third Group of Parts (miscellaneous matters bearing on both company and individual insolvency; general interpretation; final provisions).

(2) The provisions of the 1986 Act referred to in paragraph (1) shall apply to limited liability partnerships, except where the context otherwise requires, with the following modifications—

(a) references to a company shall include references to a limited liability partnership;

(b) references to a director or to an officer of a company shall include references to a member of a limited liability partnership;

(c) references to a shadow director shall include references to a shadow member;

(d) references to the 1985 Act, the Company Directors Disqualification Act 1986, the Companies Act 1989 or to any provisions of those Acts or to any provisions of the 1986 Act shall include references to those Acts or provisions as they apply to limited liability partnerships by virtue of the principal Act;

(e) references to the memorandum of association of a company and to the articles of association of a company shall include references to the limited liability partnership agreement of a limited liability partnership;

(f) the modifications set out in Schedule 3 to these Regulations; and

(g) such further modifications as the context requires for the purpose of giving effect to that legislation as applied by these Regulations.

(3) In the application of this regulation to Scotland, the provisions of the 1986 Act referred to in paragraph (1) shall not include the provisions listed in Schedule 4 to the extent specified in that Schedule.

PART 5 - AN LLP'S MEMBERS
CHAPTER 1 - REGISTER OF MEMBERS

Requirements for register of members

18. Sections 162 to 165 apply to LLPs, modified so that they read as follows—

"Register of members

162. (1) Every LLP must keep a register of its members.

(2) The register must contain the required particulars (see sections 163 and 164) of each person who is a member of the LLP.

(3) The register must be kept available for inspection—

(a) at the LLP's registered office, or

(b) at a place specified in Part 2 of the Companies (Company Records) Regulations 2008

(4) The LLP must give notice to the registrar—

(a) of the place at which the register is kept available for inspection, and

(b) of any change in that place,

unless it has at all times been kept at the LLP's registered office.

(5) The register must be open to the inspection—

(a) of any member of the LLP without charge, and

(b) of any other person on payment of the fee prescribed by regulation 2(a) of the Companies (Fees for Inspection of Company Records) Regulations 2008.

(6) If default is made in complying with subsection (1), (2) or (3) or if default is made for 14 days in complying with subsection (4), or if an inspection required under subsection (5) is refused, an offence is committed by—

(a) the LLP, and

(b) every designated member of the LLP who is in default.

(7) A person guilty of an offence under this section is liable on summary conviction to a fine not exceeding level 5 on the standard scale and, for continued contravention, a daily default fine not exceeding one-tenth of level 5 on the standard scale.

(8) In the case of a refusal of inspection of the register, the court may by order compel an immediate inspection of it.

Particulars of members to be registered: individuals

163. (1) An LLP's register of members must contain the following particulars in the case of an individual—

(a) name and any former name;

(b) a service address;

(c) the country or state (or part of the United Kingdom) in which he is usually resident;

(d) date of birth;

(e) whether he is a designated member.

(2) For the purposes of this section "name" means a person's Christian name (or other forename) and surname, except that in the case of—

(a) a peer, or

(b) an individual usually known by a title,

the title may be stated instead of his Christian name (or other forename) and surname or in addition to either or both of them.

(3) For the purposes of this section a "former name" means a name by which the individual was formerly known for business purposes.

Where a person is or was formerly known by more than one such name, each of them must be stated.

(4) It is not necessary for the register to contain particulars of a former name in the following cases—

(a) in the case of a peer or an individual normally known by a British title, where the name is one by which the person was known previous to the adoption of or succession to the title;

(b) in the case of any person, where the former name—

(i) was changed or disused before the person attained the age of 16 years, or

(ii) has been changed or disused for 20 years or more.

(5) A person's service address may be stated to be "The LLP's registered office".

Particulars of members to be registered: corporate members and firms

164. An LLP's register of members must contain the following particulars in the case of a body corporate, or a firm that is a legal person under the law by which it is governed—

(a) corporate or firm name;

(b) registered or principal office;

(c) in the case of an EEA company to which the First Company Law Directive (68/151/EEC) applies, particulars of—

(i) the register in which the company file mentioned in Article 3 of that Directive is kept (including details of the relevant state) , and

(ii) the registration number in that register;

(d) in any other case, particulars of—

(i) the legal form of the company or firm and the law by which it is governed, and

(ii) if applicable, the register in which it is entered (including details of the state) and its registration number in that register;

(e) whether it is a designated member.

Register of members' residential addresses

165. (1) Every LLP must keep a register of members' residential addresses.

(2) The register must state the usual residential address of each of the LLP's members.

(3) If a member's usual residential address is the same as his service address (as stated in the LLP's register of members), the register of members' residential addresses need only contain an entry to that effect.

This does not apply if his service address is stated to be "The LLP's registered office".

(4) If default is made in complying with this section, an offence is committed by—

    (a) the LLP, and

    (b) every designated member of the LLP who is in default.

(5) A person guilty of an offence under this section is liable on summary conviction to a fine not exceeding level 5 on the standard scale and, for continued contravention, a daily default fine not exceeding one-tenth of level 5 on the standard scale.

(6) This section applies only to members who are individuals, not where the member is a body corporate or a firm that is a legal person under the law by which it is governed.".

CHAPTER 2 - MEMBERS' RESIDENTIAL ADDRESSES: PROTECTION FROM DISCLOSURE

Members' residential addresses: protection from disclosure

19. Sections 240 to 246 apply to LLPs, modified so that they read as follows—

"Protected information

240.   (1) This Chapter makes provision for protecting, in the case of an LLP member who is an individual—

    (a) information as to his usual residential address;

    (b) the information that his service address is his usual residential address.

(2) That information is referred to in this Chapter as "protected information".

(3) Information does not cease to be protected information on the individual ceasing to be a member of the LLP.

References in this Chapter to a member include, to that extent, a former member.

Protected information: restriction on use or disclosure by LLP

241.   (1) An LLP must not use or disclose protected information about any of its members, except—

    (a) for communicating with the member concerned,

    (b) in order to comply with any requirement of this Act or of the Limited Liability Partnerships Act 2000 (c. 12) as to particulars to be sent to the registrar, or

    (c) in accordance with section 244 (disclosure under court order).

(2) Subsection (1) does not prohibit any use or disclosure of protected information with the consent of the member concerned.

Service addresses

75. Sections 1139 to 1142 apply to LLPs, modified so that they read as follows—

"Service of documents on LLP

1139. (1) A document may be served on an LLP by leaving it at, or sending it by post to, the LLP's registered office.

(2) Where an LLP registered in Scotland or Northern Ireland carries on business in England and Wales, the process of any court in England and Wales may be served on the LLP by leaving it at, or sending it by post to, the LLP's principal place of business in England and Wales, addressed to the manager or a designated member in England and Wales of the LLP.

Where process is served on an LLP under this subsection, the person issuing out the process must send a copy of it by post to the LLP's registered office.

Service of documents on members and others

1140. (1) A document may be served on—

(a) a member of an LLP, or

(b) a person appointed in relation to an LLP as a judicial factor (in Scotland) ,

by leaving it at, or sending it by post to, the member's or factor's registered address.

(2) This section applies whatever the purpose of the document in question.

(3) For the purposes of this section a person's "registered address" means any address for the time being shown as a current address in relation to that person in the part of the register available for public inspection.

(4) If notice of a change of that address is given to the registrar, a person may validly serve a document at the address previously registered until the end of the period of 14 days beginning with the date on which notice of the change is registered.

(5) Service may not be effected by virtue of this section at an address if notice has been registered of the cessation of the membership or (as the case may be) termination of the appointment in relation to which the address was registered and the address is not a registered address of the person concerned in relation to any other appointment.

(6) Nothing in this section shall be read as affecting any enactment or rule of law under which permission is required for service out of the jurisdiction.

Service addresses

1141. (1) In this Act a "service address", in relation to a person, means an address at which documents may be effectively served on that person.

   (2) The service address must be a place where—

   (a) the service of documents can be effected by physical delivery; and

   (b) the delivery of documents is capable of being recorded by the obtaining of an acknowledgment of delivery.

Requirement to give service address

1142. Any obligation under this Act to give a person's address is, unless otherwise expressly provided, to give a service address for that person.".

CCR Order 28 - Judgment Summonses
Application for judgment summons
Rule 1

(1) An application for the issue of a judgment summons may be made to the court for the district in which the debtor resides or carries on business or, if the summons is to issue against two or more persons jointly liable under the judgment or order sought to be enforced, in the court for the district in which any of the debtors resides or carries on business.

(2) The judgment creditor shall make his application by filing a request in that behalf certifying the amount of money remaining due under the judgment or order, the amount in respect of which the judgment summons is to issue and that the whole or part of any instalment due remains unpaid.

(3) The judgment creditor must file with the request all written evidence on which he intends to rely.

Mode of service

Rule 2

(1) Subject to paragraph (2), a judgment summons shall be served personally on every debtor against whom it is issued.

(2) Where the judgment creditor or the judgment creditor's solicitor gives a certificate for postal service in respect of a debtor residing or carrying on business within the district of the court, the judgment summons will, unless the district judge otherwise directs, be served on that debtor by the court sending it to the debtor by first-class post at the address stated in the request for the judgment summons and, unless the contrary is shown, the date of service is deemed to be the seventh day after the date on which the judgment summons was sent to the debtor.

(3) Where a judgment summons has been served on a debtor in accordance with paragraph (2), no order of commitment shall be made against him unless –

   (a) he appears at the hearing; or

   (b) it is made under section 110(2) of the Act.

(4) The written evidence on which the judgment creditor intends to rely must be served with the judgment summons.

Time for service
Rule 3

(1) The judgment summons and written evidence must be served not less than 14 days before the day fixed for the hearing.

(2) A notice of non-service will be sent pursuant to CPR rule 6.18 in respect of a judgment summons which has been sent by post under rule 2(2) and has been returned to the court undelivered.

(3) CPR rules 7.5 and 7.6 apply, with the necessary modifications, to a judgment summons as they apply to a claim form.

***

SECTION 5 – FAMILY COURT PROCEEDINGS

THE CHILDREN ACT 1989

Introduction

The Children Act 1989 Guidance and Regulations: Volume 1 – Court Orders
Author: Department for Children, Schools and Families
Publisher: TSO (The Stationery Office)

'The Children Act 1989 Guidance and Regulations: Volume 1 – Court Orders' provides guidance – primarily addressed to local authorities and their staff – about the court related provisions set out in the Children Act 1989 (ISBN 0105441899) . The term 'court related provisions' refers to court orders, several kinds of which are discussed in this publication. Court orders are only to be made in cases where they will contribute positively to the welfare of the child.

This publication will be of interest to Directors of Children's Services and other senior local authority managers, who together ensure that local authorities exercise their functions under the Children Act 1989 in relation to safeguarding and promoting the welfare of children.

Contents include:

- Chapter 1 – Introduction
- Chapter 2 – Parental Responsibility and Private Law Aspects of the Act
- Chapter 3 – Care and Supervision Orders
- Chapter 4 – Protection of Children
- Chapter 5 – Secure Accommodation Orders
- Annex 1 – Letter Before Proceedings: Template Letter
- Annex 2 – The Public Law Outline: Guide to Case Management in Public Law Proceedings
- Annex 3 – The Public Law Outline - Flowcharts: Court Proceedings and Pre-Proceedings
- References and Internet Links

This publication came into effect on 1 April 2008 and has replaced the 1991 edition (ISBN 9780113213719) .

Proceedings can be brought in the High Court, County Court and in the Magistrates Court. The act is not governed by the CPR; it is mainly covered by two sets of rules:

- The Family Proceedings Rules 1991(S.I. 1991 No.1247) relates to High Court and County Court proceedings. These rules can be found in Volume 2 of the Civil Court Practice 1999.

- The Family Proceedings Courts (Children Act 1989) Rules 1991 (S.I. 1991 No.1395) covers proceedings in the Magistrates Courts.

Service

Rule 4.8 of the Family Proceedings Rules 1991 reads:-

4.8. (1) Subject to the requirement in rule 4.5 (1) (b) of personal service, where service of a document is required under this Act (and not by a provision to which section 105 (8) (service of notice or other document under the act applies) it may be effected –

> (a) If the person to be served is not known by the person serving to be acting by a solicitor
>
>> (i) By delivering it to him personally, or
>>
>> (i) By delivering it at, or be sending it by first class post to his residence or his last known residence.

Note: Rule 4.6 (1) (b) refers to an order transferring proceedings from a Magistrate's Court. Section 105 (8) provides for service of any document under the act by personal service or by post. It does seem that personal service is often preferred by either instructing solicitors or certain Judges.

Rule 8 under the Family Proceedings Court (Children Act 1989) Rules 1991 covers the service of documents and is substantially the same as under the Family Proceedings Rules 1991.

8. - (1) Where service of a document is required by these Rules (and not by a provision to which section 105(8) (service of notice or other document under the Act) applies) it may be effected–

> (a) if the person to be served is not known by the person serving to be acting by solicitor–
>
>> (i) by delivering it to him personally, or
>>
>> (ii) by delivering it at, or by sending it by first-class post to, his residence or his last known residence, or
>
> (b) if the person to be served is known by the person serving to be acting by solicitor–
>
>> (i) by delivering the document at, or sending it by first-class post to, the solicitor's address for service,
>>
>> (ii) where the solicitor's address for service includes a numbered box at a document exchange, by leaving the document at that document exchange or at a document exchange which transmits documents on every business day to that document exchange, or
>>
>> (iii) by sending a legible copy of the document by facsimile transmission to the solicitor's office.

(2) In this rule, "first-class post" means first-class post which has been pre-paid or in respect of which pre-payment is not required.

(3) Where a child who is a party to any relevant proceedings is required by these Rules to serve a document, service shall be effected by–

    (a) the solicitor acting for the child,

    (b) where there is no such solicitor, the guardian ad litem, or

    (c) where there is neither such a solicitor nor a guardian ad litem, the justices' clerk.

(4) Service of any document on a child shall, subject to any direction of the justices' clerk or the court, be effected by service on–

    (a) the solicitor acting for the child,

    (b) where there is no such solicitor, the guardian ad litem, or

    (c) where there is neither such a solicitor nor a guardian ad litem, with leave of the justices' clerk or the court, the child.

(5) Where the justices' clerk or the court refuses leave under paragraph (4) (c) , a direction shall be given under paragraph (8) .

(6) A document shall, unless the contrary is proved, be deemed to have been served–

    (a) in the case of service by first-class post, on the second business day after posting, and

    (b) in the case of service in accordance with paragraph (1) (b) (ii) , on the second business day after the day on which it is left at the document exchange.

(7) At or before the first directions appointment in, or hearing of, relevant proceedings, whichever occurs first, the applicant shall file a statement that service of–

    (a) a copy of the application has been effected on each respondent, and

    (b) notice of the proceedings has been effected under rule 4(3) ;

and the statement shall indicate–

        (i) the manner, date, time and place of service, or

        (ii) where service was effected by post, the date, time and place of posting.

(8) In any relevant proceedings, the justices' clerk or the court may direct that a requirement of these Rules to serve a document shall not apply or shall be effected in such manner as the justices' clerk or court directs.

Note: "child"

    (a) means, in relation to any relevant proceedings, subject to sub-paragraph (b) , a person under the age of 18 with respect to whom the proceedings are brought, and

    (b) Where paragraph 16(1) of Schedule 1 applies, also includes a person who has reached the age of 18;

The documents most likely to be sent for service are proceedings under Section 8 of the Children Act 1989. These documents are applications for;

- **A Residence Order**: to determine with whom the child shall live.

- **A Contact Order:** to determine which person the child shall visit, stay with or have contact with.

- **A Prohibited Steps Order:** which enables the Court to order no specific steps shall be taken in regard to the child.

- **A Specific Issue Order:** whereby the Court may direct on any specific question in regard to the child.

All the above applications are made on Form CHA 10.

The document in each of the above cases comprise a set of pages (Form CHA 10) with Notice of Directions Appointment which bears a hearing date and two forms which comprise the Respondent's Reply (Form CHA 10a). A set of such documents is required to be served in respect of each child and a further set is required to accompany the Statement of Service. The notice of Directions Appointment bearing the hearing date is in the middle of such set of documents and should be brought to the attention of the person served; alternatively place as the first page.

Computation of Time

Family Proceedings Rules 1991 s.1 1991/1247

1.5 (1) Any period of time fixed by these rules, or by any rules applied by these rules, or by any decree, judgment, order or direction for doing any act shall be reckoned in accordance with the following provisions of this rule.

(2) Where the act is required to be done not less than a specified period before a specified date, the period starts immediately after the date on which the act is done and ends immediately before the specified date.

(3) Where the act is required to be done within a specified period after or from a specified date, the period starts immediately after that date.

(4) Where, apart from this paragraph, the period in question, being a period of seven days or less, would include a day which is not a business day, that day shall be excluded.

(5) Where the time so fixed for doing an act in the Court Office expires on a day on which the office is closed, and for that reason the act cannot be done on that day, the act shall be in time if done on the next day on which the office is open.

(6) In these rules "business day" means any day other than -

(a) a Saturday, Sunday, Christmas Day or Good Friday, or

(b) a bank holiday under the Banking and Financial Dealings Act 1971(d), in England and Wales.

Despite the rule in regard to a Statement of Service some solicitors (or Courts) have been requesting affidavits of service. The general form of affidavit can be adapted if necessary and the copy documents exhibited.

Proof Of Service:

Rule 4.18 reads:-

The applicant is required to file a statement of service or if necessary an affidavit of service before, or no later than the time of the first appointment for directions or the hearing. The statement must confirm that a copy of the application has been served on each respondent, and every person to whom notice of the proceedings must be given has been notified. The statement must also indicate the date and time and place of posting. A Practice Form CHA 72 is available in District Registries, County Courts and the Principal Registry of the Family Division, and may also be used in Magistrates Courts.

Time For Service:

The required time for service of documents is set out in an Appendix as follows:-

Provision under which Proceedings brought.	Minimum of days prior to hearing for service.
Proceedings under Section 8 Parental responsibility: 4 (1) (a) : 4 (3) Appointment of Guardian: 5 (1) ; 6 (7) Change of Child's Name: 13 (1) Family Assistance Order: 16 (6) Care Orders: 33 (7) Schedule 2 para 19 (1) Financial Provision: Schedule 1 Discharge Orders: Schedule 14 para 11 (3) : Schedule 14 para 16 (5)	14 days
Education Supervision Orders: 36 (1) Discharge & Variation Orders: 39 (1) : 39 (2) : 39 (3) : 39 (4) Child Assessment Order: 43 (1) Supervision Order: Schedule 3 para. 6 (3) : 15 (2) : 17 (1)	7 days
Care & Supervision Order: Parental Contact Order: Interim Order: Section 31 34 (2) : 34 (3) : 34 (4) : 34 (9) 38 (8) (b)	3 days
Child Assessment Order 43 (12)	2 days

Secure Accommodation Order: Section 25 Emergency Protection Order: 44 (1) : 44 (9) (b) 45 (4) : 45 (8) : 46 (7) : 48 (9) Recovery of Abducted Children: 50 (1) Search Warrant: 102 (1)	1 day

This Schedule is as amended by Family Proceedings (Amendment No.2) Rules 1992. The figures relate to the sections of the Children Act 1989.

When calculating the days for service any period of 7 days or less should exclude Saturday, Sunday, Bank Holidays, Christmas Day, Boxing Day, Good Friday.

Child Support Act 1991 (1991 Chapter 48)

The Child Support Act 1991 follows the Children Act 1989 and came into force in April 1993. It provides the means by which maintenance payments for children are assessed, collected and enforced after a breakdown of a relationship. Decisions are to be taken by an administrative agency rather than the Courts and to be known as Child Support Officers with provision for reviews and appeals.

The Act is to be regulated by the following Statutory Instruments:

- **Child Support (Information & Disclosure) Regulations 1992 (S.I. No 1812)**
- **Child Support (Arrears, Interest & Adjustment of Maintenance) Regulations 1992 (S.I. No 1816)**
- **Child Support (Maintenance Assessment Procedure) Regulations 1992 (S.I. No 1813)**
- **Child Support (Maintenance Assessment & Special Cases) Regulations 1992 (S.I. No 1815)**

All available from HMSO quoting the S.I. number.

The Act provides for collection and enforcement by way of deduction from earnings; liability order; enforcement by way of distress and enforcement in the County Court. Time will tell whether this Act will bring any work for the Process Server or Bailiff.

DIVORCE/DISSOLUTION/JUDICIAL SEPARATION PROCESS

Introduction

Practice in the Family Division of the High Court Divorce Registry is mainly covered by the Family Proceedings Rules 1991 and the Matrimonial Causes Act 1973 and more thoroughly dealt with in Raydens Law & Practice on Divorce and Family Matters (usually known as Rayden on Divorce) Published by Butterworth - as well as being found in other text books.

Petition

Service of a Divorce/Dissolution/Judicial Separation Petition is covered by the Family Proceedings Rules 1991.

A Petition must be served personally or by post on every respondent or co-respondent. Where service has been attempted by post and the Acknowledgment of Service has not been returned duly signed personal service is necessary.

Personal service is therefore only necessary when the Petition has been sent by post and when the Acknowledgment of Service has not been returned duly signed; where speedy service is necessary; where the solicitor feels it is unlikely the Acknowledgment of Service will be returned; when the Petitioner is unable to identify the Respondent's signature or when the Petitioner is blind.

A Petitioner **may not** effect service of a Petition but may be present at the time of service to identify the Respondent.

Family Proceedings Rules 1991

Service of Petition Rule 2.9 reads:

(1) Subject to the provision of this rule and rules 9.3 and 10.6 a copy of every petition shall be served personally or by post on every respondent or co-respondent.

(2) Service may be effected

(a) where the person to be served is a person under disability within the meaning of rule 9.1 through the Petitioner, and

(b) in any other case, through the Court or, if the Petitioner so requests, through the Petitioner.

(3) Personal service shall in no case be effected by the Petitioner himself.

(5) For the purposes of the foregoing paragraphs, a copy of a petition shall be deemed to be duly served if;

(a) an acknowledgement of service in Form M6 is signed by the party to be served or by a solicitor on his behalf and is returned to the Court office, and

(b) where the form purports to be signed by the respondent, his signature is proved at the hearing or, where the cause is undefended in the affidavit filed by the Petitioner under rule 2.24 (3).

Documents to be served on the Respondent:

1. A copy of the Petition

2. Notice of Proceedings (Form M 5)

3. Form of Acknowledgement of Service (Form M 6)

and where applicable

4. Statement of arrangements for children (Form M 4)

5. Notice of issue of Legal Aid Certificate.

Documents to be Served on the Co-Respondent:

1. A copy of the Petition

2. Notice of proceedings

3. Form of Acknowledgment of Service

Service Out Of The Jurisdiction:

Rule 10.6 of The Family Proceedings Rules 1991 reads:

1. Any document in family proceedings may be served out of England and Wales without leave.

3. The documents need not be served personally on the person required to be served so long as it is served in accordance with the law of the country in which is effected.

Identification Of Respondent:

Where personal service of the petition is effected and signature is obtained from the Respondent on the Acknowledgment of Service identification is by way of the Petitioner identifying the Respondent's signature. Where the respondent declines to sign the Acknowledgment of Service at the time of personal service some other means of identification should be available. The usual method is for the process server to be in possession of a photograph of the respondent. The photograph should be a recent one and should be sufficiently large and clear for the respondent to be identified. Care should be taken when using a "group" photograph and the Respondent should be clearly identified by describing his position in the photograph rather than marking the photograph. Such photograph must be exhibited to the affidavit of service.

Other means of identification have proved acceptable such as production of Passport or Driving Licence or Security Pass with photograph, details of which should be recited in the Affidavit of Service.

If no identification is available then the Petitioner should be present to identify the Respondent or the Petitioner should attend at a later date and identify the person who has been served as the Respondent. These facts must also be cited in the Affidavit of Service.

In the case of a third party it is not necessary to establish their identity in the same way although a verbal admission should be obtained and there is no harm in endeavouring to obtain evidence of identification at the time of service.

Minors

Rule 9.3 of the Family Proceedings Act 1991 reads:-

9.3(1) Where a document to which rule 2.9 applies (Divorce Petition) is required to be served on a person under disability within the meaning of the last foregoing rule, it shall be served

(a) in the case of a minor who is not also a patient, on his father or guardian or, if he has no father or guardian, on the person with whom he resides or in whose care he is.

Patient:

Rule 9.1 reads:

(1) in this part "patient" means a person who, by reason of mental disorder within the meaning of the Mental Health Act 1983, is incapable of managing and administering his property and affairs; "persons under disability" means a person who is a patient or a minor.

Service on a patient is set out in rule 9.3

(b) in the case of a patient:

(i) on the person (if any) who is authorised under Part VII to conduct in the name of the patient or on his behalf the proceedings in connection with which the document is to be served, or

(ii) if there is no person so authorised, on the official Solicitor if he has consented under order 9.2 (4) to be the Guardian ad Litem of the patient, or

(iii) in any other case, on the person with whom the patient resides or in whose care he is

Affidavit Of Service

An Affidavit of Service is required in cases where personal service has been carried out and where no signature has been obtained to the Acknowledgment of Service. It is important to include means of identification of the respondent.

Substituted Service:

When personal service of a petition is not possible an Order for Substituted Service can be obtained and such application is supported by an affidavit showing the attempts made to effect personal service.

Such order could provide for service by post or by way of advertisement in the press or in some cases to dispense with service.

Enquiries should be made at all known addresses; of neighbours (naming them and their addresses) of relatives and friends; place of employment clubs or associations; bankers and all other likely sources where all information concerning the party might be obtained.

Rule 2.9 (9) reads:

(9) An application for leave to substitute some other mode of service for the modes of service prescribed by paragraph (1) or to substitute notice of the proceedings by advertisement or otherwise, shall be made ex parte (without notice) by lodging an affidavit setting out the ground on which the application is made, and the form of any advertisement shall be settled by the District Judge.

(11) Where in the opinion of the District Judge it is impracticable to serve a party in accordance with any of the foregoing paragraphs or it is otherwise necessary or expedient to dispense with service of a copy of a petition on the respondent or on the other person, the District Judge may make an order dispensing with such service.

Judgment Summons:

Rule 7.4 (5) reads:

(5) Every Judgment summons shall be in Form M17 and shall be served on the debtor personally not less than 10 days before the hearing and at the time of service there shall be paid or tendered to the debtor a sum reasonably sufficient to cover his expenses in travelling to and from the Court at which he is summoned to appear.

Where service has not been effected a successive Judgment Summons may be issued within one year from the original date of issue.

An affidavit is required and a true copy of the Judgment Summons is exhibited.

Witness Summons

Rule 2.30 (1) reads:

(1) A witness summons in a cause pending in a divorce in the County Court may be issued in that Court or in the Court of trial at which the cause is to be tried.

(2) A witness summons in a cause pending in the High Court may issue out of -

    (a) the registry in which the cause is proceeding, or

    (b) if the cause is to be tried at the Royal Courts of Justice, the Principal Registry, or

    (c) if the cause is to be tried at a divorce town, the registry for that town

The FDR refer to witness statements and subpoenas. However under the CPR the term subpoena is abolished in favour of witness summons.

Personal service of a witness summons is required. It has been usual for a plain copy of the witness summons to be served, retaining the sealed copy to endorse as to service and to obtain from the witness a receipt on the back.

The practice followed the procedure adopted in regard to a writ of summons when a plain copy used to be served and the original writ retained. Recently only the original witness summons has sometimes been sent for service. In such cases it is perhaps prudent to take a copy of the witness summons to endorse and obtain a receipt from the witness on the back. Whilst, service of a sealed copy document is necessary in regard to "originating process" a witness summons is not an "originating process".

The rules in regard to Conduct Money apply and service should be effected within 12 weeks of the date of issue and not less than 4 days (or such other period that may be fixed) before the date of hearing.

CPR 34.2 states:

(1) A Witness Summons is a document issued by the Court requiring a witness to:

> a) attend Court and give evidence; or
>
> b) produce documents to the Court.

(2) A Witness Summons must be in the relevant practice form.

(3) There must be a separate Witness Summons for each Witness.

(4) A Witness Summons may require a Witness to produce documents to the Court either:-

> a) on the date fixed for a hearing; or
>
> b) on such date as the Court may direct.

(5) The only documents that a Summons under this rule can require a person to produce before a hearing are documents which that person could be required to produce at the hearing.

Service Out Of England And Wales:

Family Proceedings Rules 1991; Rule 10.6 reads:

(10) Any document in Family Proceedings may be served out of England and Wales without leave either in the manner prescribed by these rules or

> (a) where the proceedings are pending in the High Court, in accordance with RSC Order 11, rules 5 and 6 (which relate to the service of a claim abroad) or
>
> (b) where the proceedings are pending in a divorce County Court, in accordance with CCR Order 8, rules 8 to 10 (which relate to the service of process abroad) .

NOTE: CCR Order 8 has been abolished by the CPR, but by virtue of CPR Schedule 2 RSC O11.10, CPR Schedule 2 RSC O11 now applies to County Court Proceedings.

Family Proceedings Rules 1991

Under Part X Rule 10.1 reads:-

10.1 The provision of this Part apply to all family proceedings, but have effect subject to the provision of any other Part of these rules.

Applications under the Family Law Act 1996 are "family proceedings". All applications under the Children Act 1989 - with the exception of the emergency provisions in Part V - are applications in Family Proceedings.

Service on person acting in person

10.3 (1) Subject to paragraph (3) and to any other direction or order, where a document is required by these rules to be sent to any person who is acting in person, service shall be effected by sending the document by first class post to the address given by him or, if he has not given an address for service, to his last known address.

(2) Subject to paragraph (3) where no other mode of service is prescribed, directed or ordered, service may additionally be effected by delivering the document to him or by leaving it at the address specified in paragraph (1) .

(3) Where it appears to the District Judge that it is impracticable to deliver the document to the person to be served and that, if the document were left at, or sent by post to, the address specified in paragraph (1) , it would be unlikely to reach him, the District Judge may dispense with service of the document.

Generally

Changes have taken place in the rules governing work carried out in the Divorce Process mainly through the introduction of the Children Act 1989 under which proceedings in regard to children of the family can be dealt with in the High Court, County Court or Magistrate's Court.

New rules cover this law namely:

The Family Proceedings Rules 1991

(Covering High Court & County Court proceedings)

and

Family Proceedings Court (Children Act) Rules 1991 (covering proceedings in the Magistrates Court)

In April 1993 The Child Support Act came into force and relates to the maintenance of children now provided by the Children Act. Under this Act a large number of cases concerning the upbringing of children passed from the Courts into the hands of the Child Support Agency.

The Family Law Act 1996

The most important remedies for domestic violence are therefore those to be found in Part IV of the Family Law Act 1996, which comes into force in October 1997. It repeals and replaces the earlier remedies provided in the Domestic Violence and Matrimonial Proceedings Act 1976, ss.16-18 of the Domestic Proceedings and Magistrates' Courts Act 1978, and the Matrimonial Homes Act 1983, providing two specific types of order and extending the categories of persons entitled to apply for an order. The county court and the High Court retain their existing powers to grant injunctions, but only in support of some existing right.

Orders available

Where there is domestic violence, the courts may intervene to halt such violence. The court may order two forms of injunctions: a non-molestation order (section 42) restrains the defendant from interfering with the plaintiff; and an occupation order (section 33- 41) requires one party to vacate the home and not to return to it.

There is also now the Domestic Violence, Crime and Victims Act 2004 which seeks to give greater protection to victims of domestic violence. However, at the same time, the Human Rights Act 1998 will be relevant to the law on domestic violence. Particularly relevant provisions of the ECHR are Articles 1, 3, 6, 8, and 14.

Occupation Order

Occupation orders under the 1996 Act vary according to whether or not the applicant is entitled to occupy the property, and according to the applicant's relationship to the other party or parties.

Where the applicant is entitled to occupy the matrimonial home, either by virtue of the general law as a beneficial co-owner or by virtue of "matrimonial home rights", she may apply for an occupation order under s.33 against anyone with whom she is associated. An "associated person" is defined in s.62(3) as including any present or former spouse, cohabitant or recent fiancé, anyone who lives or has lived in the same household (other than by way of employment or contract), any close relative, anyone now or previously sharing parental responsibility for a child, or anyone party to the same matrimonial proceedings.

An occupation order made under s.33(3) enforces the applicant's right to enter and occupy the home and may also exclude the respondent from part or all of the home or from an area around it, suspending or restricting or terminating his own matrimonial home rights or his exercise of any other rights of occupation as may be necessary. An occupation order continues effective indefinitely, or for such period as the court may decide, but it is seen as a temporary measure until permanent arrangements can be made. These permanent arrangements may include a property adjustment order where the occupants are married and seek separation or divorce, but where they are unmarried cohabitants the court has no powers to alter the ownership or occupation rights over the property.

Non-Molestation Order

The second type of order made available by the 1996 Act is a non-molestation order, which prohibits the respondent from molesting the applicant or a relevant child. Application may be made by any "associated person" (as defined above), but a court seized of other family proceedings involving the respondent has power to make such an order of its own motion, without a formal application, if it thinks it appropriate. Almost 20 000 non-molestation orders were made by County Courts in 1996 (under the pre-1996 Act law), and an unknown number made by the Family Proceedings Courts - this is about six times the number of ouster orders (now replaced by occupation orders).

Under s.42(5), the court considering whether to make a non-molestation order (and if so, in what terms) must have regard to all the circumstances including the need to secure the health, safety and well-being of the applicant and/or any relevant child. A non-molestation order may prohibit molestation generally (which certainly includes violence but covers other conduct too) and/or identify particular prohibited acts. The order remains in effect for a specific period or indefinitely, as the court decides.

Ex-parte

Under s.45, the court may make an occupation or non-molestation order ex parte, without prior notice to the respondent, where it considers it just and convenient to do so. Before making such an order the court must consider any risk of significant harm done by the respondent to the applicant or a relevant child if the order is not made immediately, the likelihood that the applicant will be deterred or prevented from pursuing the application, and any reason to think that the respondent knows of the proceedings but is deliberately evading service. If the court does make an ex parte order, then it must soon afterwards give the respondent a chance to make representations as soon as just and convenient at a full hearing.

THE ARMED FORCES (SERVICE OF PROCESS IN MAINTENANCE PROCEEDINGS) REGULATIONS 2009

Explanatory Note (This note is not part of the Regulations)

These Regulations make provision in relation to the service of process in connection with proceedings for a maintenance order or for ancillary proceedings in connection with such an order when the person to be served is a "relevant person" within the meaning of section 355(3) (a) of the Armed Forces Act 2006.

Regulation 3 provides that service may be effected by serving the process on the commanding officer of the relevant person.

Regulation 4 provides for the circumstances in which the commanding officer may certify to the court that service is of no effect: when the relevant person is on or under orders for active service and the commanding officer considers that it would not be reasonably practicable for the relevant person to comply with the requirements set out in the process or when the relevant person is absent without leave.

Regulation 5 provides that when proceedings for a maintenance order or ancillary proceedings in connection with such an order are in a court of summary jurisdiction service of such process may only be effected if the relevant person is within the United Kingdom.

Regulation 6 provides for transitional provisions. The Secretary of State in exercise of the powers conferred by section 355 of the Armed Forces Act 2006(a), makes the following Regulations:

Citation and commencement

1. These Regulations may be cited as the Armed Forces (Service of Process in Maintenance Proceedings) Regulations 2009 and shall come into force on 31st October 2009.

Interpretation

2.- (1) In these Regulations—
"the Act" means the Armed Forces Act 2006; "maintenance order" means an order made by a court in the United Kingdom or Channel Islands or registered in or confirmed by such a court under the provisions of the Maintenance Orders (Facilities for Enforcement) Act 1920(b) or registered in such a court under Part 1 of the Maintenance Orders (Reciprocal Enforcement) Act 1972(c) or Part 1 of the Civil Jurisdiction and Judgments Act 1982(d) or Council Regulation (EEC) No 44/2001(e) being an order for the payment of any periodical or other sum specified therein for or in respect of—

> (a) the maintenance of the spouse or civil partner of the person against whom the order is made;

> (b) the maintenance of any child of that person or that person's spouse or civil partner or of any other child who has been treated by them both as a child of their family;

> (c) any costs incurred in obtaining the order; or

> (d) any costs incurred in proceedings on appeal against or for the variation, revocation or revival of any such order;

> (e) "relevant person" means a person who is a relevant person, within the meaning of section 355 of the Act, by virtue of subsection (3) (a) of that section.

(2) In the definition of "maintenance order" in paragraph (1) references to a person's spouse or civil partner include, in relation to an order made in proceedings in connection with the dissolution or annulment of a marriage or civil partnership, a person who would have been that person's spouse or civil partner if the marriage or civil partnership had subsisted.

Service of proceedings

3. Subject to regulations 4 and 5 any process served on the commanding officer of a relevant person in connection with proceedings for a maintenance order, or for the variation, revocation or revival of such an order, shall be treated as duly served on the relevant person.

Circumstances in which service of process shall be of no effect

4.- (1) This regulation applies where any process in connection with proceedings for a maintenance order, or for the variation, revocation or revival of such an order, is served on the commanding officer of a relevant person.

(2) Service of process shall be of no effect if within 21 days of the date on which the process is served upon him the commanding officer certifies to the issuing court that—

    (a) the relevant person is on active service, or is under orders for active service, and that in his opinion it would not be reasonably practicable for the relevant person to comply with the requirements stipulated in the process; or

    (b) the relevant person is absent without leave.

(3) In paragraph (2) , "active service" has the same meaning as in section 8(3) of the Act. Proceedings in a court of summary jurisdiction

5. Nothing in these Regulations shall enable process to be served in connection with proceedings in a court of summary jurisdiction unless the relevant person is within the United Kingdom.

Transitional Provisions

6.- (1) This regulation applies where prior to commencement—

    (a) process was served on a commanding officer under section 153(1) of the Army Act 1955(a) , section 153(1) of the Air Force Act 1955(b) or section 101(1) of the Naval Discipline Act 1957(c) ; and

    (b) the commanding officer had the power to certify to the issuing court under section 153(3) or (3A) of the Army Act 1955, section 153(3) or (3A) of the Air Force Act 1955 or section 101(4) or (4A) of the Naval Discipline Act 1957 that service shall be of no effect, but has not done so.

(2) Subject to paragraph (3) , where paragraph (1) applies the commanding officer may certify to the issuing court under regulation 4(2) that service shall be of no effect.

(3) The certification mentioned in paragraph (2) must occur—

    (a) within 21 days of commencement, or

    (b) by the date of the hearing stipulated in the process at which the person to be served was to attend, whichever is the earlier.

Domestic Violence Prevention Orders/Notices

The Home Office has commenced a 12 month pilot to trial a new approach to tackling domestic violence. A key strand of this will be the use of Domestic Violence Protection Orders.

NOTE: DVPN's & DVPO's are unlikely to be served by process servers but we include them here for general knowledge.

What are Domestic Violence Protection Notices and Orders?

The relevant statutory provisions are contained at sections 24-33 of the Crime and Security Act 2010 – a copy is available here http://www.legislation.gov.uk/ukpga/2010/17/contents. Domestic Violence Protection Notice (DVPN)

A DVPN is the initial notice issued by the police in order to provide emergency protection to an individual believed to be the victim of domestic violence. This notice, which must be authorised by a police superintendent, contains prohibitions that effectively bar the suspected perpetrator from returning to the victim's home or otherwise contacting the victim.

A DVPN may be issued to a person aged 18 years and over if the police superintendent has reasonable grounds for believing that:

- the individual has been violent towards, or has threatened violence towards an associated person, AND
- The issue of the DVPN is necessary to protect that person from violence or a threat of violence by the intended recipient of the DVPN

The associated person mentioned above does not have to consent to the issuing of a DVPN or DVPO.

Following an alleged breach of the DVPN, the police may arrest the individual without warrant and hold that person in custody pending the magistrates' court hearing of the DVPO application; this hearing must take place within 24 hours of the arrest for the alleged DVPN breach.

Domestic Violence Prevention Order (DVPO)

Within 48 hours of the DVPN being issued (excluding weekends and bank holidays), the police must submit an application to the magistrates' court for the DVPO. The Magistrates can make a DVPO if two conditions are met:

The court is satisfied on the balance of probabilities that the recipient has been violent towards, or has threatened violence towards, an associated person

The court thinks that making the DVPO is necessary to protect that person from violence or a threat of violence by the recipient.

A DVPO may be in force for no fewer than 14 days beginning on the day on which it was made and no more than 28 days. An individual who breaches a DVPO may be arrested without warrant and held in custody to be brought before the magistrates' court within 24 hours.

Where are they being trialled?

There are three police forces participating in the trial:

- Greater Manchester
- Wiltshire
- West Mercia

How do clients access legal aid if faced with a DVPN?

Providers with a 2010 Standard Crime Contract will be able to represent eligible clients in receipt of a DVPN. There are several routes by which clients will access advice:

- Following arrest and having been taken to the police station (from where the DVPN is almost always served), police station advice and assistance will apply and the solicitor can apply for a representation order for the DVPO hearing at the Magistrates court.

- Having been issued with a DVPN, the client may approach a 2010 Crime contract holder who could provide free standing advice and assistance away from the police station. This is subject to a means and eligibility test as set out in the Contract Specification (Part B, Section 9). The firm can subsequently apply for a representation order which will be subject to the usual 'Interests of Justice' test and means test.

The Magistrates Court duty solicitor scheme is available for clients who arrive for their court hearing without any prior representation in place. DVPOs have been added to the list of 'prescribed proceedings' for which the court duty solicitor can advise. A copy of the relevant statutory instrument is attached here: http://www.legislation.gov.uk/uksi/2011/1453/contents/made

In the event of either a breach of the DVPN or DVPO, police station advice and assistance and the Magistrates' Court duty solicitor scheme will apply in the usual way.

Clarification

Often in DV cases where the police have been called by a complainant there is a lack of substantive evidence sufficient to proceed to charge.

Current policy within the 43 Constabularies of England and Wales dictates that when the Police attend a DV incident an arrest of one party, or both, ensues. This prevents further offences being committed while the complaint is investigated.

Following arrest and interview under caution, consideration is given as to whether the matter passes what is termed a "threshold test", in other words, whether the circumstances are such that there is evidence of a criminal offence having been committed. If the test is passed, the matter is referred to the CPS for their advice on charge.

There is provision for a suspect to be retained in police custody for a "reasonable time" following interview under caution in order CPS may give advice - normally accepted as up to 3 1/2 hours, or the suspect may be bailed with conditions while CPS advice is sought. This would normally be for a week to 10 days and the conditions would be not to contact the complainant directly or indirectly, or go to the complainant's address, which may or may not be the suspect's home address (save in the latter on one occasion in company of a Police Officer to collect personal possessions)

Where bail with conditions are granted, a measure of protection is thereby given to the complainant in that if the conditions are breached, the suspect is liable to further arrest.

If CPS advice is gained whilst the suspect remains in Police custody and that advice is to charge, the suspect may either be remanded in police custody and placed before the next available court or may be granted Court bail with conditions similar to above. Again, some measure of protection is thereby given to the complainant.

However, where either the matter does not pass the "threshold" test, or the CPS advice is that there is insufficient evidence to charge and the result for the Police would be "no further action", consideration may now be given by Police in Greater Manchester, Wiltshire and Mercia to invoke a Domestic Violence Protection Notice. In such cases, the officers dealing with the case must satisfy a Police Superintendent that the complainant remains at real and substantial risk from further DV from the suspect. If that Superintendent is satisfied that a DVPN is appropriate, he can authorise such a notice to be served on the suspect before they leave the Police Station. The notice bars the suspect from any contact with the complainant or their return to the complainant's address, normally their own home address for a period of 48 hours. It is explained that within the following 48 hours the Police will make application to the Magistrates' Court for a Domestic Violence Protection Order and that he has the right to be present and represented at Court to make application to oppose the order. If he does not attend Court, the Court will grant the order in his absence. If he does attend, the Court will decide whether to grant an order according to the representations made by the Police and his Solicitor

A DVPO may be granted for not less than 14 days and not more than 28 days, thus providing a "breathing space" for the complainant to make alternative arrangements as required, whether that is to apply in the Civil Court for a Non-Molestation Order and Occupation Order or other appropriate action.

Should the suspect breach the DVPN or DVPO he is subject to arrest and potential imprisonment.

A DVPN / DVPO is specifically designed to provide a measure of protection for a DV complainant in cases where there is insufficient evidence for the Police to take formal action, but where a risk is recognised and accepted as existing.

***

SECTION 6 – MAGISTRATES & CROWN COURT PROCEEDINGS

MAGISTRATE'S COURT PROCESS

Introduction

Butterworths Stone's Justices' Manual is relied upon each year by thousands of professionals to provide the most reliable and current coverage of the legislative changes affecting magistrates' courts.

With the accompanying CD-ROM, Stone's provides comprehensive coverage of all existing, new and amended legislation affecting the magistrates' courts and hundreds of new cases that set precedents or clarify particular principles of law.

As part of the subscription an updating CD-ROM is provided in October.

Butterworths Supplement to Stone's Justices' Manual is also included in the subscription price, published in October. Butterworths Supplement to Stone's Justices' Manual 2012 is a valuable addition to the Stone's service, with recent cases and legislation included, as well as updated and new commentary on relevant changes to the law of the magistrates' court.

Fully cross-referenced to the main work, the Supplement ensures your Butterworths Stone's Justice Manual 2012 is updated with the latest developments.

Service Of Summons

Magistrate's Courts Rule 1981

Rule 99 reads:

99. (1) Service of a summons issued by a justice of the peace on a person other than a corporation may be effected—

    (a) by delivering it to the person to whom it is directed; or

    (b) by leaving it for him with some person at his last known or usual place of abode; or

    (c) by sending it by post in a letter addressed to him at his last known or usual place of abode.

(2) […]1

(3) Service for the purposes of the Act of 1980 of a summons issued by a justice of the peace on a corporation may be effected by delivering it at, or sending it by post to, the registered office of the corporation, if that office is in the United Kingdom, or, if there is no registered office in the United Kingdom, any place in the United Kingdom where the corporation trades or conducts its business.

(4) Paragraph (3) shall have effect in relation to a document (other than a summons) issued by a justice of the peace as it has effect in relation to a summons so issued, but with the substitution of references to England and Wales for the references to the United Kingdom.

(5) Any summons or other document served in manner authorised by the preceding provisions of this rule shall, for the purposes of any enactment other than the Act of 1980 or these Rules requiring a summons or other document to be served in any particular manner, be deemed to have been as effectively served as if it had been served in that manner; and nothing in this rule shall render invalid the service of a summons or other document in that manner.

(6) Sub-paragraph (c) of paragraph (1) shall not authorise the service by post of—

> (a) a summons requiring the attendance of any person to give evidence or produce a document or thing; or

> (b) a summons issued under any enactment relating to the liability of members of the naval, military or air forces of the Crown for the maintenance of their [husbands, wives or civil partners, as the case may be,] 2 and children, whether legitimate or illegitimate.

(7) In the case of a summons issued on an application for an order under section 16 or 17(1) of the Act of 1978 (powers of court to make orders for the protection of a party to a marriage or a child of the family) service of the summons shall not be effected in manner authorised by sub-paragraph

> (b) or (c) of paragraph (1) unless a justice of the peace is satisfied by evidence on oath that prompt personal service of the summons is impracticable and allows service to be effected in such manner.

(8) Where this rule or any other of these Rules provides that a summons or other document may be sent by post to a person's last known or usual place of abode that rule shall have effect as if it provided also for the summons or other document to be sent in the manner specified in the rule to an address given by that person for that purpose.

(9) This rule shall not apply to a judgment summons. [4] 3

Notes

1 Revoked by Magistrates' Courts (Miscellaneous Amendments) Rules 1993/1183 rule 3(h) (May 24, 1993)
2 Word substituted by Magistrates' Courts (Miscellaneous Amendments) Rules 2005/2930 Sch.1 para.8 (December
5, 2005)
3 Superseded in relation to criminal matters as authorised by Criminal Procedure Rules 2005/384 Pt 2 rule 2.1 (April
4, 2005)
4 In relation to criminal matters: SI 1981/552 rule 99 is substantively re-enacted by SI 2005/384 rule 4.1.

Commencement

rule 99.(1) -(9) : July 6, 1981 save as proceedings commenced before July 6, 1981

PROOF OF SERVICE

Rule 67 reads:

67.(1) The service on any person of a summons, process notice or document required or authorised to be served in any proceedings before a Magistrates Court, and the handwriting or seal of a Justice of the Peace or other person on any warrant, summons notice, process or documents issued or made in any such proceedings, may be proved in any legal proceedings by a document purporting to be a solemn declaration in the prescribed form made before a Justice of the Peace, Commissioner of Oaths, Clerk of a Magistrate's Court or Registrar of a County Court or a Sheriff or Sheriff's Clerk (in Scotland) or a Clerk of Petty Sessions (in Northern Ireland).

(2) The service of any process or other document required or authorised to be served, the proper addressing, pre-paying and posting or registration for the purpose of service of a letter containing such a document, and the place, date and time of posting or registration of any such letter, may be proved in any proceedings before a Magistrate's Court by a document purporting to be a certificate signed by the person by whom the service was effected or the letter posted or registered.

(3) Reference in paragraph (2) to the service of any process shall, in their application to a witness summons, be construed as including reference to the payment or tender to the witness of his costs and expenses.

MAGISTRATES' COURTS ACT 1980
Part IV - Witnesses and Evidence
Procuring attendance of witness

97 Summons to witness and warrant for his arrest.

(1) Where a justice of the peace is satisfied that—

(a) any person in England or Wales is likely to be able to give material evidence, or produce any document or thing likely to be material evidence, at the summary trial of an information or hearing of a complaint [F2or of an application under the Adoption and Children Act 2002 (c. 38)] by a magistrates' court, and

(b) it is in the interests of justice to issue a summons under this subsection to secure the attendance of that person to give evidence or produce the document or thing, the justice shall issue a summons directed to that person requiring him to attend before the court at the time and place appointed in the summons to give evidence or to produce the document or thing.

(2) If a justice of the peace is satisfied by evidence on oath of the matters mentioned in subsection (1) above, and also that it is probable that a summons under that subsection would not procure the attendance of the person in question, the justice may instead of issuing a summons issue a warrant to arrest that person and bring him before such a court as aforesaid at a time and place specified in the warrant; but a warrant shall not be issued under this subsection where the attendance is required for the hearing of a complaint [F3or of an application under the Adoption and Children Act 2002 (c. 38).

(2A) A summons may also be issued under subsection (1) above if the justice is satisfied that the person in question is outside the British Islands but no warrant shall be issued under subsection (2) above unless the justice is satisfied by evidence on oath that the person in question is in England or Wales.

(2B) A justice may refuse to issue a summons under subsection (1) above in relation to the summary trial of an information if he is not satisfied that an application for the summons was made by a party to the case as soon as reasonably practicable after the accused pleaded not guilty.

(2C) In relation to the summary trial of an information, subsection (2) above shall have effect as if the reference to the matters mentioned in subsection (1) above included a reference to the matter mentioned in subsection (2B) above.

(3) On the failure of any person to attend before a magistrates' court in answer to a summons under this section, if—

> (a) the court is satisfied by evidence on oath that he is likely to be able to give material evidence or produce any document or thing likely to be material evidence in the proceedings; and
>
> (b) it is proved on oath, or in such other manner as may be prescribed, that he has been duly served with the summons, and that a reasonable sum has been paid or tendered to him for costs and expenses; and
>
> (c) it appears to the court that there is no just excuse for the failure, the court may issue a warrant to arrest him and bring him before the court at a time and place specified in the warrant.

(4) If any person attending or brought before a magistrates' court refuses without just excuse to be sworn or give evidence, or to produce any document or thing, the court may commit him to custody until the expiration of such period not exceeding [F6one month] as may be specified in the warrant or until he sooner gives evidence or produces the document or thing [F7or impose on him a fine not exceeding £2,500] or both.

(5) A fine imposed under subsection (4) above shall be deemed, for the purposes of any enactment, to be a sum adjudged to be paid by a conviction.

The Criminal Procedure Rules 2011

Part 4 as in force 3 October 2011

PART 4
SERVICE OF DOCUMENTS

When this Part applies

4.1. The rules in this Part apply to the service of every document in a case to which these Rules apply, subject to any special rules in other legislation (including other Parts of these Rules) or in the Practice Direction.

Methods of service

4.2.-   (1) A document may be served by any of the methods described in rules 4.3 to 4.6 (subject to rule 4.7), or in rule 4.8.

> (2) Where a document may be served by electronic means, the general rule is that the person serving it will use that method.

Service by handing over a document

4.3.- (1) A document may be served on—
(a) an individual by handing it to him or her;
(b) a corporation by handing it to a person holding a senior position in that corporation;
(c) an individual or corporation who is legally represented in the case by handing it to that representative;
(d) the prosecution by handing it to the prosecutor or to the prosecution representative;
(e) the court officer by handing it to a court officer with authority to accept it at the relevant court office; and
(f) the Registrar of Criminal Appeals by handing it to a court officer with authority to accept it at the Criminal Appeal Office.

(2) If an individual is under 18, a copy of a document served under paragraph (1) (a) must be handed to his or her parent, or another appropriate adult, unless no such person is readily available.

[Note. Certain legislation treats a body that is not a corporation as if it were one for the purposes of rules about service of documents. See for example section 143 of the Adoption and Children Act 2002( ) .]

Service by leaving or posting a document

4.4.- (1) A document may be served by leaving it at the appropriate address for service under this rule or by sending it to that address by first class post or by the equivalent of first class post.

(2) The address for service under this rule on—

(a) an individual is an address where it is reasonably believed that he or she will receive it;
(b) a corporation is its principal office, and if there is no readily identifiable principal office then any place where it carries on its activities or business;
(c) an individual or corporation who is legally represented in the case is that representative's office;
(d) the prosecution is the prosecutor's office;
(e) the court officer is the relevant court office; and
(f) the Registrar of Criminal Appeals is the Criminal Appeal Office, Royal Courts of Justice, Strand, London, WC2A 2LL.

[Note. In addition to service in England and Wales for which these rules provide, service outside England and Wales may be allowed under other legislation. See—

(a) section 39 of the Criminal Law Act 1977( ) (service of summons, etc. in Scotland and Northern Ireland) ;
(b) section 1139(4) of the Companies Act 2006( ) (service of copy summons, etc. on company's registered office in Scotland and Northern Ireland) ;
(c) sections 3, 4, 4A and 4B of the Crime (International Co-operation) Act 2003( ) (service of summons, etc. outside the United Kingdom) and rules 32.1 and 32.2; and
(d) section 1139(2) of the Companies Act 2006 (service on overseas company) .]

Service through a document exchange

4.5. A document may be served by document exchange (DX) where—
    (a) the person to be served—
        (i) has given a DX box number, and
        (ii) has not refused to accept service by DX; or
    (b) the person to be served is legally represented in the case and the representative has given a DX box number.

Service by electronic means

4.6.- (1) A document may be served by electronic means where—
    (a) the person to be served—
        (i) has given an electronic address, and
        (ii) has not refused to accept service by that method; or
    (b) the person to be served is legally represented in the case and the representative has given an electronic address.

(2) Where a document is served under this rule the person serving it need not provide a paper copy as well.

Documents that must be served by specified methods

4.7.- (1) The documents listed in paragraph (2) may be served—
    (a) on an individual, only under rule 4.3(1) (a) (handing over) or rule 4.4(1) and (2) (a) (leaving or posting) ; and
    (b) on a corporation, only under rule 4.3(1) (b) (handing over) or rule 4.4(1) and (2) (b) (leaving or posting) .

(2) Those documents are—
    (a) a summons, requisition or witness summons;
    (b) notice of an order under section 25 of the Road Traffic Offenders Act 1988( ) ;
    (c) a notice of registration under section 71(6) of that Act( ) ;
    (d) notice of a hearing to review the postponement of the issue of a warrant of detention or imprisonment under section 77(6) of the Magistrates' Courts Act 1980( ) ;
    (e) notice under section 86 of that Act( ) of a revised date to attend a means inquiry;
    (f) any notice or document served under Part 19 (Bail in magistrates' courts and the Crown Court) ;
    (g) notice under rule 37.15(a) of when and where an adjourned hearing will resume;
    (h) notice under rule 42.5(3) of an application to vary or discharge a compensation order;
    (i) notice under rule 42.10(2) (c) of the location of the sentencing or enforcing court;
    (j) a collection order, or notice requiring payment, served under rule 52.2(a) .

(3) An application or written statement, and notice, under rule 62.9 alleging contempt of court may be served—
    (a) on an individual, only under rule 4.3(1) (a) (by handing it to him or her) ;
    (b) on a corporation, only under rule 4.3(1) (b) (by handing it to a person holding a senior position in that corporation) .

Service by person in custody

4.8.- (1) A person in custody may serve a document by handing it to the custodian addressed to the person to be served.

(2) The custodian must—
    (a) endorse it with the time and date of receipt;
    (b) record its receipt; and
    (c) forward it promptly to the addressee.

Service by another method

4.9.- (1) The court may allow service of a document by a method—
    (a) other than those described in rules 4.3 to 4.6 and in rule 4.8;
    (b) other than one specified by rule 4.7, where that rule applies.

(2) An order allowing service by another method must specify—
    (a) the method to be used; and
    (b) the date on which the document will be served.

Date of service

4.10.- (1) A document served under rule 4.3 or rule 4.8 is served on the day it is handed over.

(2) Unless something different is shown, a document served on a person by any other method is served—
    (a) in the case of a document left at an address, on the next business day after the day on which it was left;
    (b) in the case of a document sent by first class post or by the equivalent of first class post, on the second business day after the day on which it was posted or despatched;
    (c) in the case of a document served by document exchange, on the second business day after the day on which it was left at the addressee's DX or at a correspondent DX;
    (d) in the case of a document transmitted by electronic means, on the next business day after it was transmitted; and
    (e) in any case, on the day on which the addressee responds to it, if that is earlier.

(3) Unless something different is shown, a document produced by a court computer system is to be taken as having been sent by first class post, or by the equivalent of first class post, to the addressee on the business day after the day on which it was produced.

(4) Where a document is served on or by the court officer, 'business day' does not include a day on which the court office is closed.

Proof of service

4.11. The person who serves a document may prove that by signing a certificate explaining how and when it was served.

Court's power to give directions about service

4.12.- (1) The court may specify the time as well as the date by which a document must be—
    (a) served under rule 4.3 or rule 4.8; or
    (b) transmitted by electronic means, if it is served under rule 4.6.

(2) The court may treat a document as served if the addressee responds to it even if it was not served in accordance with the rules in this Part.

***

SECTION 7 – SCOTTISH PROCESS PROCEEDINGS

INTRODUCTION

A Messenger-at-Arms is an officer of the Court of Session which is the supreme civil court in Scotland. A Messenger-at-Arms can travel anywhere in Scotland and can serve documents and enforce court orders of the supreme court.

A Sheriff Officer is an officer of the regional civil court. Scotland is geographically divided into six Sheriffdoms and 49 local sheriff court districts. Unlike a Messenger-at-Arms, a Sheriff Officer can only operate in the geographical area for which he holds a commission.

Process from both the Higher Courts and Sheriff's Courts is served by either Messengers at Arms or Sheriff's Officers. These are persons in the employ of private firms, but who are commissioned by the Sheriff's Principal. To obtain such a commission, the applicant is obliged to complete a three year study period followed by a written/oral examination. Commissions are granted by each Court for service of documents within said Court's jurisdiction. So in theory a Process Server wanting to serve process throughout Scotland should obtain a Commission from every Court in Scotland, however Multiple Commissions are granted. Further details can be obtained from The Society of Messengers at Arms and Sheriff's Officers, telephone number 0131-225-9110 or their website www.smaso.org.

The Witness Rule

The development of the rules of the Court of Session and the Sheriff Court in Scotland have resulted in there being different requirements, between the courts, concerning the service of documents originating in Scotland upon addressees furth Scotland, but within the other legal jurisdictions of the UK.

In relation to the Sheriff Court, rule 5.5(1) (a) (i) of the Ordinary Cause Rules 1993 specifies that a document shall be served "in accordance with the rules for personal service under the domestic law of the place in which service is to be executed" - if at a known residence or place of business in England, Wales, Northern Ireland, the Isle of Man, and the Channel Islands.

Rule 5.7(2) (a) (ii) of the Summary Cause Rules 2002 and rule 6.5(2) (a) (ii) of the Small Claim Rules 2002 complete the relevant Sheriff Court rules, by making the same provision for this so-called "personal service". (In fact, "personal service", in Scots law, does not mean what it is here intended to mean, i.e. service by delivery, by the hand of a process server. Its strict meaning is service upon the addressee, personally apprehended by the appropriate officer of court.)

These rules mean that there is no requirement for a witness to be present when a sheriff court document is served by a process server outside Scotland, but within another legal jurisdiction of the UK.

The Court of Session (the supreme civil court in Scotland), however, has not made a separate rule devoted to the question of how to serve documents on those addressees who are furth of Scotland, but within the other legal jurisdictions of the UK. Rule 16.3 of the Rules of the Court of Session 1994 deals with service by messenger-at-arms. At rule 16.3(6) it states: "In the application of this rule to service in a part of the United Kingdom furth of Scotland, reference to a messenger-at-arms shall be construed as a reference to a person entitled to serve Supreme Court writs in that part."

This construction means that the other parts of the rule - originally dealing only with service by messenger-at-arms (and, almost invariably, with service within Scotland) - apply when a process server in another part of the UK is serving the document. In particular, rule 16.3(2) applies: "Such service shall be witnessed by one witness who shall sign the certificate of service (which shall state his name, occupation and address) ".

The result of this is that when a process server in another part of the UK is instructed to serve a document from the Court of Session he needs to be accompanied by a person to act as witness.

The Society believes that this difference in procedure between the Court of Session and the Sheriff Court has resulted from the unforeseen consequences of inserting subsection (6) to rule 16.3

It should be noted that the current sheriff court rules do conform to the general principle of citation: that service should be in accordance with the domestic law of the place in which service is to be executed, and not by reference to the rules for service of the jurisdiction within which the document was issued.

NOTE I: IT IS ILLEGAL FOR ANYONE ELSE BUT MESSENGER-AT-ARMS AND SHERIFF OFFICERS TO SERVE PROCESS IN SCOTLAND.

NOTE II: WHEN EFFECTING SERVICE OF DOCUMENTS IN ENGLAND & WALES ISSUED BY THE SHERIFF SCOTTISH COURTS IT WILL BE NOT BE NECESSARY FOR THE PROCESS SERVER TO BE ACCOMPANIED BY A WITNESS UNLESS OTHERWISE INSTRUCTED.

NOTE III: WHEN EFFECTING SERVICE OF DOCUMENTS IN ENGLAND & WALES ISSUED BY THE COURT OF SESSION IT WILL BE NECESSARY FOR THE PROCESS SERVER TO BE ACCOMPANIED BY A WITNESS.

NOTE IV: THE WITNESS CAN BE ANYONE EXCEPT A PARTY TO THE ACTION.

SERVICE OF PROCESS FROM SCOTLAND UNDER MAINTENANCE ORDERS ACT 1950

The procedure is covered by section 15 of the above Act.

Section 15

(2) A summons or writ may be endorsed under this section, in England by a Justice of the Peace, in Scotland by a Sheriff, and in Northern Ireland by a resident Magistrate: and the endorsement shall be made in the form numbered 1 in the Second Schedule of this Act, or any form to the like effect.

(3) In any proceedings in which a summons or writ is served under this section, the service may be proved by means of a declaration made in the form numbered 2 in the Second Schedule to this Act, or any form to the like effect, before a Justice of the Peace, Sheriff or resident Magistrate, as the case may be.

(4) Nothing in this section shall be construed as authorising the service of a summons or writ otherwise than personally.

(3) Section four of the Summary Jurisdiction (Process) Act 1881, shall not apply to any process which may be served under this section; and nothing in this section or in any other enactment shall be construed as authorising the execution in one part of the United Kingdom of a warrant for the arrest of a person who fails to appear in answer to any such process issued in another part of the United Kingdom.

Service of the claim form where the permission of the court is not required – Scotland and Northern Ireland

6.32 (1) The claimant may serve the claim form on a defendant in Scotland or Northern Ireland where each claim made against the defendant to be served and included in the claim form is a claim which the court has power to determine under the 1982 Act and –

(a) no proceedings between the parties concerning the same claim are pending in the courts of any other part of the United Kingdom; and

(b)

(i) the defendant is domiciled in the United Kingdom;

(ii) the proceedings are within paragraph 11 of Schedule 4 to the 1982 Act; or

(iii) the defendant is a party to an agreement conferring jurisdiction, within paragraph 12 of Schedule 4 to the 1982 Act.

(2) The claimant may serve the claim form on a defendant in Scotland or Northern Ireland where each claim made against the defendant to be served and included in the claim form is a claim which the court has power to determine under any enactment other than the 1982 Act notwithstanding that –

(a) the person against whom the claim is made is not within the jurisdiction; or

(b) the facts giving rise to the claim did not occur within the jurisdiction.

Service of the claim form where the permission of the court is not required – out of the United Kingdom

6.33 (1) The claimant may serve the claim form on the defendant out of the United Kingdom where each claim against the defendant to be served and included in the claim form is a claim which the court has power to determine under the 1982 Act or the Lugano Convention and –

(a) no proceedings between the parties concerning the same claim are pending in the courts of any other part of the |United Kingdom or any other Convention territory; and

(b)

(i) the defendant is domiciled in the United Kingdom or in any Convention territory;

(ii) the proceedings are within article 16 of Schedule 1 to the 1982 Act or article 22 of the Lugano Convention; or

(iii) the defendant is a party to an agreement conferring jurisdiction, within article 17 of Schedule 1 to the 1982 Act or article 23 of the Lugano Convention.

(2) The claimant may serve the claim form on a defendant out of the United Kingdom where each claim made against the defendant to be served and included in the claim form is a claim which the court has power to determine under the Judgments Regulation and –

    (a) no proceedings between the parties concerning the same claim are pending in the courts of any other part of the United Kingdom or any other Member State; and

    (b)

        (i) the defendant is domiciled in the United Kingdom or in any Member State;

        (ii) the proceedings are within article 22 of the Judgments Regulation; or

        (iii) the defendant is a party to an agreement conferring jurisdiction, within article 23 of the Judgments Regulation.

(3) The claimant may serve the claim form on a defendant out of the United Kingdom where each claim made against the defendant to be served and included in the claim form is a claim which the court has power to determine other than under the 1982 Act or the Lugano Convention or the Judgments Regulation, notwithstanding that –

    (a) the person against whom the claim is made is not within the jurisdiction; or

    (b) the facts giving rise to the claim did not occur within the jurisdiction.

Service of the claim form on a defendant in Scotland or Northern Ireland

(2) Where the claimant serves on a defendant in Scotland or Northern Ireland under rule 6.32, the period –

    (a) for filing an acknowledgment of service or admission is 21 days after service of the particulars of claim; or

    (b) for filing a defence is –

        (i) 21 days after service of the particulars of claim; or

        (ii) where the defendant files an acknowledgment of service, 35 days after service of the particulars of claim.

N.B. Part 7 provides that particulars of claim must be contained in or served with the claim form or served separately on the defendant within 14 days after service of the claim form.

SAMPLE AFFIDAVITS

Where the process originates from Scotland, and is for service in the UK, an affidavit of service is set out on the following page. Also included are examples of an Endorsement of Summons and Declaration of Service.

COURT OF SESSION (SCOTLAND)

Pursuer

against

Defender

AFFIDAVIT OF SERVICE

I, ...of .... and I, ... of .... both Process Servers acting under the direction of .... Solicitors for the above-named Pursuer, jointly and severally make Oath and say:

AND I .... for myself say:

1.   THAT a true copy of the summons issued herein at Edinburgh on the .... day of .... 2000, together with a Notice of Defender in an action of Divorce where it is stated there has been 5 years non-cohabitation on Form 15C dated the .... day of .... of ....2000, by delivering the same into his hands personally before and in the presence of .... the second Deponent to this Affidavit of Service.

2.   THAT the Defender .... so served was identified to me by .... immediately prior to service being effected upon him.

    or: produced to me his Driving Licence bearing number ....

    (or Passport Number .... expiring on ....)

AND I .... for myself say:

3.   THAT the service effected as aforesaid was duly effected in my presence and I remained present while Mr .... drew the Defender's attention to the contents of all the documents served upon him and I heard the Defender inform Mr .... that he would give the documents to his Solicitor.

SWORN by the first-named deponent	)
at in the	)
County of , England, this	)
day of 2012	)

Before me,

A Solicitor empowered to administer Oaths

SWORN by the second-named deponent)

at   in the)

County of   , England, this   )

day of   2012   )

Before me,

A Solicitor empowered to administer Oaths.

Endorsement Of Summons

I, A.B., a justice of the peace [sheriff] [resident magistrate] for the [county] of , hereby authorise the service of this summons [writ] in England [Scotland] [Northern Ireland] under section fifteen of the Maintenance Orders Act, 1950.

Given under my hand this day of , 2012 .

Declaration as to Service

I, C.D. of hereby declare that on the day of 19 , I served E.F. of with the summons [writ] now shown to me and marked "A' by delivering a true copy to him.

(Signed) C.D.

Declared before me this day of   , 2012 .

A.B.

Justice of the Peace [sheriff] [resident magistrate] for the [county] of .

***

SECTION 8 - FOREIGN PROCESS PROCEEDINGS
(HAGUE, EU CONVENTION & INFORMAL)

Introduction

From time to time the process server may receive process from abroad for service. Normally all originating solicitors provide full instructions as to service and quite often enclose a draft form of affidavit of service. If doubt arises as to which documents are to be served and which should be retained, sight of the original letter of instructions from those instructing you sometimes clarifies the position.

Affidavits are usually prepared on good quality A4 paper and are usually required to be Notarized (Sworn) before a Notary Public – Occasionally some Solicitors are authorised to Swear Affidavits in respect of particular countries; i.e. Australia or South Africa.

A photograph to cover identification is usually required in matrimonial cases and a signature is usually required on the original document or on the form of acknowledgement. If a photograph is not available some other form of identification should be obtained at the time of service such as production of Passport, Driving Licence or other official document. Many US States require a description of the Party served to be included on the Affidavit (sometimes referred to as a Return of Service)

In some cases special instructions need to be complied with inasmuch as certain questions have to be put to the person served and the answers to such questions recorded and deposed to in the affidavit of service.

Affidavits of service for American process vary from State to State and most need to be sworn before a Notary Public or authenticated at the U.S. Embassy.

There are three routes that service from abroad may take.

- Hague Service Convention
- Rogatory Letter
- Informal Service

It is important that if you are instructed either directly or via a Lawyer that you are aware of these routes.

Hague Service Convention

The Convention on the Service Abroad of Judicial and Extrajudicial Documents in Civil or Commercial Matters, more commonly called the Hague Service Convention, is a multilateral treaty which was signed in The Hague on 15 November 1965 by members of the Hague Conference on Private International Law. It allows service of process of judicial documents from one signatory state to another without use of consular and diplomatic channels. The issue of international service had been previously addressed as part of the 1905 Civil Procedure Convention which was also signed in The Hague, which did not command wide support and was ratified by only 22 countries.

The Hague Service Convention established a more simplified means for parties in signatory states to effect service in other contracting states. Under the convention, each contracting state is required to designate a "Central Authority" to accept incoming requests for service. A "Judicial Officer" who is competent to serve process in the state of origin is permitted to send request for service directly to the "Central Authority" of the state where service is to be made. Upon receiving the request, the Central Authority in the receiving state arranges for service in a manner permitted within the receiving state, typically through a local court to the defendant's residence. Once service is effected, the "Central Authority" sends a certificate of service to the "Judicial Officer' who made the request. Parties are required to use three standardized forms:

- a request for service
- a summary of the proceedings
- a certificate of service.

The main benefits of the Hague Service Convention over Letters Rogatory is that it is faster (requests generally take 2 - 4 months rather than 6 - 12 months), it uses standardized forms which should be recognized by authorities in signatory countries, and in most cases, it is cheaper because service can be effected by the local attorney without hiring a foreign lawyer to advise on how to serve.

The Hague Service Convention does not prohibit a receiving state from permitting international service by other methods otherwise authorized by local law (for example, service directly by mail or personal service by a person otherwise authorized to service process in the foreign country). For example, in the United Kingdom, service can often be made by a process server.

Letter Rogatory

A letter rogatory or letter of request is a formal request from a court to a foreign court for some type of judicial assistance. The most common remedies sought by letters rogatory are service of process and taking of evidence.

Courts may serve documents only to individuals within the court's jurisdiction. One exception to this rule is countries that invoke universal jurisdiction, granting their courts ubiquitous domain. Therefore a person seeking to take an action against a person in another country will need to seek assistance from the judicial authorities in the other country. This is of course assuming the court in his own country has jurisdiction to hear the case matter.

The use of letters rogatory for purposes of service of process to initiate court action is now largely confined to the Americas, as between countries in Europe, Asia, and North America, service of process is effected without resort to letters rogatory, under the provisions of the Hague Service Convention.

In the past, letters rogatory could not usually be transmitted directly between the applicable courts, and had to be transmitted via consular or diplomatic channels, which could make the whole process very slow.

There have been various international conventions in regard to service of process and taking of evidence. One of the earliest conventions to simplify the procedure of Letters Rogatory was the 1905 Civil Procedure Convention, signed at The Hague. Drafted only in French, it was only ratified by 22 countries.

Later conventions, created after the institution of the Hague Conference on Private International Law, drafted in both English and French commanded more support. The Hague Service Convention, ratified in 1965, enabled designated authorities in each of the signatory states to transmit documents for service to each other, bypassing the diplomatic route. This convention has been ratified by 60 states including the United Kingdom and the United States, neither of whom had ratified the 1905 convention.

For countries not signed up to any convention, the letter rogatory is still used. So for example, a plaintiff in the United Kingdom which is signed up to the Hague Service Convention would still need to issue a letter rogatory to Chile, as the latter has not signed the Convention.

Informal Service (Service in Person by Agent)

If personal service is desired in countries which are not party to the Hague Service Convention, the most expeditious method may be to retain the services of a local process server as long as that country's laws do not specifically make it illegal.

This is also a form of service recognized under the Hague Convention, but, again, not all signatories permit its use within their territory. With the cooperation of a local process server, service is accomplished face to face.

In some countries which are a signatory to the Hague Service Convention, the Informal Service route is still open. The Civil Procedure Rules provides for personal service in the United Kingdom as follows;

IV Service of the Claim Form and other documents out of the jurisdiction

Scope of this Section

6.30   This Section contains rules about –

    (a) service of the claim form and other documents out of the jurisdiction;

    (b) when the permission of the court is required and how to obtain that permission; and

    (c) the procedure for service.

N.B. 'Jurisdiction' is defined in rule 2.3(1).

Interpretation

6.31   (1) For the purposes of this Section –

    (a) 'the Hague Convention' means the Convention on the service abroad of judicial and extrajudicial documents in civil or commercial matters signed at the Hague on 15 November 1965[7];

    (b) 'the 1982 Act' means the Civil Jurisdiction and Judgments Act 1982[8];

    (c) 'Civil Procedure Convention' means the Brussels and Lugano Conventions (as defined in section 1(1) of the 1982 Act) and any other Convention (including the Hague Convention) entered into by the United Kingdom regarding service out of the jurisdiction;

(d) 'the Judgments Regulation' means Council Regulation (EC) No. 44/2001 of 22 December 2000 on jurisdiction and the recognition and enforcement of judgments in civil and commercial matters9, as amended from time to time and as applied by the Agreement made on 19 October 2005 between the European Community and the Kingdom of Denmark on jurisdiction and the recognition and enforcement of judgments in civil and commercial matters10;

(e) 'the Service Regulation' means Regulation (EC) No. 1393/2007 of the European Parliament and of the Council of 13 November 2007 on the service in the Member States of judicial and extrajudicial documents in civil or commercial matters (service of documents) 11, and repealing Council Regulation (EC) No. 1348/200012, as amended from time to time and as applied by the Agreement made on 19 October 2005 between the European Community and the Kingdom of Denmark on the service of judicial and extrajudicial documents on civil and commercial matters13;

(f) 'Commonwealth State' means a state listed in Schedule 3 to the British Nationality Act 198114;

(g) 'Contracting State' has the meaning given by section 1(3) of the 1982 Act;

(h) 'Convention territory' means the territory or territories of any Contracting State to which the Brussels or Lugano Conventions (as defined in section 1(1) of the 1982 Act) apply; and

(i) 'domicile' is to be determined –

(i) in relation to a Convention territory, in accordance with sections 41 to 46 of the 1982 Act; and

(ii) in relation to a Member State, in accordance with the Judgments Regulation and paragraphs 9 to 12 of Schedule 1 to the Civil Jurisdiction and Judgments Order 200115.

(j) 'the Lugano Convention' means the Convention on jurisdiction and the recognition and enforcement of judgments in civil and commercial matters, between the European Community and the Republic of Iceland, the Kingdom of Norway, the Swiss Confederation and the Kingdom of Denmark and signed by the European Community on 30th October 2007.

Service of the claim form on a defendant in a Convention territory within Europe or a Member State

(3) Where the claimant serves the claim form on a defendant in a Convention territory within Europe or a Member State under rule 6.33, the period –

(a) for filing an acknowledgment of service or admission, is 21 days after service of the particulars of claim; or

(b) for filing a defence is –

(i) 21 days after service of the particulars of claim; or

(ii) where the defendant files an acknowledgment of service, 35 days after service of the particulars of claim.

Service of the claim form on a defendant in a Convention territory outside Europe

(4) Where the claimant serves the claim form on a defendant in a Convention territory outside Europe under rule 6.33, the period –

(a) for filing an acknowledgment of service or admission, is 31 days after service of the particulars of claim; or

(b) for filing a defence is –

(i) 31 days after service of the particulars of claim; or

(ii) where the defendant files an acknowledgment of service, 45 days after service of the particulars of claim.

Service on a defendant elsewhere

(5) Where the claimant serves the claim form under rule 6.33 in a country not referred to in paragraph (3) or (4), the period for responding to the claim form is set out in Practice Direction 6B.

Service of the claim form where the permission of the court is required

6.36 In any proceedings to which rule 6.32 or 6.33 does not apply, the claimant may serve a claim form out of the jurisdiction with the permission of the court if any of the grounds set out in paragraph 3.1 of Practice Direction 6B apply.

Practice Direction 6b – Service out of the Jurisdiction

This Practice Direction supplements Section IV of CPR Part 6

Scope of this Practice Direction

1.1 This Practice Direction supplements Section IV (service of the claim form and other documents out of the jurisdiction) of Part 6.

Service out of the jurisdiction where permission of the court is not required

2.1 Where rule 6.34 applies, the claimant must file practice form N510 when filing the claim form.

Service out of the jurisdiction where permission is required

3.1 The claimant may serve a claim form out of the jurisdiction with the permission of the court under rule 6.36 where –

General Grounds

(1) A claim is made for a remedy against a person domiciled within the jurisdiction.
(2) A claim is made for an injunction(GL) ordering the defendant to do or refrain from doing an act within the jurisdiction.
(3) A claim is made against a person ('the defendant') on whom the claim form has been or will be served (otherwise than in reliance on this paragraph) and –
    (a) there is between the claimant and the defendant a real issue which it is reasonable for the court to try; and
    (b) the claimant wishes to serve the claim form on another person who is a necessary or proper party to that claim.
(4) A claim is an additional claim under Part 20 and the person to be served is a necessary or proper party to the claim or additional claim.

Claims for interim remedies

(5) A claim is made for an interim remedy under section 25(1) of the Civil Jurisdiction and Judgments Act 1982.

Claims in relation to contracts

(6) A claim is made in respect of a contract where the contract –
    (a) was made within the jurisdiction;
    (b) was made by or through an agent trading or residing within the jurisdiction;
    (c) is governed by English law; or
    (d) contains a term to the effect that the court shall have jurisdiction to determine any claim in respect of the contract.
(7) A claim is made in respect of a breach of contract committed within the jurisdiction.

(8) A claim is made for a declaration that no contract exists where, if the contract was found to exist, it would comply with the conditions set out in paragraph (6).

Claims in tort

(9) A claim is made in tort where
- (a) damage was sustained within the jurisdiction; or
- (b) the damage sustained resulted from an act committed within the jurisdiction.

Enforcement

(10) A claim is made to enforce any judgment or arbitral award.

Claims about property within the jurisdiction

(11) The whole subject matter of a claim relates to property located within the jurisdiction.

Claims about trusts etc.

(12) A claim is made for any remedy which might be obtained in proceedings to execute the trusts of a written instrument where –
- (a) the trusts ought to be executed according to English law; and
- (b) the person on whom the claim form is to be served is a trustee of the trusts.

(13) A claim is made for any remedy which might be obtained in proceedings for the administration of the estate of a person who died domiciled within the jurisdiction.

(14) A probate claim or a claim for the rectification of a will.

(15) A claim is made for a remedy against the defendant as constructive trustee where the defendant's alleged liability arises out of acts committed within the jurisdiction.

(16) A claim is made for restitution where the defendant's alleged liability arises out of acts committed within the jurisdiction.

Claims by HM Revenue and Customs

(17) A claim is made by the Commissioners for H.M. Revenue and Customs relating to duties or taxes against a defendant not domiciled in Scotland or Northern Ireland.

Claim for costs order in favour of or against third parties

(18) A claim is made by a party to proceedings for an order that the court exercise its power under section 51 of the Senior Courts Act 1981 to make a costs order in favour of or against a person who is not a party to those proceedings.

Rule 48.2 sets out the procedure where the court is considering whether to exercise its discretion to make a costs order in favour of or against a non-party.

Admiralty claims

(19) A claim is –
- (a) in the nature of salvage and any part of the services took place within the jurisdiction; or
- (b) to enforce a claim under section 153, 154, 175 or 176A of the Merchant Shipping Act 1995.

Claims under various enactments

(20) A claim is made
- (a) under an enactment which allows proceedings to be brought and those proceedings are not covered by any of the other grounds referred to in this paragraph; or
- (b) under the Directive of the Council of the European Communities dated 15 March 1976 No. 76/308/EEC, where service is to be effected in a Member State of the European Union.

Documents to be filed under rule 6.43(2) (c)

4.1 A party must provide the following documents for each party to be served out of the jurisdiction –
(1) a copy of the particulars of claim if not already contained in or served with the claim form and any other relevant documents;
(2) a duplicate of the claim form, a duplicate of the particulars of claim (if not already contained in or served with the claim form), copies of any documents accompanying the claim form and copies of any other relevant documents;
(3) forms for responding to the claim; and
(4) any translation required under rule 6.45 in duplicate.

4.2 Some countries require legalisation of the document to be served and some require a formal letter of request which must be signed by the Senior Master. Any queries on this should be addressed to the Foreign Process Section (Room E02) at the Royal Courts of Justice.

Service in a Commonwealth State or British overseas territory

5.1 The judicial authorities of certain Commonwealth States which are not a party to the Hague Convention require service to be in accordance with rule 6.42(1) (b) (i) and not 6.42(3) . A list of such countries can be obtained from the Foreign Process Section (Room E02) at the Royal Courts of Justice.

5.2 The list of British overseas territories is contained in Schedule 6 to the British Nationality Act 1981. For ease of reference, these are –

    (a) Anguilla;

    (b) Bermuda;

    (c) British Antarctic Territory;

    (d) British Indian Ocean Territory;

    (e) British Virgin Islands;

    (f) Cayman Islands;

    (g) Falkland Islands;

    (h) Gibraltar;

    (i) Montserrat;

    (j) Pitcairn, Henderson, Ducie and Oeno;

    (k) St. Helena and Dependencies;

    (l) South Georgia and the South Sandwich Islands;

    (m) Sovereign Base Areas of Akrotiri and Dhekelia; and

    (n) Turks and Caicos Islands.

Further information

7.2 Further information concerning service out of the jurisdiction can be obtained from the Foreign Process Section, Room E02, Royal Courts of Justice, Strand, London WC2A 2LL (telephone: 020 7947 6691) .

Table

Place or country	Number of days
Afghanistan	23
Albania	25
Algeria	22
Andorra	21
Angola	22
Anguilla	31
Antigua and Barbuda	23
Antilles (Netherlands)	31
Argentina	22
Armenia	21
Ascension Island	31
Australia	25
Austria	21
Azerbaijan	22
Azores	23
Bahamas	22
Bahrain	22
Balearic Islands	21
Bangladesh	23
Barbados	23
Belarus	21
Belgium	21
Belize	23
Benin	25
Bermuda	31
Bhutan	28
Bolivia	23
Bosnia and Herzegovina	21
Botswana	23
Brazil	22
British Virgin Islands	31
Brunei	25

Bulgaria	23
Burkina Faso	23
Burma	23
Burundi	22
Cambodia	28
Cameroon	22
Canada	22
Canary Islands	22
Cape Verde	25
Caroline Islands	31
Cayman Islands	31
Central African Republic	25
Chad	25
Chile	22
China	24
China (Hong Kong)	31
China (Macau)	31
China (Taiwan)	23
China (Tibet)	34
Christmas Island	27
Cocos (Keeling) Islands	41
Colombia	22
Comoros	23
Congo (formerly Congo Brazzaville or French Congo)	25
Congo (Democratic Republic)	25
Corsica	21
Costa Rica	23
Croatia	21
Cuba	24
Cyprus	31
Czech Republic	21
Denmark	21
Djibouti	22

Dominica	23
Dominican Republic	23
East Timor	25
Ecuador	22
Egypt	22
El Salvador	25
Equatorial Guinea	23
Eritrea	22
Estonia	21
Ethiopia	22
Falkland Islands and Dependencies	31
Faroe Islands	31
Fiji	23
Finland	24
France	21
French Guyana	31
French Polynesia	31
French West Indies	31
Gabon	25
Gambia	22
Georgia	21
Germany	21
Ghana	22
Gibraltar	31
Greece	21
Greenland	31
Grenada	24
Guatemala	24
Guernsey	21
Guinea	22
Guinea-Bissau	22
Guyana	22
Haiti	23
Holland (Netherlands)	21

Honduras	24
Hungary	22
Iceland	22
India	23
Indonesia	22
Iran	22
Iraq	22
Ireland (Republic of)	21
Ireland (Northern)	21
Isle of Man	21
Israel	22
Italy	21
Ivory Coast	22
Jamaica	22
Japan	23
Jersey	21
Jordan	23
Kazakhstan	21
Kenya	22
Kiribati	23
Korea (North)	28
Korea (South)	24
Kosovo	21
Kuwait	22
Kyrgyzstan	21
Laos	30
Latvia	21
Lebanon	22
Lesotho	23
Liberia	22
Libya	21
Liechtenstein	21
Lithuania	21
Luxembourg	21

Macedonia	21
Madagascar	23
Madeira	31
Malawi	23
Malaysia	24
Maldives	26
Mali	25
Malta	21
Mariana Islands	26
Marshall Islands	32
Mauritania	23
Mauritius	22
Mexico	23
Micronesia	23
Moldova	21
Monaco	21
Mongolia	24
Montenegro	21
Montserrat	31
Morocco	22
Mozambique	23
Namibia	23
Nauru	36
Nepal	23
Netherlands	21
Nevis	24
New Caledonia	31
New Zealand	26
New Zealand Island Territories	50
Nicaragua	24
Niger (Republic of)	25
Nigeria	22
Norfolk Island	31
Norway	21

Oman (Sultanate of)	22
Pakistan	23
Palau	23
Panama	26
Papua New Guinea	26
Paraguay	22
Peru	22
Philippines	23
Pitcairn, Henderson, Ducie and Oeno Islands	31
Poland	21
Portugal	21
Portuguese Timor	31
Puerto Rico	23
Qatar	23
Reunion	31
Romania	22
Russia	21
Rwanda	23
Sabah	23
St. Helena	31
St. Kitts and Nevis	24
St. Lucia	24
St. Pierre and Miquelon	31
St. Vincent and the Grenadines	24
Samoa (U.S.A. Territory) (See also Western Samoa)	30
San Marino	21
Sao Tome and Principe	25
Sarawak	28
Saudi Arabia	24
Scotland	21
Senegal	22
Serbia	21
Seychelles	22

Sierra Leone	22
Singapore	22
Slovakia	21
Slovenia	21
Society Islands (French Polynesia)	31
Solomon Islands	29
Somalia	22
South Africa	22
South Georgia (Falkland Island Dependencies)	31
South Orkneys	21
South Shetlands	21
Spain	21
Spanish Territories of North Africa	31
Sri Lanka	23
Sudan	22
Surinam	22
Swaziland	22
Sweden	21
Switzerland	21
Syria	23
Tajikistan	21
Tanzania	22
Thailand	23
Togo	22
Tonga	30
Trinidad and Tobago	23
Tristan Da Cunha	31
Tunisia	22
Turkey	21
Turkmenistan	21
Turks & Caicos Islands	31
Tuvalu	23
Uganda	22
Ukraine	21

United Arab Emirates	22
United States of America	22
Uruguay	22
Uzbekistan	21
Vanuatu	29
Vatican City State	21
Venezuela	22
Vietnam	28
Virgin Islands – U.S.A	24
Wake Island	25
Western Samoa	34
Yemen (Republic of)	30
Zaire	25
Zambia	23
Zimbabwe	22

Article 7

The standard terms in the model annexed to the present Convention shall in all cases be written either in French or in English. They may also be written in the official language, or in one of the official languages, of the State in which the documents originate.

The corresponding blanks shall be completed either in the language of the State addressed or in French or in English.

15. Reason For Non-Service Of Document

15.1. address unknown
15.2. addressee cannot be located
15.3. document could not be served before the date or time limit stated in point 6.2.
15.4. other (please specify)

The document is annexed to this certificate.

> Done at ...   Date ...
> Signature and/or stamp ...

Regulation (EC) No 1393/2007 of the European Parliament and of the Council of 13 November 2007

On the service in the Member States of judicial and extrajudicial documents in civil or commercial matters (service of documents), and repealing Council Regulation (EC) No 1348/2000

This regulation can be found in full at:

http://eur-lex.europa.eu/LexUriServ/LexUriServ.do?uri=CELEX:32007R1393:EN:HTML

The European Parliament And The Council Of The European Union,

Having regard to the Treaty establishing the European Community, and in particular Article 61(c) and Article 67(5), second indent, thereof,

Having regard to the proposal from the Commission,

Having regard to the opinion of the European Economic and Social Committee [1],

Acting in accordance with the procedure laid down in Article 251 of the Treaty [2],

Whereas:

(1) The Union has set itself the objective of maintaining and developing the Union as an area of freedom, security and justice, in which the free movement of persons is assured. To establish such an area, the Community is to adopt, among others, the measures relating to judicial cooperation in civil matters needed for the proper functioning of the internal market.

(2) The proper functioning of the internal market entails the need to improve and expedite the transmission of judicial and extrajudicial documents in civil or commercial matters for service between the Member States.

(3) The Council, by an Act dated 26 May 1997 [3], drew up a Convention on the service in the Member States of the European Union of judicial and extrajudicial documents in civil or commercial matters and recommended it for adoption by the Member States in accordance with their respective constitutional rules. That Convention has not entered into force. Continuity in the results of the negotiations for conclusion of the Convention should be ensured.

(4) On 29 May 2000 the Council adopted Regulation (EC) No 1348/2000 on the service in the Member States of judicial and extrajudicial documents in civil or commercial matters [4]. The main content of that Regulation is based on the Convention.

(5) On 1 October 2004 the Commission adopted a report on the application of Regulation (EC) No 1348/2000. The report concludes that the application of Regulation (EC) No 1348/2000 has generally improved and expedited the transmission and the service of documents between Member States since its entry into force in 2001, but that nevertheless the application of certain provisions is not fully satisfactory.

(6) Efficiency and speed in judicial procedures in civil matters require that judicial and extrajudicial documents be transmitted directly and by rapid means between local bodies designated by the Member States. Member States may indicate their intention to designate only one transmitting or

receiving agency or one agency to perform both functions, for a period of five years. This designation may, however, be renewed every five years.

(7) Speed in transmission warrants the use of all appropriate means, provided that certain conditions as to the legibility and reliability of the document received are observed. Security in transmission requires that the document to be transmitted be accompanied by a standard form, to be completed in the official language or one of the official languages of the place where service is to be effected, or in another language accepted by the Member State in question.

(8) This Regulation should not apply to service of a document on the party's authorised representative in the Member State where the proceedings are taking place regardless of the place of residence of that party.

(9) The service of a document should be effected as soon as possible, and in any event within one month of receipt by the receiving agency.

(10) To secure the effectiveness of this Regulation, the possibility of refusing service of documents should be confined to exceptional situations.

(11) In order to facilitate the transmission and service of documents between Member States, the standard forms set out in the Annexes to this Regulation should be used.

(12) The receiving agency should inform the addressee in writing using the standard form that he may refuse to accept the document to be served at the time of service or by returning the document to the receiving agency within one week if it is not either in a language which he understands or in the official language or one of the official languages of the place of service. This rule should also apply to the subsequent service once the addressee has exercised his right of refusal. These rules on refusal should also apply to service by diplomatic or consular agents, service by postal services and direct service. It should be established that the service of the refused document can be remedied through the service on the addressee of a translation of the document.

(13) Speed in transmission warrants documents being served within days of receipt of the document. However, if service has not been effected after one month has elapsed, the receiving agency should inform the transmitting agency. The expiry of this period should not imply that the request be returned to the transmitting agency where it is clear that service is feasible within a reasonable period.

(14) The receiving agency should continue to take all necessary steps to effect the service of the document also in cases where it has not been possible to effect service within the month, for example, because the defendant has been away from his home on holiday or away from his office on business. However, in order to avoid an open-ended obligation for the receiving agency to take steps to effect the service of a document, the transmitting agency should be able to specify a time limit in the standard form after which service is no longer required.

(15) Given the differences between the Member States as regards their rules of procedure, the material date for the purposes of service varies from one Member State to another. Having regard to such situations and the possible difficulties that may arise, this Regulation should provide for a system where it is the law of the Member State addressed which determines the date of service. However, where according to the law of a Member State a document has to be served within a particular period, the date to be taken into account with respect to the applicant should be that determined by the law of that Member State. This double date system exists only in a limited number of Member States. Those Member States which apply this system should communicate this to the Commission, which should publish the information in the Official Journal of the

European Union and make it available through the European Judicial Network in Civil and Commercial Matters established by Council Decision 2001/470/EC [5].

(16) In order to facilitate access to justice, costs occasioned by recourse to a judicial officer or a person competent under the law of the Member State addressed should correspond to a single fixed fee laid down by that Member State in advance which respects the principles of proportionality and non-discrimination. The requirement of a single fixed fee should not preclude the possibility for Member States to set different fees for different types of service as long as they respect these principles.

(17) Each Member State should be free to effect service of documents directly by postal services on persons residing in another Member State by registered letter with acknowledgement of receipt or equivalent.

(18) It should be possible for any person interested in a judicial proceeding to effect service of documents directly through the judicial officers, officials or other competent persons of the Member State addressed, where such direct service is permitted under the law of that Member State.

(19) The Commission should draw up a manual containing information relevant for the proper application of this Regulation, which should be made available through the European Judicial Network in Civil and Commercial Matters. The Commission and the Member States should do their utmost to ensure that this information is up to date and complete especially as regards contact details of receiving and transmitting agencies.

(20) In calculating the periods and time limits provided for in this Regulation, Regulation (EEC, Euratom) No 1182/71 of the Council of 3 June 1971 determining the rules applicable to periods, dates and time limits [6] should apply.

(21) The measures necessary for the implementation of this Regulation should be adopted in accordance with Council Decision 1999/468/EC of 28 June 1999 laying down the procedures for the exercise of implementing powers conferred on the Commission [7].
(22) In particular, power should be conferred on the Commission to update or make technical amendments to the standard forms set out in the Annexes. Since those measures are of general scope and are designed to amend/delete non-essential elements of this Regulation, they must be adopted in accordance with the regulatory procedure with scrutiny provided for in Article 5a of Decision 1999/468/EC.

(23) This Regulation prevails over the provisions contained in bilateral or multilateral agreements or arrangements having the same scope, concluded by the Member States, and in particular the Protocol annexed to the Brussels Convention of 27 September 1968 [8] and the Hague Convention of 15 November 1965 [9] in relations between the Member States party thereto. This Regulation does not preclude Member States from maintaining or concluding agreements or arrangements to expedite or simplify the transmission of documents, provided that they are compatible with this Regulation.

(24) The information transmitted pursuant to this Regulation should enjoy suitable protection. This matter falls within the scope of Directive 95/46/EC of the European Parliament and of the Council of 24 October 1995 on the protection of individuals with regard to the processing of personal data and on the free movement of such data [10], and of Directive 2002/58/EC of the European Parliament and of the Council of 12 July 2002 concerning the processing of personal data and the protection of privacy in the electronic communications sector (Directive on privacy and electronic communications) [11].

(25) No later than 1 June 2011 and every five years thereafter, the Commission should review the application of this Regulation and propose such amendments as may appear necessary.

(26) Since the objectives of this Regulation cannot be sufficiently achieved by the Member States and can therefore, by reason of the scale or effects of the action, be better achieved at Community level, the Community may adopt measures, in accordance with the principle of subsidiarity as set out in Article 5 of the Treaty. In accordance with the principle of proportionality, as set out in that Article, this Regulation does not go beyond what is necessary in order to achieve those objectives.

(27) In order to make the provisions more easily accessible and readable, Regulation (EC) No 1348/2000 should be repealed and replaced by this Regulation.

(28) In accordance with Article 3 of the Protocol on the position of the United Kingdom and Ireland, annexed to the Treaty on European Union and to the Treaty establishing the European Community, the United Kingdom and Ireland are taking part in the adoption and application of this Regulation.

(29) In accordance with Articles 1 and 2 of the Protocol on the position of Denmark, annexed to the Treaty on European Union and to the Treaty establishing the European Community, Denmark does not take part in the adoption of this Regulation and is not bound by it or subject to its application,

HAVE ADOPTED THIS REGULATION:

Chapter I
General Provisions
Article 1
Scope

1. This Regulation shall apply in civil and commercial matters where a judicial or extrajudicial document has to be transmitted from one Member State to another for service there. It shall not extend in particular to revenue, customs or administrative matters or to liability of the State for actions or omissions in the exercise of state authority (acta iure imperii).

2. This Regulation shall not apply where the address of the person to be served with the document is not known.

3. In this Regulation, the term "Member State" shall mean the Member States with the exception of Denmark.

Article 2
Transmitting and receiving agencies

1. Each Member State shall designate the public officers, authorities or other persons, hereinafter referred to as "transmitting agencies", competent for the transmission of judicial or extrajudicial documents to be served in another Member State.

2. Each Member State shall designate the public officers, authorities or other persons, hereinafter referred to as "receiving agencies", competent for the receipt of judicial or extrajudicial documents from another Member State.

3. A Member State may designate one transmitting agency and one receiving agency, or one agency to perform both functions. A federal State, a State in which several legal systems apply or a State with autonomous territorial units shall be free to designate more than one such agency. The designation shall have effect for a period of five years and may be renewed at five-year intervals.

4. Each Member State shall provide the Commission with the following information:

    (a) the names and addresses of the receiving agencies referred to in paragraphs 2 and 3;
    (b) the geographical areas in which they have jurisdiction;
    (c) the means of receipt of documents available to them; and
    (d) the languages that may be used for the completion of the standard form set out in Annex I.

Member States shall notify the Commission of any subsequent modification of such information.

Article 3
Central body

Each Member State shall designate a central body responsible for:

    (a) supplying information to the transmitting agencies;

    (b) seeking solutions to any difficulties which may arise during transmission of documents for service;

    (c) forwarding, in exceptional cases, at the request of a transmitting agency, a request for service to the competent receiving agency.

A federal State, a State in which several legal systems apply or a State with autonomous territorial units shall be free to designate more than one central body.

Chapter II
Judicial Documents
Section 1
Transmission and service of judicial documents

Article 4

1. Judicial documents shall be transmitted directly and as soon as possible between the agencies designated pursuant to Article 2.

2. The transmission of documents, requests, confirmations, receipts, certificates and any other papers between transmitting agencies and receiving agencies may be carried out by any appropriate means, provided that the content of the document received is true and faithful to that of the document forwarded and that all information in it is easily legible.

3. The document to be transmitted shall be accompanied by a request drawn up using the standard form set out in Annex I. The form shall be completed in the official language of the Member State addressed or, if there are several official languages in that Member State, the official language or one of the official

languages of the place where service is to be effected, or in another language which that Member State has indicated it can accept. Each Member State shall indicate the official language or languages of the institutions of the European Union other than its own which is or are acceptable to it for completion of the form.

4. The documents and all papers that are transmitted shall be exempted from legalisation or any equivalent formality.

5. When the transmitting agency wishes a copy of the document to be returned together with the certificate referred to in Article 10, it shall send the document in duplicate.

Article 5
Translation of documents

1. The applicant shall be advised by the transmitting agency to which he forwards the document for transmission that the addressee may refuse to accept it if it is not in one of the languages provided for in Article 8.

2. The applicant shall bear any costs of translation prior to the transmission of the document, without prejudice to any possible subsequent decision by the court or competent authority on liability for such costs.

Article 6
Receipt of documents by receiving agency

1. On receipt of a document, a receiving agency shall, as soon as possible and in any event within seven days of receipt, send a receipt to the transmitting agency by the swiftest possible means of transmission using the standard form set out in Annex I.

2. Where the request for service cannot be fulfilled on the basis of the information or documents transmitted, the receiving agency shall contact the transmitting agency by the swiftest possible means in order to secure the missing information or documents.

3. If the request for service is manifestly outside the scope of this Regulation or if non-compliance with the formal conditions required makes service impossible, the request and the documents transmitted shall be returned, on receipt, to the transmitting agency, together with the notice of return using the standard form set out in Annex I.

4. A receiving agency receiving a document for service but not having territorial jurisdiction to serve it shall forward it, as well as the request, to the receiving agency having territorial jurisdiction in the same Member State if the request complies with the conditions laid down in Article 4(3) and shall inform the transmitting agency accordingly using the standard form set out in Annex I. That receiving agency shall inform the transmitting agency when it receives the document, in the manner provided for in paragraph 1.

Article 7
Service of documents

1. The receiving agency shall itself serve the document or have it served, either in accordance with the law of the Member State addressed or by a particular method requested by the transmitting agency, unless that method is incompatible with the law of that Member State.

2. The receiving agency shall take all necessary steps to effect the service of the document as soon as possible, and in any event within one month of receipt. If it has not been possible to effect service within one month of receipt, the receiving agency shall:

(a) immediately inform the transmitting agency by means of the certificate in the standard form set out in Annex I, which shall be drawn up under the conditions referred to in Article 10(2) ; and

(b) continue to take all necessary steps to effect the service of the document, unless indicated otherwise by the transmitting agency, where service seems to be possible within a reasonable period of time.

Article 8
Refusal to accept a document

1. The receiving agency shall inform the addressee, using the standard form set out in Annex II, that he may refuse to accept the document to be served at the time of service or by returning the document to the receiving agency within one week if it is not written in, or accompanied by a translation into, either of the following languages:

   (a) a language which the addressee understands;

   or

   (b) the official language of the Member State addressed or, if there are several official languages in that Member State, the official language or one of the official languages of the place where service is to be effected.

2. Where the receiving agency is informed that the addressee refuses to accept the document in accordance with paragraph 1, it shall immediately inform the transmitting agency by means of the certificate provided for in Article 10 and return the request and the documents of which a translation is requested.

3. If the addressee has refused to accept the document pursuant to paragraph 1, the service of the document can be remedied through the service on the addressee in accordance with the provisions of this Regulation of the document accompanied by a translation into a language provided for in paragraph 1. In that case, the date of service of the document shall be the date on which the document accompanied by the translation is served in accordance with the law of the Member State addressed. However, where according to the law of a Member State, a document has to be served within a particular period, the date to be taken into account with respect to the applicant shall be the date of the service of the initial document determined pursuant to Article 9(2) .

4. Paragraphs 1, 2 and 3 shall also apply to the means of transmission and service of judicial documents provided for in Section 2.

5. For the purposes of paragraph 1, the diplomatic or consular agents, where service is effected in accordance with Article 13, or the authority or person, where service is effected in accordance with Article 14, shall inform the addressee that he may refuse to accept the document and that any document refused must be sent to those agents or to that authority or person respectively.

Article 9
Date of service

1. Without prejudice to Article 8, the date of service of a document pursuant to Article 7 shall be the date on which it is served in accordance with the law of the Member State addressed.

2. However, where according to the law of a Member State a document has to be served within a particular period, the date to be taken into account with respect to the applicant shall be that determined by the law of that Member State.

3. Paragraphs 1 and 2 shall also apply to the means of transmission and service of judicial documents provided for in Section 2.

Article 10
Certificate of service and copy of the document served

1. When the formalities concerning the service of the document have been completed, a certificate of completion of those formalities shall be drawn up in the standard form set out in Annex I and addressed to the transmitting agency, together with, where Article 4(5) applies, a copy of the document served.

2. The certificate shall be completed in the official language or one of the official languages of the Member State of origin or in another language which the Member State of origin has indicated that it can accept. Each Member State shall indicate the official language or languages of the institutions of the European Union other than its own which is or are acceptable to it for completion of the form.

Article 11
Costs of service

1. The service of judicial documents coming from a Member State shall not give rise to any payment or reimbursement of taxes or costs for services rendered by the Member State addressed.

2. However, the applicant shall pay or reimburse the costs occasioned by:

(a) recourse to a judicial officer or to a person competent under the law of the Member State addressed;

(b) the use of a particular method of service.

Costs occasioned by recourse to a judicial officer or to a person competent under the law of the Member State addressed shall correspond to a single fixed fee laid down by that Member State in advance which respects the principles of proportionality and non-discrimination. Member States shall communicate such fixed fees to the Commission.

Section 2
Other means of transmission and service of judicial documents

Article 12
Transmission by consular or diplomatic channels

Each Member State shall be free, in exceptional circumstances, to use consular or diplomatic channels to forward judicial documents, for the purpose of service, to those agencies of another Member State which are designated pursuant to Articles 2 or 3.

Article 13
Service by diplomatic or consular agents

1. Each Member State shall be free to effect service of judicial documents on persons residing in another Member State, without application of any compulsion, directly through its diplomatic or consular agents.

2. Any Member State may make it known, in accordance with Article 23(1), that it is opposed to such service within its territory, unless the documents are to be served on nationals of the Member State in which the documents originate.

Article 14
Service by postal services

Each Member State shall be free to effect service of judicial documents directly by postal services on persons residing in another Member State by registered letter with acknowledgement of receipt or equivalent.

Article 15
Direct service

Any person interested in a judicial proceeding may effect service of judicial documents directly through the judicial officers, officials or other competent persons of the Member State addressed, where such direct service is permitted under the law of that Member State.

Chapter III
Extrajudicial Documents
Article 16
Transmission

Extrajudicial documents may be transmitted for service in another Member State in accordance with the provisions of this Regulation.

Chapter IV
Final Provisions
Article 17
Implementing rules

Measures designed to amend non-essential elements of this Regulation relating to the updating or to the making of technical amendments to the standard forms set out in Annexes I and II shall be adopted in accordance with the regulatory procedure with scrutiny referred to in Article 18(2).

Article 18

Committee

1. The Commission shall be assisted by a committee.

2. Where reference is made to this paragraph, Article 5a(1) to (4), and Article 7 of Decision 1999/468/EC shall apply, having regard to the provisions of Article 8 thereof.

Article 19
Defendant not entering an appearance

1. Where a writ of summons or an equivalent document has had to be transmitted to another Member State for the purpose of service under the provisions of this Regulation and the defendant has not appeared, judgment shall not be given until it is established that:

>(a) the document was served by a method prescribed by the internal law of the Member State addressed for the service of documents in domestic actions upon persons who are within its territory; or

>(b) the document was actually delivered to the defendant or to his residence by another method provided for by this Regulation;
>and that in either of these cases the service or the delivery was effected in sufficient time to enable the defendant to defend.

2. Each Member State may make it known, in accordance with Article 23(1), that the judge, notwithstanding the provisions of paragraph 1, may give judgment even if no certificate of service or delivery has been received, if all the following conditions are fulfilled:
>(a) the document was transmitted by one of the methods provided for in this Regulation;

>(b) a period of time of not less than six months, considered adequate by the judge in the particular case, has elapsed since the date of the transmission of the document;

>(c) no certificate of any kind has been received, even though every reasonable effort has been made to obtain it through the competent authorities or bodies of the Member State addressed.

3. Notwithstanding paragraphs 1 and 2, the judge may order, in case of urgency, any provisional or protective measures.

4. When a writ of summons or an equivalent document has had to be transmitted to another Member State for the purpose of service under the provisions of this Regulation and a judgment has been entered against a defendant who has not appeared, the judge shall have the power to relieve the defendant from the effects of the expiry of the time for appeal from the judgment if the following conditions are fulfilled:

>   (a) the defendant, without any fault on his part, did not have knowledge of the document in sufficient time to defend, or knowledge of the judgment in sufficient time to appeal; and

>   (b) the defendant has disclosed a prima facie defence to the action on the merits.

An application for relief may be filed only within a reasonable time after the defendant has knowledge of the judgment.

Each Member State may make it known, in accordance with Article 23(1), that such application will not be entertained if it is filed after the expiry of a time to be stated by it in that communication, but which shall in no case be less than one year following the date of the judgment.

5. Paragraph 4 shall not apply to judgments concerning the status or capacity of persons.

Article 20
Relationship with agreements or arrangements to which Member States are party

1. This Regulation shall, in relation to matters to which it applies, prevail over other provisions contained in bilateral or multilateral agreements or arrangements concluded by the Member States, and in particular Article IV of the Protocol to the Brussels Convention of 1968 and the Hague Convention of 15 November 1965.

2. This Regulation shall not preclude individual Member States from maintaining or concluding agreements or arrangements to expedite further or simplify the transmission of documents, provided that they are compatible with this Regulation.

3. Member States shall send to the Commission:

>   (a) a copy of the agreements or arrangements referred to in paragraph 2 concluded between the Member States as well as drafts of such agreements or arrangements which they intend to adopt; and

>   (b) any denunciation of, or amendments to, these agreements or arrangements.

Article 21
Legal aid

This Regulation shall not affect the application of Article 23 of the Convention on civil procedure of 17 July 1905, Article 24 of the Convention on civil procedure of 1 March 1954 or Article 13 of the Convention on international access to justice of 25 October 1980 between the Member States party to those Conventions.

Article 22
Protection of information transmitted

1. Information, including in particular personal data, transmitted under this Regulation shall be used by the receiving agency only for the purpose for which it was transmitted.

2. Receiving agencies shall ensure the confidentiality of such information, in accordance with their national law.

3. Paragraphs 1 and 2 shall not affect national laws enabling data subjects to be informed of the use made of information transmitted under this Regulation.

4. This Regulation shall be without prejudice to Directives 95/46/EC and 2002/58/EC.

Article 23
Communication and publication

1. Member States shall communicate to the Commission the information referred to in Articles 2, 3, 4, 10, 11, 13, 15 and 19. Member States shall communicate to the Commission if, according to their law, a document has to be served within a particular period as referred to in Articles 8(3) and 9(2).

2. The Commission shall publish the information communicated in accordance with paragraph 1 in the Official Journal of the European Union with the exception of the addresses and other contact details of the agencies and of the central bodies and the geographical areas in which they have jurisdiction.

3. The Commission shall draw up and update regularly a manual containing the information referred to in paragraph 1, which shall be available electronically, in particular through the European Judicial Network in Civil and Commercial Matters.

Article 24
Review

No later than 1 June 2011, and every five years thereafter, the Commission shall present to the European Parliament, the Council and the European Economic and Social Committee a report on the application of this Regulation, paying special attention to the effectiveness of the agencies designated pursuant to Article 2 and to the practical application of Article 3(c) and Article 9. The report shall be accompanied if need be by proposals for adaptations of this Regulation in line with the evolution of notification systems.

Article 25
Repeal

1. Regulation (EC) No 1348/2000 shall be repealed as from the date of application of this Regulation.

2. References made to the repealed Regulation shall be construed as being made to this Regulation and should be read in accordance with the correlation table in Annex III.

Article 26
Entry into force

This Regulation shall enter into force on the 20th day following its publication in the Official Journal of the European Union.

It shall apply from 13 November 2008 with the exception of Article 23 which shall apply from 13 August 2008.

This Regulation shall be binding in its entirety and directly applicable in the Member States in accordance with the Treaty establishing the European Community.
Done at Strasbourg, 13 November 2007.
For the European Parliament
The President
H.-G. Pöttering
For the Council
The President
M. LOBO ANTUNES

N.B. On 25 October 1980 the Fourteenth Session adopted a Recommendation on information to accompany judicial and extrajudicial documents to be sent or served abroad in civil or commercial matters (Proceedings of the Fourteenth Session, Tome I, Miscellaneous matters, p. 67; idem, Tome IV, Judicial co-operation, p. 339; Practical Handbook on the Operation of the Hague Service Convention, Appendix 3, p. 129).

Hague Convention of 15 November 1965 on the Service Abroad of Judicial and Extrajudicial Documents in Civil or Commerce Matters

The outline on the Hague Service Convention can be downloaded as a PDF document from:
http://www.hcch.net/upload/outline14e.pdf

Hague Service Convention - model forms

Model Form annexed to the Convention (Request, Certificate, Summary with Warning) can be downloaded in PDF or WORD format from http://www.hcch.net/index_en.php?act=text.display&tid=47

Convention On The Service Abroad Of Judicial And Extrajudicial Documents In Civil Or Commercial Matters

(Concluded 15 November 1965)

The States signatory to the present Convention,

Desiring to create appropriate means to ensure that judicial and extrajudicial documents to be served abroad shall be brought to the notice of the addressee in sufficient time,

Desiring to improve the organisation of mutual judicial assistance for that purpose by simplifying and expediting the procedure,

Have resolved to conclude a Convention to this effect and have agreed upon the following provisions:

Article 1

The present Convention shall apply in all cases, in civil or commercial matters, where there is occasion to transmit a judicial or extrajudicial document for service abroad.

This Convention shall not apply where the address of the person to be served with the document is not known.

Chapter I - Judicial Documents
Article 2

Each Contracting State shall designate a Central Authority which will undertake to receive requests for service coming from other Contracting States and to proceed in conformity with the provisions of Articles 3 to 6.

Each State shall organise the Central Authority in conformity with its own law.

Article 3

The authority or judicial officer competent under the law of the State in which the documents originate shall forward to the Central Authority of the State addressed a request conforming to the model annexed to the present Convention, without any requirement of legalisation or other equivalent formality.

The document to be served or a copy thereof shall be annexed to the request. The request and the document shall both be furnished in duplicate.

Article 4

If the Central Authority considers that the request does not comply with the provisions of the present Convention it shall promptly inform the applicant and specify its objections to the request.

Article 5

The Central Authority of the State addressed shall itself serve the document or shall arrange to have it served by an appropriate agency, either -

> a) by a method prescribed by its internal law for the service of documents in domestic actions upon persons who are within its territory, or

> b) by a particular method requested by the applicant, unless such a method is incompatible with the law of the State addressed.

Subject to sub-paragraph (b) of the first paragraph of this Article, the document may always be served by delivery to an addressee who accepts it voluntarily.

If the document is to be served under the first paragraph above, the Central Authority may require the document to be written in, or translated into, the official language or one of the official languages of the State addressed.

That part of the request, in the form attached to the present Convention, which contains a summary of the document to be served, shall be served with the document.

Article 6

The Central Authority of the State addressed or any authority which it may have designated for that purpose, shall complete a certificate in the form of the model annexed to the present Convention.

The certificate shall state that the document has been served and shall include the method, the place and the date of service and the person to whom the document was delivered. If the document has not been served, the certificate shall set out the reasons which have prevented service.

The applicant may require that a certificate not completed by a Central Authority or by a judicial authority shall be countersigned by one of these authorities.

The certificate shall be forwarded directly to the applicant.

Article 7

The standard terms in the model annexed to the present Convention shall in all cases be written either in French or in English. They may also be written in the official language, or in one of the official languages, of the State in which the documents originate.

The corresponding blanks shall be completed either in the language of the State addressed or in French or in English.

Article 8

Each Contracting State shall be free to effect service of judicial documents upon persons abroad, without application of any compulsion, directly through its diplomatic or consular agents.

Any State may declare that it is opposed to such service within its territory, unless the document is to be served upon a national of the State in which the documents originate.

Article 9

Each Contracting State shall be free, in addition, to use consular channels to forward documents, for the purpose of service, to those authorities of another Contracting State which are designated by the latter for this purpose.

Each Contracting State may, if exceptional circumstances so require, use diplomatic channels for the same purpose.

Article 10

Provided the State of destination does not object, the present Convention shall not interfere with -

a) the freedom to send judicial documents, by postal channels, directly to persons abroad,

b) the freedom of judicial officers, officials or other competent persons of the State of origin to effect service of judicial documents directly through the judicial officers, officials or other competent persons of the State of destination,

c) the freedom of any person interested in a judicial proceeding to effect service of judicial documents directly through the judicial officers, officials or other competent persons of the State of destination.

Article 11

The present Convention shall not prevent two or more Contracting States from agreeing to permit, for the purpose of service of judicial documents, channels of transmission other than those provided for in the preceding Articles and, in particular, direct communication between their respective authorities.

Article 12

The service of judicial documents coming from a Contracting State shall not give rise to any payment or reimbursement of taxes or costs for the services rendered by the State addressed.

The applicant shall pay or reimburse the costs occasioned by --

a) the employment of a judicial officer or of a person competent under the law of the State of destination,

b) the use of a particular method of service.

Article 13

Where a request for service complies with the terms of the present Convention, the State addressed may refuse to comply therewith only if it deems that compliance would infringe its sovereignty or security.

It may not refuse to comply solely on the ground that, under its internal law, it claims exclusive jurisdiction over the subject-matter of the action or that its internal law would not permit the action upon which the application is based.

The Central Authority shall, in case of refusal, promptly inform the applicant and state the reasons for the refusal.

Article 14

Difficulties which may arise in connection with the transmission of judicial documents for service shall be settled through diplomatic channels.

Article 15

Where a writ of summons or an equivalent document had to be transmitted abroad for the purpose of service, under the provisions of the present Convention, and the defendant has not appeared, judgment shall not be given until it is established that -

> a) the document was served by a method prescribed by the internal law of the State addressed for the service of documents in domestic actions upon persons who are within its territory, or
>
> b) the document was actually delivered to the defendant or to his residence by another method provided for by this Convention, and that in either of these cases the service or the delivery was effected in sufficient time to enable the defendant to defend.

Each Contracting State shall be free to declare that the judge, notwithstanding the provisions of the first paragraph of this Article, may give judgment even if no certificate of service or delivery has been received, if all the following conditions are fulfilled -

> a) the document was transmitted by one of the methods provided for in this Convention,
>
> b) a period of time of not less than six months, considered adequate by the judge in the particular case, has elapsed since the date of the transmission of the document,
>
> c) no certificate of any kind has been received, even though every reasonable effort has been made to obtain it through the competent authorities of the State addressed.

Notwithstanding the provisions of the preceding paragraphs the judge may order, in case of urgency, any provisional or protective measures.

Article 16

When a writ of summons or an equivalent document had to be transmitted abroad for the purpose of service, under the provisions of the present Convention, and a judgment has been entered against a defendant who has not appeared, the judge shall have the power to relieve the defendant from the effects of the expiration of the time for appeal from the judgment if the following conditions are fulfilled -

> a) the defendant, without any fault on his part, did not have knowledge of the document in sufficient time to defend, or knowledge of the judgment in sufficient time to appeal, and
>
> b) the defendant has disclosed a prima facie defence to the action on the merits.

An application for relief may be filed only within a reasonable time after the defendant has knowledge of the judgment.

Each Contracting State may declare that the application will not be entertained if it is filed after the expiration of a time to be stated in the declaration, but which shall in no case be less than one year following the date of the judgment.

This Article shall not apply to judgments concerning status or capacity of persons.

Chapter II - Extrajudicial Documents
Article 17

Extrajudicial documents emanating from authorities and judicial officers of a Contracting State may be transmitted for the purpose of service in another Contracting State by the methods and under the provisions of the present Convention.

Chapter III - General Clauses
Article 18

Each Contracting State may designate other authorities in addition to the Central Authority and shall determine the extent of their competence.

The applicant shall, however, in all cases, have the right to address a request directly to the Central Authority.

Federal States shall be free to designate more than one Central Authority.

Article 19

To the extent that the internal law of a Contracting State permits methods of transmission, other than those provided for in the preceding Articles, of documents coming from abroad, for service within its territory, the present Convention shall not affect such provisions.

Article 20

The present Convention shall not prevent an agreement between any two or more Contracting States to dispense with -

    a) the necessity for duplicate copies of transmitted documents as required by the second paragraph of Article 3,

    b) the language requirements of the third paragraph of Article 5 and Article 7,

    c) the provisions of the fourth paragraph of Article 5,

    d) the provisions of the second paragraph of Article 12.

Article 21

Each Contracting State shall, at the time of the deposit of its instrument of ratification or accession, or at a later date, inform the Ministry of Foreign Affairs of the Netherlands of the following -

    a) the designation of authorities, pursuant to Articles 2 and 18,

    b) the designation of the authority competent to complete the certificate pursuant to Article 6,

    c) the designation of the authority competent to receive documents transmitted by consular channels, pursuant to Article 9.

Each Contracting State shall similarly inform the Ministry, where appropriate, of -

    a) opposition to the use of methods of transmission pursuant to Articles 8 and 10,

    b) declarations pursuant to the second paragraph of Article 15 and the third paragraph of Article 16,

    c) all modifications of the above designations, oppositions and declarations.

Article 22

Where Parties to the present Convention are also Parties to one or both of the Conventions on civil procedure signed at The Hague on 17th July 1905, and on 1st March 1954, this Convention shall replace as between them Articles 1 to 7 of the earlier Conventions.

Article 23

The present Convention shall not affect the application of Article 23 of the Convention on civil procedure signed at The Hague on 17th July 1905, or of Article 24 of the Convention on civil procedure signed at The Hague on 1st March 1954.

These Articles shall, however, apply only if methods of communication, identical to those provided for in these Conventions, are used.

Article 24

Supplementary agreements between Parties to the Conventions of 1905 and 1954 shall be considered as equally applicable to the present Convention, unless the Parties have otherwise agreed.

Article 25

Without prejudice to the provisions of Articles 22 and 24, the present Convention shall not derogate from Conventions containing provisions on the matters governed by this Convention to which the Contracting States are, or shall become, Parties.

Article 26

The present Convention shall be open for signature by the States represented at the Tenth Session of the Hague Conference on Private International Law.

It shall be ratified, and the instruments of ratification shall be deposited with the Ministry of Foreign Affairs of the Netherlands.

Article 27

The present Convention shall enter into force on the sixtieth day after the deposit of the third instrument of ratification referred to in the second paragraph of Article 26.

The Convention shall enter into force for each signatory State which ratifies subsequently on the sixtieth day after the deposit of its instrument of ratification.

Article 28

Any State not represented at the Tenth Session of the Hague Conference on Private International Law may accede to the present Convention after it has entered into force in accordance with the first paragraph of Article 27. The instrument of accession shall be deposited with the Ministry of Foreign Affairs of the Netherlands.

The Convention shall enter into force for such a State in the absence of any objection from a State, which has ratified the Convention before such deposit, notified to the Ministry of Foreign Affairs of the Netherlands within a period of six months after the date on which the said Ministry has notified it of such accession.

In the absence of any such objection, the Convention shall enter into force for the acceding State on the first day of the month following the expiration of the last of the periods referred to in the preceding paragraph.

Article 29

Any State may, at the time of signature, ratification or accession, declare that the present Convention shall extend to all the territories for the international relations of which it is responsible, or to one or more of them. Such a declaration shall take effect on the date of entry into force of the Convention for the State concerned.

At any time thereafter, such extensions shall be notified to the Ministry of Foreign Affairs of the Netherlands.

The Convention shall enter into force for the territories mentioned in such an extension on the sixtieth day after the notification referred to in the preceding paragraph.

Article 30

The present Convention shall remain in force for five years from the date of its entry into force in accordance with the first paragraph of Article 27, even for States which have ratified it or acceded to it subsequently.

If there has been no denunciation, it shall be renewed tacitly every five years.

Any denunciation shall be notified to the Ministry of Foreign Affairs of the Netherlands at least six months before the end of the five year period.

It may be limited to certain of the territories to which the Convention applies.

The denunciation shall have effect only as regards the State which has notified it. The Convention shall remain in force for the other Contracting States.

Article 31

The Ministry of Foreign Affairs of the Netherlands shall give notice to the States referred to in Article 26, and to the States which have acceded in accordance with Article 28, of the following -

a) the signatures and ratifications referred to in Article 26;

b) the date on which the present Convention enters into force in accordance with the first paragraph of Article 27;

c) the accessions referred to in Article 28 and the dates on which they take effect;

d) the extensions referred to in Article 29 and the dates on which they take effect;

e) the designations, oppositions and declarations referred to in Article 21;

f) the denunciations referred to in the third paragraph of Article 30.

In witness whereof the undersigned, being duly authorised thereto, have signed the present Convention.

Done at The Hague, on the 15th day of November, 1965, in the English and French languages, both texts being equally authentic, in a single copy which shall be deposited in the archives of the Government of the Netherlands, and of which a certified copy shall be sent, through the diplomatic channel, to each of the States represented at the Tenth Session of the Hague Conference on Private International Law.

N.B. On 25 October 1980 the Fourteenth Session adopted a Recommendation on information to accompany judicial and extrajudicial documents to be sent or served abroad in civil or commercial matters (Proceedings of the Fourteenth Session, Tome I, Miscellaneous matters, p. 67; idem, Tome IV, Judicial co-operation, p. 339; Practical Handbook on the Operation of the Hague Service Convention, Appendix 3, p. 129).

Sample Affidavits

The forms of affidavit of service set out here are either from draft affidavits which have accompanied instructions or copies of affidavits which have been sworn and which appear to have been acceptable. It must be remembered that these affidavits are purely a guide and that from time to time the practice in all Courts changes.

If no affidavit of service is available to suit the process an affidavit should be prepared showing when and where the process was served, specifying the process and headed up according to the original.

IN THE FAMILY COURT OF AUSTRALIA AT ADELAIDE

                                                                            No   of 2012

IN THE MARRIAGE OF

....   Husband

      and

....   Wife

I,   of   in the County of   , England, Process Server, make Oath and say as follows:-

1.   THAT I am authorised and empowered to effect service of Process of the Supreme Court of Judicature in England.

2.   THAT I did on .... the .... day of ....2000 at ....o'clock in the ....noon at .... in the County of ....England, duly serve upon ....the respondent in this cause a sealed copy of the Application for Dissolution of Marriage and Form of Acknowledgement of Service by delivering the same personally to her.

3.   THAT at the time and place of service the said respondent admitted her full name as .... and identified herself from her Australian Passport No ....

4.   AT my request the said respondent signed the Acknowledgement of Service which is now produced and shown to me marked 'A'.

SWORN at   )

in the COUNTY of   )

England, this   day of   )

                                2012   )

        Before me,

A Notary Public

IN THE SUPREME COURT OF ONTARIO

BETWEEN:

Petitioner

and

Respondent

AFFIDAVIT OF SERVICE

I, ... of .... in the County of .... , England, Process Server make Oath and say:

1. I DID on .... day the ....day of .... 2012 personally serve, at approximately ....am/pm the attached Notice of Petition and Petition for Divorce, by delivering true copies of the same to and leaving the same with the said Respondent on the day last aforesaid at ....

2. UPON the said copies so served as aforesaid were endorsed at the time of such service true copies of all the endorsements appearing upon the original Notice of Petition for Divorce and Petition for Divorce.

3. AT the time of such service, I requested the said Respondent to complete and sign the Acknowledgement of Service endorsed on the said Notice of Petition for Divorce and my request was complied with and I witnessed the signature on page 3 of the Notice of Petition for Divorce.

4. MY means of knowledge as to the identity of the person so served was as follows:

The Respondent acknowledged that she was the person named as Respondent in the Petition for Divorce and used the following method of identification:

She produced for my inspection her Canadian Passport - or

I asked in the area and neighbours pointed out the Respondent to me - or

I recognised her from a photograph supplied to me.

SWORN at   )

in the County of   )

England, this   day of   2012   )

Before me,

A Notary Public.

CANADIAN PRINTED FORM OF AFFIDAVIT OF SERVICE

IN THE COURT OF SUPREME/COUNTY

BETWEEN:

                                                                                                        Plaintiff

                                                                             - and -

                                                                                                        Defendant

AFFIDAVIT OF SERVICE

I,   of   in the County of   England, Process Server make Oath and say as follows:

1.   THAT I did on .... day the .... day of ....2012 personally serve ....the Defendant ....at .... with the .... (name document) by delivering a true copy of the same to, and leaving the same with .... (name and address of person with whom the papers were left)

SWORN at   )

in the County of   )

England, this   day of   )

                              2012   )

           Before me,

A Notary Public.

IN THE CIRCUIT COURT OF THE ELEVENTH

JUDICIAL CIRCUIT OF FLORIDA IN AND FOR

DADE COUNTY

Case No

GENERAL JURISDICTION DIVISION

CIVIL ACTIONS SUMMONS

.... Plaintiff

- v -

.... Defendants

I, of in the County of ...., England, Process

Server acting under the direction of .... of .... Solicitors for the Plaintiff, make

Oath and say:

1. THAT I did on .... the .... day of ....2012 at ....in the County of .... England, personally serve .... and .... each with the Civil Action Summons and Complaint issued herein.

2. THERE is now produced and shown to me copies of each of the Civil Action Summonses so served by me.

SWORN at)

in the County of)

England, this day of)

2012)

Before me,

A Notary Public.

IN THE HIGH COURT OF THE STATE OF SINGAPORE ISLAND OF SINGAPORE

Suit No   of

BETWEEN:

Plaintiff

- and -

Defendant

I, ... of .... in the County of .... England, Process Server, make Oath and say as follows:

1. I AM authorised and empowered to effect service of the process of the Supreme Court of Judicature in England.

2. THAT I did on .... the .... day of .... 2012, at .... in the County of .... England, duly serve the Defendant .... with a true copy of the concurrent Writ of Summons issued in this action, and bearing date the .... day of .... 2012, the original of which is now produced and shown to me marked 'A'.

3. THAT I did at the same time and place of service hand to the said Defendant .... a true copy of the Order of Court made in this action and dated the .... day of .... 2012, a sealed copy of which is now produced and shown to me marked 'B'.

4. THAT at my request the said Defendant signed a form of receipt endorsed on each of the original documents now produced and shown to me marked 'A' and 'B', and which he dated the .... day of .... 2012.

SWORN at   )

in the County of   )

England, this   day of   )

                       2012   )

        Before me,

A Notary Public.

IN THE HIGH COURT OF ZIMBABWE HELD AT HARARE

Case No   2012

IN THE MATTER BETWEEN:

....   Plaintiff

- and -

....   Defendant

I,   of   in the County of   , England, Process Server make Oath and say as follows:

1.   THAT on the .... day of .... 2012, I effected service of the Citation by Edict, Plaintiff's Intendit, Court Order granting leave to sue by Edictal Citation, and Notice of Set Down for Trial, all in connection with the above matter, by handling copies thereof personally to .... at .... England, at the same time exhibiting to her the originals and explaining to her the nature of exigency thereof.

SWORN at   )

in the County of   )

England, this   day of   )

                        2012   )

    Before me,

A Notary Public.

IN THE SUPREME COURT OF SOUTH AFRICA

(................................ LOCAL DIVISION)

IN THE MATTER BETWEEN:

                                                                Plaintiff

- and -

                                                               Defendant

I, ... of .... in the County of .... England, Process Server,

make Oath and say as follows:

1.   THAT an Office copy of the Edictal Citation issued in this matter and bearing date the .... day of .... 2012 was duly served by me on the Defendant (born) .... at .... England, by delivering the same personally to the said Defendant .... (born) ....

2.   THAT at the time such service as aforesaid the said Defendant .... (born) .... admitted to me that she was the Defendant in this action and at my request signed an Acknowledgement of Service upon her and I now produce the said Acknowledgement of Service marked 'A' signed by the said Defendant.

3.   THAT the original of the said Edictal Citation is now produced to me marked 'B'.

SWORN at   )

in the County of   )

this   day of   2012   )

       Before me

A Notary Public.

AFFIDAVIT OF PERSONAL SERVICE (PRINTED FORM) NEW YORK

Family Court

Return Date

State of New York

Part

County of

Docket No

I, ... being duly sworn, depose and say:

1. That I am over the age of 18 years and not a party to the above action, and reside at .... England.

2. On the .... day of ....2012 at .... at (time) .... I personally served the summons (and petition) (or order to show cause) on .... respondent in the above mentioned action, by delivering to and leaving copies of each with .... at said time and place.

3. I knew the person so served to be .... the person named in said summons as the respondent in the action by reason of his admission of identity.

4. Description of person served:

Sex .... colour of skin .... hair .... approx age .... approx height .... approx weight .... other identifying features (wearing a moustache) ....

SWORN before me this   )

day of   2012   )

A Notary Public.

SECTION 9 - AFFIDAVITS, STATEMENTS OF SERVICE AND CERTIFICATES OF SERVICE

INTRODUCTION

Under the CPR affidavits will be required far less frequently than before. In most cases an unsworn statement will suffice. As a general rule, however, any order for service with a penal notice endorsed upon it will require an affidavit of service. Unless the rules specifically require an affidavit to be sworn or the Court requires an affidavit to be sworn the additional cost of swearing an affidavit may not be allowed on taxation of costs.

High Court Practice

Any such affidavit which needs to be specially prepared should be on A4 paper and if more than one page, should be on double A4 paper and the back should be endorsed.

Practice Direction 32 – Evidence

This Practice Direction supplements CPR Part 32

Deponent

2. A deponent is a person who gives evidence by affidavit or affirmation.

Heading

3.1. The affidavit should be headed with the title of the proceedings where the proceedings are between several parties with the same status, it is sufficient to identify the parties as follows:

	Number
A.B. (and others)	Claimants/Applicants
C.D. (and others)	Defendants/Respondents
	(as appropriate)

3.2 At the top right hand corner of the first page (and on the backsheet) there should be clearly written:

(1) the party on whose behalf it is made.

(2) the initials and surname of the deponent.

(3) the number of the affidavit in relation to that deponent.

(4) the identifying initials and number of each exhibit referred to, and

(5) the date sworn.

Body of Affidavit

4.1. The affidavit must, if practicable, be in the deponent's own words, the affidavit should be expressed in the first person and the deponent should:

(1) commence "I (full name) of (address) state on oath ...",

(2) if giving evidence in his professional, business or other occupational capacity, give the address at which he works in (1) above, the position he holds and the name of this firm or employer,

(3) give his occupation or, if he has none, his description, and

(4) state if he is a party to the proceedings or employed by a party to the proceedings, if it be the case.

4.2 An affidavit must indicate:

(1) which of the statements in it are made from the deponent's own knowledge and which are matters of information or belief, and

(2) the source for any matters of information or belief.

4.3 Where a deponent:

(1) refers to an exhibit or exhibits, he should state "there is now shown to me marked "...." the (description of exhibit) ", and

(2) makes more than one affidavit (to which there are exhibits) in the same proceedings, the numbering of the exhibits should run consecutively throughout and not start again with each affidavit.

Jurat

5.1 The jurat of an affidavit is a statement set out at the end of the document which authenticates the affidavit.

5.2 It must:

(1) be signed by all deponents,

(2) be completed and signed by the person before whom the affidavit was sworn whose name and qualification must be printed beneath his signature,

(3) contain the full address of the person before whom the affidavit was sworn, and

(4) follow immediately on from the text and not to be put on a separate page.

Format of Affidavits

6.1　An affidavit should:

(1) be produced on durable quality A.4 paper with a 3.5 cm margin,

(2) be fully legible and should normally be typed on one side of the paper only,

(3) where possible, be bound securely in a manner which would not hamper filing, or otherwise each page should be endorsed with the case number and should bear the initials of the deponent and of the person before whom it was sworn,

(4) have the pages numbered consecutively as a separate document (or as one of several documents contained in a file),

(5) be divided into numbered paragraphs,

(6) have all numbers, including dates, expressed in figures, and

(7) give in the margin the reference to any document or documents mentioned.

6.2 It is usually convenient for an affidavit to follow the chronological sequence of events or matters dealt with; each paragraph of an affidavit should as far as possible be confined to a distinct portion of the subject.

Inability of Deponent to read or sign Affidavit

7.1 Where an affidavit is sworn by a person who is unable to read or sign it, the person before whom the affidavit is sworn must certify in the jurat that:

(1) he read the affidavit to the deponent,

(2) the deponent appeared to understand it, and

(3) the deponent signed or made his mark, in his presence.

7.2 If that certificate is not included in the jurat, the affidavit may not be used in evidence unless the Court is satisfied that it was read to the deponent and that he appeared to understand it. Two versions of the form of jurat with the certificate are set out in the Annex 1 to this practice direction and are detailed hereto.

Example 1.

Certificate to be used where a deponent to an affidavit is unable to read or sign it

Sworn at......... this day of....................Before me, I having first read over the contents of this affidavit to the deponent (if there are exhibits, add "and explained the nature and effect of the exhibits referred to in it") who appeared to understand it and approved its content as accurate, and made his mark on the affidavit in my presence.

Or, (after, Before me) the witness to the mark of the deponent having been first sworn that he had read over etc. (as above) and that he saw him make his mark on the affidavit (Witness must sign) .

Example 2.

Certificate to be used where a deponent to an affirmation is unable to read or sign it

Affirmed at ………… this day of ………… Before me, I having first read over the contents of this affirmation to the deponent (if there are exhibits, add "and explained the nature and effect of the exhibits referred to in it") who appeared to understand it and approved its content as accurate, and made his mark on the affirmation in my presence.

Or, (after, Before me) the witness to the mark of the deponent having been first sworn that he had read over etc. (as above) and that he saw him make his mark on the affirmation (Witness must sign) .

Alterations to Affidavits

8.1 Any alteration to an affidavit must be initialled by both the deponent and the person before whom the affidavit was sworn.

8.2 An affidavit which contains an alteration that has not been initialled may be filed or used in evidence only with the permission of the Court.

Who may administer oaths and take Affidavits

9.1 Only the following may administer oaths and take affidavits:

    (1) Commissioners for oaths,

    (2) Practising Solicitors,

    (3) other persons specified by Statute,

    (4) certain officials of the Supreme Court,

    (5) a Circuit Judge or District Judge,

    (6) any justice of the peace, and

    (7) certain officials of any County Court appointed by the Judge of that Court for the purpose.[7]

9.2 An affidavit must be sworn before a person independent of the parties or their representatives.

Filing of Affidavits

10.1 If the Court directs that an affidavit is to be filed,[8] it must be filed in the Court or Division, or Office or Registry of the Court or Division where the action in which it was or is to be used, is proceeding or will proceed.

10.2 Where an affidavit is in a foreign language:

    (1) the party wishing to rely on it

        (a) must have it translated, and

        (b) must file the foreign language affidavit with the Court, and

(2) the translator must make and file with the Court an affidavit verifying the translation and exhibiting both the translation and a copy of the foreign language affidavit.

    1 Commissioner for Oaths Act 1889 and 1891.

    2 S.81 of the Solicitors Act 1974.

    3 S.65 of the Administration of Justice Act 1985 s.113 of the Courts and Legal Services Act 1990 and the Commissioners for Oaths (Prescribed Bodies) Regulations 1994 and 1995.

    4 S.2 of the Commissioners for Oaths Act 1889.

    5 S.58 of the County Courts Act 1984.

    6 S.58 as above.

    7 S.58 as above.

    8 Rules 32.1(3) and 32.4(b) .

Exhibits

Manner of Exhibiting Documents

11.1 A document used in conjunction with an affidavit should be:

    (1) produced to and verified by the deponent, and remain separate from the affidavit, and

    (2) identified by a declaration of the person before whom the affidavit was sworn.

11.2 The declaration should be headed with the name of the proceedings in the same way as the affidavit.

11.3 The first page of each exhibit should be marked:

    (1) as in paragraph 3.2 above, and

    (2) with the exhibit mark referred to in the affidavit.

Letters

12.1 Copies of individual letters should be collected together with exhibited in a bundle or bundles. They should be arranged in chronological order with the earliest at the top, and firmly secured.

12.2 When a bundle of correspondence is exhibited, the exhibit should have a front page attached stating that the bundle consists of original letters and copies. They should be arranged and secured as above and numbered consecutively.

Other documents

13.1 Photocopies instead of original documents may be exhibited provided the original are made available for inspection by the other parties before the hearing and by the Judge at the hearing.

13.2 Court documents must not be exhibited (official copies of such documents prove themselves).

13.3 Where an exhibit contains more than one document, a front page should be attached setting out a list of the documents contained in the exhibit; the list should contain the dates of the documents.

Exhibits other than documents

14.1 Items other than documents should be clearly marked with an exhibit number or letter in such a manner that the mark cannot become detached from the exhibit.

14.2 Small items may be placed in a container and the container appropriately marked.

General provisions

15.1 Where an exhibit contains more than one document:

> (1) the bundle should not be stapled but should be securely fastened in a way that does not hinder the reading of the documents, and

> (2) the pages should be numbered consecutively at bottom centre.

15.2 Every page of an exhibit should be clearly legible; typed copies of illegible documents should be included, paginated with "a" numbers.

15.3 Where affidavits and exhibits have become numerous, they should be put into separate bundles and the pages numbered consecutively throughout.

15.4 Where on account of their bulk the service of exhibits or copies of exhibits on the other parties would be difficult or impracticable, the directions of the Court should be sought as to arrangements for bringing the exhibits to the attention of the other parties and as to their custody pending trial.

Affirmations

16. All provisions in this or any other practice direction relating to affidavits apply to affirmations with the following exceptions:

> (1) the deponent should commence "I (name) of (address) do solemnly and sincerely affirm ....", and in the Jurat the word "sworn" is replaced by the word "affirmed".

Administration Of Oaths And Taking Of Affidavits

Section 81 of the Solicitors Act 1974 reads:

> (1) Subject to the provisions of this section, every solicitor who holds a practising certificate which is in force shall have the powers conferred on a Commissioner for Oaths by the Commissioners for Oaths Act 1889 and 1891 and Section 24 of the Stamp Duties Management Act 1891; and any reference to such a Commissioner in an enactment passed or instrument (including an enactment made after the passing of this Act) shall include a reference to such a solicitor unless the context otherwise requires.
>
> (2) A Solicitor shall not exercise the powers conferred by this section in a proceeding in which he is solicitor to any of the parties, or in which he is interested.
>
> (3) A Solicitor before whom any oath or affidavit is taken or made shall state in the jurat or attestation at which place and on what date the oath or affidavit is taken or made.
>
> (4) A document containing such a statement and purporting to be sealed or signed by a solicitor shall be admitted in evidence without proof of the seal or signature, and without proof that he is a solicitor or that he holds a practising certificate which is in force.

The importance of correctly preparing an affidavit of service cannot be too strongly stressed. This applies especially to the use of printed forms of affidavit. The unnecessary portions of the form should be deleted and a tick placed in the margin so the solicitor may spot the deletion and initial in the margin.

The subject is fully covered by CPR 32PD as previously mentioned.

County Court Practice
Introduction

Most forms of affidavit required to be used in the County Court are obtainable from the County Court.

Section 58 of the County Court Act 1984 states:

58. (1) An affidavit to be used in a county court may be sworn before—

 (a) the judge or registrar of any court; or

 (b) any justice of the peace; or

 (c) an officer of any court appointed by the judge of that court for the purpose,

as well as before a commissioner for oaths or any other person authorised to take affidavits under the Commissioners for Oaths Acts 1889 and 1891.

> (2) An affidavit sworn before a judge or registrar or before any such officer may be sworn without the payment of any fee.

General Notes On Affidavits

Experience of handling numerous affidavits of service prompts the following observations in regard to affidavits of service prepared by process servers:

1. The careful preparation of the affidavit of service is essential. An affidavit which is incorrect or does not comply with the rules, can delay, cause unnecessary expense and spoil a job otherwise well done.

2. An affidavit of service should be sworn at the earliest opportunity and returned or filed at once.

3. The description 'Process Server' should come after the name and address of the deponent and NOT after the deponent's name - as is so often seen.

4. The jurat of the affidavit should be properly completed showing the actual address of swearing. The name of the town is insufficient.

5. The signature of the solicitor before whom the affidavit is sworn should be legible or a rubber stamp or printed name should appear under it.

6. The affidavit should be endorsed in all High Court matters, i.e. the backsheet completed.

7. All alterations or erasure in the affidavit should be initialled by the solicitor in the margin.

8. All affidavits should be marked at the top right hand corner of the first page showing:

   (a) the party on whose behalf it is filed

   (b) the initial and surname of the deponent

   (c) the number of the affidavit in relation to the deponent

   (d) the date sworn

9. When preparing an affidavit of service the exact place of service should be stated, i.e. "at the corner of Blank Street and Black Avenue" or: "at or outside No.28 Blank Street" or: "in room No.305 on the third floor of City House". The Bankruptcy Court pay particular attention to the exact place of service especially in large office blocks or complexes.

10. When preparing an affidavit of attempts the source of information should be recited in the affidavit and made clear, i.e. "I was informed by an adult male at No.23 Blank Street".

11. Affidavits should never end on one page with the jurat following overleaf. The text should be carried over the page even by only one word.

12. Any affidavit altered after it has been sworn requires to be re-sworn and a fresh jurat prepared.

Certificates and Statements of Service

Under the Civil Procedure Rules, proof of service in many instances can be by Certificate or Statement of Service which do not need to be sworn. Your instructing Solicitor will specify whether an Affidavit, Certificate or Statement of Service is required. Affidavits will become increasingly rare. However, it is important to remember that any documents for service endorsed with a penal notice will require to be served personally and an Affidavit of Service will need to be sworn.

WITNESS STATEMENTS
Heading

17.1 The witness statement should be headed with the title of the proceedings (see paragraph 4 of Practice Direction 7A and paragraph 7 of Practice Direction 20) ; where the proceedings are between several parties with the same status it is sufficient to identify the parties as follows:

Number:

A.B. (and others)   Claimants/Applicants

C.D. (and others)   Defendants/Respondents

(as appropriate)

17.2 At the top right hand corner of the first page there should be clearly written:

    (1) the party on whose behalf it is made,

    (2) the initials and surname of the witness,

    (3) the number of the statement in relation to that witness,

    (4) the identifying initials and number of each exhibit referred to, and

    (5) the date the statement was made.

Body of Witness Statement

18.1 The witness statement must, if practicable, be in the intended witness's own words, the statement should be expressed in the first person and should also state:

    (1) the full name of the witness,

    (2) his place of residence or, if he is making the statement in his professional, business or other occupational capacity, the address at which he works, the position he holds and the name of his firm or employer,

    (3) his occupation, or if he has none, his description, and

    (4) the fact that he is a party to the proceedings or is the employee of such a party if it be the case.

18.2 A witness statement must indicate:

    (1) which of the statements in it are made from the witness's own knowledge and which are matters of information or belief, and

(2) the source for any matters of information or belief.

18.3 An exhibit used in conjunction with a witness statement should be verified and identified by the witness and remain separate from the witness statement.

18.4 Where a witness refers to an exhibit or exhibits, he should state 'I refer to the (description of exhibit) marked '...''.

18.5 The provisions of paragraphs 11.3 to 15.4 (exhibits) apply similarly to witness statements as they do to affidavits.

18.6 Where a witness makes more than one witness statement to which there are exhibits, in the same proceedings, the numbering of the exhibits should run consecutively throughout and not start again with each witness statement.

Format of Witness Statement

19.1 A witness statement should:

(1) be produced on durable quality A4 paper with a 3.5cm margin,

(2) be fully legible and should normally be typed on one side of the paper only,

(3) where possible, be bound securely in a manner which would not hamper filing, or otherwise each page should be endorsed with the case number and should bear the initials of the witness,

(4) have the pages numbered consecutively as a separate statement (or as one of several statements contained in a file),

(5) be divided into numbered paragraphs,

(6) have all numbers, including dates, expressed in figures, and

(7) give the reference to any document or documents mentioned either in the margin or in bold text in the body of the statement.

19.2 It is usually convenient for a witness statement to follow the chronological sequence of the events or matters dealt with, each paragraph of a witness statement should as far as possible be confined to a distinct portion of the subject.

Statement of Truth

20.1 A witness statement is the equivalent of the oral evidence which that witness would, if called, give in evidence; it must include a statement by the intended witness that he believes the facts in it are true[13].

20.2 To verify a witness statement the statement of truth is as follows:

'I believe that the facts stated in this witness statement are true'.

20.3 Attention is drawn to rule 32.14 which sets out the consequences of verifying a witness statement containing a false statement without an honest belief in its truth.

(Paragraph 3A of Practice Direction 22 sets out the procedure to be followed where the person who should sign a document which is verified by a statement of truth is unable to read or sign the document.)

Alterations to witness statements

22.1 Any alteration to a witness statement must be initialled by the person making the statement or by the authorised person where appropriate (see paragraph 21).

22.2 A witness statement which contains an alteration that has not been initialled may be used in evidence only with the permission of the court.

Filing of witness statements

23.1 If the court directs that a witness statement is to be filed14, it must be filed in the court or Division, or Office or Registry of the court or Division where the action in which it was or is to be used, is proceeding or will proceed.

23.2 Where the court has directed that a witness statement in a foreign language is to be filed:

> (1) the party wishing to rely on it must –
>
>> (a) have it translated, and
>>
>> (b) file the foreign language witness statement with the court, and
>
> (2) the translator must make and file with the court an affidavit verifying the translation and exhibiting both the translation and a copy of the foreign language witness statement.

Certificate of court officer

24.1 Where the court has ordered that a witness statement is not to be open to inspection by the public or that words or passages in the statement are not to be open to inspection the court officer will so certify on the statement and make any deletions directed by the court under rule 32.13(4).

Defects in affidavits, witness statements and exhibits

25.1 Where:

> (1) an affidavit,
>
> (2) a witness statement, or
>
> (3) an exhibit to either an affidavit or a witness statement,

does not comply with Part 32 or this practice direction in relation to its form, the court may refuse to admit it as evidence and may refuse to allow the costs arising from its preparation.

25.2

Permission to file a defective affidavit or witness statement or to use a defective exhibit may be obtained from a judge17 in the court where the case is proceeding.

STATEMENTS OF CASE

26.1 A statement of case may be used as evidence in an interim application provided it is verified by a statement of truth.

26.2 To verify a statement of case the statement of truth should be set out as follows:

'[I believe][the (party on whose behalf the statement of case is being signed) believes] that the facts stated in the statement of case are true'.

26.3 Attention is drawn to rule 32.14 which sets out the consequences of verifying a witness statement containing a false statement without an honest belief in its truth.

(For information regarding statements of truth see Part 22 and Practice Direction 22.)

(Practice Directions 7A and 17 provide further information concerning statements of case.)

Sample Affidavits

There are various affidavits, Statements, Certificates of Service and letters referred to throughout the Guide, and samples of these are annexed hereto.

Letter of Appointment

Dear Sir (or Madam),

I have been directed to serve you with a .... issued in the above action.

I have to inform you that I will attend at your address, as below, on .... the .... day of .... 2012 at .... am/pm for the purpose of serving you personally with such............................

Should the above appointment prove inconvenient I will endeavour to attend any other reasonable appointment you may suggest. It is my duty to inform you that should you fail to attend the above appointment, or any other made in lieu thereof, application will be made to the Court for an Order for Substituted Service of the said .... by way of advertisement in the daily press or in such other manner as the Court may direct and you may be liable for the costs of such application.

Yours faithfully,

Process Server

.........Affidavit of....................
Sworn on the ....day of 2012
Exhibit marked 'A'
Sworn on Behalf of the ....

AFFIDAVIT OF SERVICE OF CLAIM FORM (PERSONAL)

IN THE HIGH COURT OF JUSTICE
QUEEN'S BENCH DIVISION   2012   No.

BETWEEN:

Claimant

-and-

Defendant

I, ... of ....in the County of..Process Server, make Oath and say as follows:

1. I DID on .... day, the .... day of .... 2012 at .... personally serve .... the above-named Defendant (or one of the above-named Defendants) with a true copy of the Claim Form in this action.

2. THE said copy Claim Form was duly sealed with the seal of the Court office out of which it was issued and was accompanied by a prescribed Form of Acknowledgement of Service.

3. A true copy of the Claim Form so served as aforesaid is exhibited hereto marked 'A'.

SWORN at   )

in the County of   )
)
this   day of   2012   )
      Before me,

A Solicitor empowered to administer Oaths.

..........Affidavit of...........................

Sworn on the ....day of 2012

Exhibit marked 'A'

Sworn on Behalf of the ....

AFFIDAVIT OF SERVICE OF CLAIM FORM BY INSERTION THROUGH THE LETTERBOX

IN THE HIGH COURT OF JUSTICE
QUEEN'S BENCH DIVISION

BETWEEN: Claimant

- and -

Defendant

I, of in the County of , Process Server, make Oath and say as follows:

1. THAT I did serve the above-named Defendant .... with a true copy of the Claim Form in this action by inserting the same through the letterbox for the address of the said Defendant, on day, the day of 2012, enclosed in a sealed envelope duly and properly addressed to the said Defendant at ....

2. THE said copy was duly sealed with the seal of the Court office out of which it was issued and was accompanied by a prescribed form of Acknowledgment of Service.

3. THAT in my opinion the said Claim Form, so inserted through the letterbox for the address of the Defendant will have come to his knowledge within seven days after the said date of such insertion thereof.

4. THERE is now produced and shown to me marked 'A' a true copy of the Claim Form so served by me as aforesaid.

SWORN at)
in the County of)
this day of 2012)

Before me,

A Solicitor empowered to administer Oaths.

..........Affidavit of..............................

Sworn on the ....day of 2012

Exhibit marked 'A'

Sworn on Behalf of the ....

AFFIDAVIT OF SERVICE ON MANAGER OF PARTNERSHIP

IN THE HIGH COURT OF JUSTICE

QUEEN'S BENCH DIVISION   2012   No

BETWEEN: Claimant

- and -

Defendant

I, ...of .... ,

Process Server, make Oath and say as follows:

1. I DID on.....................day, the .... day of ....2012, at .... being the principal place of business of the above-named Defendant Partnership within the jurisdiction of this Honourable Court, personally serve .... (the insertion of the name is not essential) the person having at the time of such service the control or management of the said partnership business there, with a true copy of the Claim Form in this action.

2. THE said copy Claim Form was duly sealed with the seal of the Court office out of which it was issued and was accompanied by a prescribed form of Acknowledgment of Service.

3. I DID at the time of the said service deliver to the person so served as aforesaid a notice in writing that the said Claim Form was served upon him as the person having control or management of the partnership business of the said Defendant Firm.

4. THERE is now produced and shown to me marked 'A' a true copy of the Claim Form so served by me as aforesaid.

SWORN at   )

in the County of   )

this   day of   2012   )

Before me,

A Solicitor empowered to administer Oaths.

.........Affidavit of.........................

Sworn on the ....day of 2012

Exhibit marked 'A'

Sworn on Behalf of the ....

AFFIDAVIT OF SERVICE ON A PARTNER IN A FIRM

IN THE HIGH COURT OF JUSTICE

QUEEN'S BENCH DIVISION   2012   No

BETWEEN:

Claimant

- and -

Defendant

I, ... of ....

in the County of .... , Process Server, make Oath and say as follows:

1. I DID on .... day, the .... day of .... 2012 at .... personally serve ...., a partner in the above-named Defendant Firm .... with a true copy of the Claim Form in this action.

2. THE said copy Claim Form was duly sealed with the seal of the Court office out of which it was issued and was accompanied by a prescribed form of Acknowledgement of Service.

3. THERE is now produced and shown to me marked 'A' a true copy of the Claim Form so served by me as aforesaid.

SWORN at   )

in the County of   )

this   day of   2012   )
       Before me,

A Solicitor empowered to administer Oaths.

........Affidavit of..........................
Sworn on the ....day of 2012
Exhibit marked 'A'
Sworn on Behalf of the ....

AFFIDAVIT OF SERVICE OF CLAIM FORM
ON AN ENGLISH LIMITED COMPANY

IN THE HIGH COURT OF JUSTICE
QUEEN'S BENCH DIVISION   2012   No.

BETWEEN: Claimant

-and-

                                                                                Defendant

I, ... of ....
in the County of   , Process Server, make an Oath and say as follows:

1. I DID on .... day, the .... day of .... 2012 (date of posting) serve the above-named Defendants with a true copy of the Claim Form in this action, by (leaving the same at ....)
or: (sending the same by ordinary post First Class Mail in an envelope duly pre-paid and properly addressed to the company at ....) which is the registered office of the said company.

2. THE said copy Claim Form was duly sealed with the seal of the Court office out of which it was issued and was accompanied by a prescribed form of Acknowledgement of Service.

3. A true copy of the Claim Form so served as aforesaid is exhibited hereto marked 'A'.

SWORN at   )
)
in the County of   )

this   day of   2012   )
            Before me,

A Solicitor empowered to administer Oaths.

........Affidavit of........................
Sworn on the ....day of 2012
Exhibit marked 'A'
Sworn on Behalf of the ....

**AFFIDAVIT OF SERVICE OF CLAIM FORM ON
A LOCAL AUTHORITY**

IN THE HIGH COURT OF JUSTICE
QUEEN'S BENCH DIVISION   2012   No.

BETWEEN: Claimant

                                      -and-

                                                                          Defendant

I, ... of ....
in the County of.............................. , Process Server, make an Oath and say as follows:

1. I DID on .... day, the..................... day of .... 2012, at .... personally serve .... (Mayor or Chairman, Town Clerk as the case may be) being the head officer of the above-named Defendant corporation, with a true copy of the Claim Form in this action.

2. THE said copy Claim Form was duly sealed with the seal of the Court office out of which it was issued and was accompanied by a prescribed form of Acknowledgement of Service.

3. A true copy of the Claim Form so served as aforesaid is exhibited hereto marked 'A'.

SWORN at   )
in the County of   )
)
this   day of   2012   )
      Before me,

        A Solicitor empowered to administer Oaths.

..........Affidavit of..........................
Sworn on the ....day of 2012
Exhibit marked 'A'
Sworn on Behalf of the ....

GENERAL FORM OF AFFIDAVIT OF SERVICE

IN THE HIGH COURT OF JUSTICE
QUEEN'S BENCH DIVISION   2012   No

BETWEEN:

                                                                                            Claimant

                                              - and -

                                                                                            Defendant

I, ... of ....
in the County of ...., Process Server, make Oath and say as follows:

1. THAT I did on .... day, the .... day .... of 2012 at .... personally, serve the above-named Defendant .... with a true copy of the .... issued in this action and dated the   day of 2012.

2. THERE is now produced and shown to me marked "A" the original (or copy as the case may be) of the said .... so served by me.

SWORN at   )
in the County of   )

this   day of   2012   )

    Before me,
    A Solicitor empowered to administer Oaths.

..........Affidavit of..........…............
Sworn on the ....day of 2012
Exhibit marked 'A'
Sworn on Behalf of the ....

AFFIDAVIT OF SERVICE OF A WITNESS SUMMONS

IN THE HIGH COURT OF JUSTICE
QUEEN'S BENCH DIVISION   2012   No.

BETWEEN:

                                                                                Claimant

-and-

                                                                                Defendant

I, ... of ....
in the County of .... , Process Server acting under the direction of
.... of...................................., Solicitors for the above-named
.... make Oath and say as follows:

1. THAT I did on .... day, the .... day of .... 2012 at ....personally serve .... with a true copy of Witness Summons issued herein.

2. THAT at the time of service I paid (or tendered) to the said .... the sum of £......... by way of conduct money.

3. A true copy of the Witness Summons so served by me is now produced and shown to me marked 'A'.

SWORN at   )
)
in the County of   )
)
this   day of   2012   )
       Before me,

A Solicitor empowered to administer Oaths.

........Affidavit of........................

Sworn on the ....day of 2012

Exhibit marked 'A'

Sworn on Behalf of the ....

AFFIDAVIT OF SERVICE OF APPLICATION NOTICE

IN THE HIGH COURT OF JUSTICE

QUEEN'S BENCH DIVISION   2012   No

BETWEEN: Claimant

- and -

Defendant

_____

I, ... of ....

in the County of ...., Process Server make Oath and say as follows:

1. I DID on   day, the   day of   2012 , before/after the hour of four in the afternoon (12 noon if a Saturday) serve .... Solicitor for the above named .... in this action with a true copy of the Application Notice now produced and shown to me marked 'A' by leaving it at .... being the address for service in this action, with his clerk there.

SWORN at   )

in the County of   )

this   day of   2012   )

Before me,

A Solicitor empowered to administer Oaths.

.........Affidavit of..........................

Sworn on the ....day of 2012

Sworn on Behalf of the ....

SPECIMEN AFFIDAVIT WHERE MADE BY TWO DEPONENTS (OR MORE)

IN THE HIGH COURT OF JUSTICE

QUEEN'S BENCH DIVISION   2012 No

BETWEEN:

Claimant

- and -

Defendant

We (Deponent one) .... of .... in the County of ...., and (Deponent two) .... of .... in the County of ...., both process Servers acting under the direction of .... of .... Solicitor for the above named Claimant jointly and severally make Oath and say:

AND I (Deponent one) for myself say:

1. That being directed to effect service of the Claim Form issued in this action on the Defendant ...., I did on .... day, the .... day of .... 2012, attend at the address of the Defendant .... situate at .... and where I saw an adult female who informed me that the said Defendant was seldom to be found at that address and in fact did not reside there and that he would not be calling again for at least two weeks.

AND I (Deponent two) for myself say:

2. THAT being directed to effect service of the Claim Form in this action on the Defendant .... I did on .... day, the .... of .... 2012 attend at the address of the said Defendant situate at .... and when I saw an adult male who informed me the said Defendant was not then within and although he did not live at that address called from time to time. In answer to my further enquiry the said adult male informed me the Defendant would receive any letter I cared to send to him at that address.

3. THAT I did on .... day, the .... day of .... 2012, send to the Defendant .... at his address .... a letter by first class pre-paid post, enclosed with such letter being a copy of the Claim Form issued in this action and which letter omitting formal parts ran as follows:

(here quote the text of the appointment letter)

4. THAT I duly attended at the address of the said Defendant in accordance with my written appointment and when I saw an adult male who informed me that the Defendant was not then within but that he had been at the address earlier that day and had received all letters arriving for him at that address. I was further informed no message had been left for me and it was not known when the said Defendant would next be calling although he usually called once a week.

5. My letter addressed to the said defendant has not been returned to me through the post or at all.

   AND WE .... (Deponent one)

   and .... (Deponent two) jointly say:

6. THAT we have made reasonable efforts to effect personal service of the Claim Form herein but we have been unable to meet with the said Defendant for the purpose of serving him personally and we verily believe the said Defendant has received notice of the said Claim Form and is deliberately evading service thereof.

7. THE said Claim form was duly sealed with the seal of the Court office out of which it was issued and was accompanied by a prescribed form of Acknowledgment of Service.

8. We crave leave that an order be made for service of the said Claim Form by sending a copy together with form of Acknowledgment of Service, by first class pre-paid post addressed to the Defendant .... at the only known address for him ....

SWORN by the first named deponent)

....

at)

in the County of)

this   day of   2012)

   Before me,

   A Solicitor empowered to administer Oaths.

SWORN by the second-named deponent)

at)

in the County of)

this   day of   2012)

   Before me,

A Solicitor empowered to administer Oaths.

.........Affidavit of.........…..............

Sworn on the ....day of 2012

Sworn on Behalf of the ....

AFFIDAVIT OF APPLICATION FOR SERVICE BY AN ALTERNATIVE METHOD

IN THE HIGH COURT OF JUSTICE

QUEEN'S BENCH DIVISION						2012 No.

BETWEEN											Claimant

- and -

Defendant

I, ... of ....

in the County of ...., Process Server acting under the direction of

.... of .... Solicitor for the above-named Claimant, make Oath

and say as follows:

1. HAVING been directed by.. to serve the above-named Defendant with a copy of the Claim Form in this action which has been duly sealed with the seal of the Court Office out of which the Claim Form was issued, accompanied by a prescribed form of Acknowledgement of Service, I did on .... day, the .... day of .... 2012 attend for the purpose of serving a copy of the said Claim Form at........................

    (describe efforts to effect service and quote text of appointment letter)

2. I HAVE made all reasonable efforts and used all due means in my power to serve the said copy Claim Form accompanied by an Acknowledgement of Service but I have not been able to do so.

SWORN at   )
)
in the County of   )
)
this   day of   2012   )

Before me,

A Solicitor empowered to administer Oaths.

........Affidavit of............................
Sworn on the ....day of...... 2012
Exhibit marked 'A'
Sworn on Behalf of the ....

AFFIDAVIT OF SERVICE OF DUPLICATE ORDER

IN THE HIGH COURT OF JUSTICE
CHANCERY DIVISION   2012 No

BETWEEN: Claimant

- and -

                                                                                                              Defendant

I,.. of ....
in the County of .... , Process Server acting under the direction of
.... Solicitors for the above-named Claimant make Oath and say as follows:

1.   THAT I did on .... day, the......................day of .... 2012, at .... in the above-named (each of the above-named Defendants if more than one) Defendant with a true copy of the order dated the .... day of .... issued in this action.

(Add if be the case)

2.   The copy of the said order so served by me as aforesaid had endorsed thereon when so served the following words, that is to say:

   TAKE NOTICE that if you the within-named ...., neglect to obey this Order by the time therein limited you will be liable to process of execution for the purpose of compelling you to obey the same Order.

3.   There is now produced and shown to me marked "A" a bundle containing a copy of the Claim Form and Affidavit so served by me.

SWORN at   )
in the County of   )
this   day of   2012   )
         Before me,

A Solicitor empowered to administer Oaths.

……..Affidavit of……...……………
Sworn on the ……..day of ……..2012
Exhibit marked 'A'
Sworn on Behalf of the …………….

AFFIDAVIT OF SERVICE OF NOTICE OF APPLICATION

IN THE HIGH COURT OF JUSTICE
CHANCERY DIVISION   2012 No
BETWEEN: Claimant

- and -

Defendant

_____

I, ……………… of ………………… in the County of ……………… , Process Server acting under the direction of……………… of ……………… Solicitors for the above-named Claimant, make Oath and say as follows:

1. I DID on …………… day the …………… day of ………… 2012, personally serve the above-named Defendant ……………… with a true copy of the Application Notice a copy of which is now produced and shown to me marked "A" by delivering the same into his hands and leaving the same with him at ……………….

2. THAT I did at the same time and place of service hand to the said Defendant ……………… a copy of the Affidavit of ……………… sworn on the …………… day of 2012, together with copy of the exhibit therein referred to as 'ABC1'. I also handed to the defendant a copy of the Affidavit of ……………… sworn on the ……………… day of ………2012, together with copy of the exhibit therein referred to as 'ABC2'.

SWORN at   )
in the County of   )
this   day of   2012   )
    Before me,

    A Solicitor empowered to administer Oaths.

........Affidavit of.........................
Sworn on the ....day of 2012
Sworn on Behalf of the ....

AFFIDAVIT OF SERVICE OF PART 8 CLAIM FORM

IN THE HIGH COURT OF JUSTICE

.... DIVISION   2012 No

BETWEEN: Claimant

- and -

                                                                                           Defendant

I, ... of ....

in the County of .... , Process Server acting under the direction of .... of Solicitors for the above-named Claimant make Oath and say as follows:

1. I DID on .... day the .... day of .... 2012, at .... personally serve .... the Defendant herein (each of - if more than one) with a true copy of the Part 8 Claim Form in this action.

2. THE said copy Part 8 Claim Form was duly sealed with the seal of the Court office out of which it was issued and was accompanied by a prescribed form of Acknowledgment of Service.

   (Add a further paragraph if applicable)

3. THE copy of the Part 8 Claim Form so served as aforesaid bore on the face thereof due notice to the person served therewith of the place where he was required to attend and the day and hour of such attendance, or if such a date and place has not been fixed at a date time and place to be fixed.

SWORN at   )
in the County of   )
this   day of   2012   )
        Before me,
            A Solicitor empowered to administer Oaths.

........Affidavit of........................
Sworn on the ....day of 2012
Exhibit marked 'A'
Sworn on Behalf of the ....

AFFIDAVIT OF SERVICE OF CLAIM FORM
UNDER ORDER 113

IN THE HIGH COURT OF JUSTICE

QUEEN'S BENCH DIVISION   2012 No.

IN THE MATTER of 29 Blank Street, London, N

BETWEEN

          GREEN PROPERTIES LIMITED   Claimant

- and -

GEORGE BLACK and
PERSONS UNKNOWN   Defendant

I, ... of ....
in the County of ...., Process Server acting under the direction of......................of..........................Solicitors for the above-named Claimants, make Oath and say as follows:

1. THAT I did on..................day the............day of .... 2012 attend at 29 Blank Street, London, N   and where I personally served the above-named Defendant George Black with a sealed copy of the Claim Form issued herein together with a copy of the Affidavit of......................................sworn herein on the ....day of .... 2012.

2. THAT on the same day I inserted through the letter-box of the said premises 29 Blank Street, London, N , a sealed copy of the said Claim Form together with a copy of the Affidavit of.................... sworn herein on the................day of 2012, in a sealed transparent envelope addressed to "the occupiers".

3. THAT I did on the same day affix to the main door of the said premises 29 Blank Street, London, N. a sealed copy of the Claim Form, together with a copy of the Affidavit of .... sworn herein on the ....day of .... 2012, enclosed in a sealed transparent envelope addressed to "the occupiers".

                                                            cont'd........

4. THE said Claim Form so served by me was duly sealed with the seal of the Court Office out of which it was issued and bore on the face thereof due notice to the person served therewith of the place where he was required to attend and the day and hour of such attendance.

5. THERE is now produced and shown to me marked "A" a bundle containing a copy of the Part 8 Claim Form and Affidavit so served by me.

SWORN at   )
)
in the County of   )
)
this   day of   2012   )

    Before me,

    A Solicitor empowered to administer Oaths.

Filed on behalf of the Claimant
Statement of..................
Exhibits "A"
Dated.......................

STATEMENT OF SERVICE OF A CLAIM FORM

BETWEEN.. **CLAIMANT**

and

.... **DEFENDANT**

I,..........................of...........................in the County of ...., Process Server acting under the instructions of..in the County of ....
Solicitors, will state as follows:

1. THAT I did on the .... day of ....2012 at.. serve the above named Defendant with a copy of the above mentioned Claim Form, duly sealed with the seal of the Court,

2. The said Claim Form was accompanied by a prescribed Form of Acknowledgement of Service.

3. A true copy of the said Claim Form is now produced and shown to me marked "A".

4. I believe that the facts stated in this Statement are true.

Signed......................................

Dated this............... day of 2012

Certificate of service

In the	
Claim No.	
Claimant	
Defendant	

On the .... (insert date)

the .... (insert title or description of documents served)

a copy of which is attached to this notice was served on (insert name of person served, including position i.e. partner, director, if appropriate)

....

Tick as appropriate

☐ by first class post ☐ Document Exchange

☐ by delivering to or leaving ☐ by handing it to or leaving it with

☐ by fax machine (............... time sent)
(you may want to enclose a copy of the transmission sheet)

☐ by e-mail

☐ by other means (please specify)

at (insert address where service effected. Include fax or DX number or e-mail address)

being the defendant's:

☐ residence ☐ registered office

☐ place of business ☐ other (please specify) ....

The date of service is therefore deemed to be ....(insert date - see over for guidance)

N215 Certificate of service (4.99)

Notes for guidance

Please note these notes are only a guide and are not exhaustive. If you are in doubt you should refer to Part 6 of the rules.

Where to serve

Nature of party to be served	Place of service
Individual	• Usual or last known residence
Proprietor of business	• Usual or last known residence: or • Place of business or last known place of business
Individual who is suing or being sued in the name of a firm	• Usual or last know residence: or • Principal or last known place of business of the firm
Corporation (incorporated in England and Wales) other than a company)	• Principal office of the corporation: or • any place within the jurisdiction where the corporation carries on its activities and which has a real connection with the claim
Company registered in England and Wales	• Principal office of the company or corporation; or • any place of business of the company within the jurisdiction which has a real connection with the claim

Personal Service - A document is served personally on an individual by leaving it with that individual. A document is served personally on a company or other corporation by leaving it with a person holding a senior position within the company or corporation. In the case of a partnership, you must leave it with either a partner or a person having control or management at the principal place of business. Where a solicitor is authorised to accept service on behalf of a party, service must be effected on the solicitor, unless otherwise ordered.

Deemed Service - (Part 6.7 (1) . A document which is served in accordance with these rules or any relevant practice direction shall be deemed to be served on the day shown in the following table.

Method of service	Deemed day of service
First class post	The second day after it was posted
Document exchange	The second day after it was left at the document exchange
Delivering the document to or leaving it at a permitted address	The day after it was delivered to or left at the permitted address
Fax	If it was transmitted on a business day before 4 p.m., on that day, or otherwise on the business day after the day on which it was transmitted
Other electronic method	The second day after the day on which it was transmitted

- If a document (other than a claim form) is served after 5 p.m. on a business day, or at any time on a Saturday, Sunday or a bank holiday, the document shall, for the purpose of calculating any period of time after service of the document, be treated as having been served on the next business day.

- In this context "business day" means any day except Saturday, Sunday or a bank holiday; and "bank holiday" includes Christmas Day and Good Friday.

Service of documents on children and patients. - The rules relating to service on children and patients are contained in Part 6.6 of the rules.

Claim Forms - The general rules about service are subject to the special rules about service of claim forms contained in rules 6.12 to 6.16

STATEMENT OF SERVICE

Family Law Act 1996

Case number

Applicant
Ref.

The Court at which your case is being heard

Respondent
Ref.

You must
- **give details of service of the application on each of the other parties**
- give details of service on the mortgagee or landlord of the dwelling-house (if appropriate)
- file this form with the Court on or before the first Directions Appointment or Hearing of the Proceedings

You should if the person's solicitor was served, give his or her name and address

You must indicate the manner, date, time and place of service
or where service was effected by post, the date, time and place of posting

Name and address of person served	Means of identification of person, and how, when and where served	Prescribed forms served

I have served [application] [Notice of Proceedings] as stated above.
I am the [applicant] [solicitor for the applicant] [other] (*state*)

Signed: Date:

SAMPLE AFFIDAVITS

Examples of the various Affidavits referred to in the County Court section are annexed hereto.

……..Affidavit of……………….........

Sworn on the ……..day of ……..2012

Exhibit marked 'A'

Sworn on Behalf of the ....

AFFIDAVIT OF SERVICE OF CLAIM FORM

IN THE   COUNTY COURT   CASE NO

BETWEEN   Claimant
                                        - and -
                                                                    Defendant

I,…………………….. of ……………….. in the County of ……………. Process Server, make Oath and say as follows:

1. That I am over 16 years of age and employed by …………of …………Solicitors for the above-named Claimant.

2. That I did on the ……..day of …………. 2012 serve the Claim Form a copy of which is attached and marked 'A' on …………………..

   (a) by delivering the same to the said Defendant personally at……………………………………………………………………………………….
   (the following paragraph to be adapted if the Defendant is a partnership)
   (b) by delivering it at …………..to …………… who stated that he was a partner in the Defendant firm (or: carried on) or: who stated that he carried on) business in the name of the Defendant firm or:
   (c) by delivering it at ………………….. to a person who did not give his name but   stated that he (was a partner) (or: carried on business in the name of) the Defendant firm or:
   (d) by delivering it at ………………….. being the principal place of business of the Defendant firm within the district of this Court to ………the person who had or appeared to have the control or management of the business there:

   Registered Company:

   by leaving it at ………………….. the address stated in the Claim Form to be the registered office of the Defendant company.

   SWORN at   County Court   )
   in the County of   )
   this   day of   2012   )
                 Before me.

   Officer of the Court appointed by the Judge to take Affidavits.

   This Affidavit is filed on behalf of the Claimant.

........Affidavit of.........................
Sworn on the ....day of 2012
Exhibit marked 'A'
Sworn on Behalf of the ....

GENERAL FORM OF AFFIDAVIT

IN THE   COUNTY COURT   CASE NO

BETWEEN:

                                                    Claimant
                          - and -
                                                    Defendant

I, ... of .... in the County of .... Process Server, make Oath and say as follows:

1. That I am a person employed by .... of ....Solicitor(s) for the above named Claimant, and that I am over sixteen years of age.

2. That I did on the .... day of .... 2012 at .... duly serve .... with a .... a true copy thereof is hereto exhibited marked 'A', by delivering the same to h.... personally.

    (Add if necessary)

3. That I paid (or tendered) to the said .... at the same time and place the sum of £ .... for h..... expenses in travelling to and from the Court.

SWORN at   County Court   )

in the County of   )

this   day of   2012   )

    Before me,

    Officer of the Court appointed by the Judge to take Affidavits.

This Affidavit is filed on behalf of the Claimant.

........Affidavit of.........................
Sworn on the ....day of 2012
Exhibit marked 'A'
Sworn on Behalf of the ....

AFFIDAVIT OF SERVICE OF WITNESS SUMMONS

IN THE   COUNTY COURT   CASE NO

BETWEEN   Claimant

- and -

Defendant

I, ...of ....in the County of...............
Process Server, make Oath and say as follows:

1. That I am a person acting under the direction of ....of ....Solicitor(s) for the above-named.......... and I am over 16 years of age.

2. That I did on the .... day of ....2012 at .... duly serve .... with a Witness Summons, a true copy of which is hereto exhibited marked 'A' by delivering the same to h.. personally.

3. That I paid (or tendered) to the said .... at the same time and place, the sum of £ ....for h.. expenses (and loss of time) .

SWORN at   )
)
in the County of   )
)
this   day of   2012   )

      Before me.

Officer of the Court appointed by the Judge to take Affidavits.

This Affidavit is filed on behalf of the ....

........Affidavit of..........................
Sworn on the ....day of 2012
Exhibit marked 'A'
Sworn on Behalf of the ....

AFFIDAVIT OF SERVICE OF NOTICE OF APPLICATION FOR INJUNCTION

IN THE   COUNTY COURT   CASE NO

BETWEEN   Claimant

- and -

Defendant

I, ... of .... in the County of .... Process Server acting under the direction of .... of .... Solicitors for the above-named Claimant make Oath and say as follows:

1. That I am over sixteen years of age.

2. That I did on .... the ....day of ....2012 at .... personally serve the Defendant with the Notice of Application issued herein and dated the ....day of .... 2012 and for hearing on the ....day of .... 2012 together with copy Affidavit of the Claimant sworn herein on the .... day of .... 2012 together with exhibit. (Add any other documents served.)

3. There is now produced and shown to me marked 'A' a bundle containing copies of the said documents so served by me.

SWORN at   )
)
in the County of   )
)
this   day of   2012   )

   Before me.

Officer of the Court appointed by the Judge to take Affidavits.

This Affidavit is filed on behalf of the Claimant.

..........Affidavit of..........................
Sworn on the ....day of 2012

Exhibit marked 'A'
Sworn on Behalf of the ....

AFFIDAVIT OF SERVICE OF ORDER OF INJUNCTION

IN THE   COUNTY COURT   CASE NO

BETWEEN   Petitioner

- and -

Respondent

I, ... of .... in the County of .... Process Server acting under the direction of .... of .... Solicitors for the above-named Petitioner, make Oath and say:

1. That I am over sixteen years of age:

2. That I did on .... the ....day of .... 2012 at ....personally serve the above-named Respondent with an Order made herein on the ....day of .... 2012 a copy of which is exhibited hereto and marked 'A'

3. The said Order so served as aforesaid had endorsed thereon the following words, that is to say:

   "Take notice that unless you obey the directions contained in this Order you will be guilty of contempt of Court and will be liable to be committed to prison".

SWORN at   )
)
in the County of   )
)
this   day of   2012   )

Before me.

Officer of the Court appointed by the Judge to take Affidavits.

..........Affidavit of...........................
Sworn on the ....day of 2012
Exhibit Marked 'A'
Sworn on Behalf of the ....

SPECIMEN AFFIDAVIT IN SUPPORT OF ORDER FOR SERVICE BY AN ALTERNATIVE METHOD

IN THE   COUNTY COURT   CASE NO

BETWEEN   Thomas Black   Claimant

                              - and -

                            James White   Defendant

I,............................ of .... in the County of .... Process Server acting under the direction of .... of .... Solicitors for the above-named Claimant, make Oath and say as follows:

1. That I am over sixteen years of age.

2. That being directed to effect personal service of the Claim Form issued in this action (a copy of which is hereto exhibited and marked 'A') on the Defendant James White. I did on .... the .... day of .... 2012 attend at the only known address at which to communicate with the said Defendant James White, namely, that of his bankers Barclays Bank PLC situate at 10 High Street Blanktown and when I saw an adult male clerk who in answer to my enquiry informed me the said Defendant James White had an account at that branch and that any letter I cared to address to the said Defendant James White would be forwarded to him at his address in England but that such address could not be divulged.

3. Accordingly, I handed to the said adult male clerk a letter enclosed in a sealed envelope, duly stamped with a first class stamp and addressed to the said Defendant James White and which he promised to forward to the said Defendant to his address in England. Such letter, omitting formal parts ran as follows:

(Here quote the text of the usual appointment letter sent to the Defendant)

4. That I duly attended at the address of the Defendant's bankers in accordance with my written appointment and when I saw the same adult male clerk seen on my previous call and who informed me the Defendant was not present at the bank but that my letter had been forwarded to the Defendant to his address in England but that such address could not be divulged.

5. That I have made reasonable efforts to meet with the Defendant to effect personal service of the said Claim Form but I have been unable to meet with the Defendant and I verily believe the said Defendant has received notice of the said Claim Form and is deliberately evading personal service thereof. My letter addressed to the said Defendant had not been returned through the post or at all.

6. I am informed and verily believe the said Defendant is no longer at the address shown on the said Claim Form as is shown by the bailiff's return and I crave leave that an Order be made for service of the said Claim Form by sending a copy by first class prepaid post addressed to the Defendant James White at the only known address at which to communicate with him, namely c/o Barclays Bank PLC 10 High Street Blanktown.

Alternatively:

6. That on the .... day of................ 2012 I attended at the address of the said defendant situate at .... (the address on the Claim Form) and when I saw an adult female who informed me the said Defendant no longer lived at that address and that he left the address three months ago without leaving any forwarding address.

7. I crave leave that an order be made for service of the said Claim Form by sending a copy by first class prepaid post addressed to the Defendant James White at the only known address at which to communicate with him namely c/o Barclays Bank PLC 10 High Street Blanktown.

SWORN at   County Court   )

in the County of   )

this   day of   2012   )

    Before me,

    Officer of the Court appointed by the Judge to take Affidavits.

This affidavit is filed on behalf of the Claimant

..........Affidavit of..........................
Sworn on the ....day of 2012

Exhibit marked 'A'
Sworn on Behalf of the ....

AFFIDAVIT OF SERVICE OF PART 8 CLAIM

IN THE   COUNTY COURT   CASE NO

BETWEEN   Claimant

                                                                  - and -

                                                                                     Defendant

I, ... of .... in the County of .... Process Server acting under the direction of .... of .... Solicitors for the above-named Claimant make Oath and say:

1.   That I am over sixteen years of age.

2.   That I did on .... the ....day of .... 2012 attend at .... in the County of .... and when I saw an adult male occupant who informed me the Defendant James White was not then within. He declined to give his name and I served him with a copy of the Part 8 Claim issued in this action together with a copy of the Affidavit of John Brown sworn herein on the .... day of .... 2012 (together with exhibits).

3.   That I did on the same day affix to the front door of the said premises .... (add if necessary: 'and also to the rear door of the said premises') copies of the Part 8 Claim herein together with copy Affidavit of the said John Brown (and exhibits) enclosed in a sealed transparent envelope addressed to the 'occupiers'.

4.   That I also, on the same day, placed a copy of the said Part 8 Claim issued herein together with a copy Affidavit of John Brown in a sealed transparent envelope addressed to the 'occupiers' through the letter box of the said premises together with a further envelope addressed to the Defendant James White containing a copy of the Part 8 Claim and Affidavit of John Brown.

5.   There is now produced and shown to me marked 'A' a bundle containing copies of the said Part 8 Claim and Affidavit of John Brown (and exhibits) so served by me.

SWORN at   )
)
in the County of   )
)
this   day of   2012   )

        Before me,
        Officer of the Court appointed by the Judge to take Affidavits.

STATEMENT OF SERVICE

Family Law Act 1996

Case number

Applicant
Ref.

The Court at which your case is being heard

Respondent
Ref.

You must
- **give details of service of the application on each of the other parties**
- give details of service on the mortgagee or landlord of the dwelling house (if appropriate)
- file this form with the Court on or before the first Directions Appointment or Hearing of the Proceedings

You should — if the person's solicitor was served, give his or her name and address

You must indicate the manner, date, time and place of service
or where service was effected by post, the date, time and place of posting

Name and address of person served	Means of identification of person, and how, when and where served	Prescribed forms served

I have served [application] [Notice of Proceedings] as stated above.
I am the [applicant] [solicitor for the applicant] [other] (*state*)

Signed: Date:

Statement of............................
Exhibits "A"
Dated...
Filed on behalf of the Claimant

STATEMENT OF SERVICE OF A CLAIM FORM

BETWEEN .... CLAIMANT

AND

.... DEFENDANT

I,.............................of.............................in the County of ...., Process Server acting under the instructions of...in the County of .... Solicitors for the Claimant will state as follows:

1. THAT I did on ....the day of......................2012 at.. .... personally serve the above named Defendant with a copy of the above mentioned Claim Form, duly sealed with the seal of the Court.

2. A true copy of the said Claim Form is now produced and shown to me marked "A".

3. I believe that the facts stated in this Statement are true.

Signed....................................

Dated this............... day of 2012

.... Affidavit of ....
Sworn on the .... day of 2012
Exhibit (s) marked
Filed on behalf of the................................

IN THE .... **COUNTY COURT**   **CASE No**

Between: ....   **Applicant**

....

....   **Respondent**

IN THE MATTER OF .... **(A CHILD)**

I, ... of .... Process Server acting under the direction of ....of .... Solicitors acting on behalf of the above named Applicant make Oath and say as follows:

1) That I am over sixteen years of age.

2) That I did on .... the .... day of ....2012 at .... personally serve the above named respondent with a .... issued herein and dated the .... day of .... 2012 (list any additional documents served) true copies of which are exhibited hereto marked 'A'.

Sworn at   )
)
This   day of   2012   )
)
Before me   )
)
                   Solicitor   )

Filed on behalf of the Creditor
First Statement of…………
………………………………….
Exhibits "A"
Dated……………………….
Filed………………………..

STATEMENT OF SERVICE OF STATUTORY DEMAND

RE:……………………………………………..

IN BANKRUPTCY

DATE OF STATUTORY DEMAND …………………………..

I,……………………………………… of,………………………………. in the County of ………………………………., Process Server, acting in the employ of………………………………..in the County of ……..……….. Solicitors for the Creditors, will state as follows:

THAT I did on………………… the …………day of………………2012 before/after 1700 hours (*if a Saturday at*……………*hours*) personally serve the above named Debtor with the Demand dated………………………… by handing the Demand to him/her personally at…………………………………………..

1. A copy of the Demand is now shown to me marked "A".

2. I believe that the facts stated in this Statement are true.

Signed……………………………………………………….

Dated this…………… Day of…………………………2012

Filed on behalf of the Creditor
First Statement of.............
Exhibits "A"
Dated........................
Filed.............................

EXHIBIT

"A"

RE..

IN BANKRUPTCY

DATE OF STATUTORY DEMAND............................

This is the document marked "A" referred to in the Statement

of...

Dated this.........................day of........................ 2012

Signed...

APPOINTMENT LETTER FOR STATUTORY DEMAND

Dear Sir,

_____

I have been directed to serve you with a Statutory Demand issued under the Insolvency Act 1986.

I have already attended at your address without meeting with you.

I have to inform you that I will attend at your address, as below, on ……………………….day, the……………….day of……………………2012 at …………a.m./…………p.m. for the purpose of serving you personally with such Statutory Demand.

Should the above appointment prove inconvenient, I will endeavour to attend any other reasonable appointment you may suggest.

It is my duty to inform you that should you fail to attend the above appointment or any other made in lieu thereof, substituted service of the said Statutory Demand shall be deemed to have been effected by way of advertisement in the daily press or by insertion of same through your letter box.

Yours faithfully,

Process Server.

..........Affidavit of..........................
Sworn on the ....day of 2012
Exhibit marked 'A'
Sworn on Behalf of the ....

AFFIDAVIT OF SUBSTITUTED SERVICE OF STATUTORY DEMAND

(Title)

Date of Statutory Demand ....

I, ... of ....
of .... Solicitors acting for the Creditor, make Oath and say as follows:

1. That on ....(date) ....an attempt was made to serve the Demand on the above-named debtor by attending at .... the address of the above named debtor and where I met with an adult female who stated she was the wife of the debtor and that he was out and she did not know the time of his return. In answer to my enquiry she informed me the said debtor continued to reside at the address but she could not say when would be the best time to meet with him.

2. That I did on .... the .... day of ....2012 send to the debtor at his address .... a letter by first class prepaid post which letter omitting formal parts ran as follows:

   (Here quote the full text of the appointment letter)

3. That I duly attended at the address of the debtor in accordance with my letter of appointment and when I again met with the wife of the debtor who informed me the said debtor was not then within and she could not say when he would be home. In answer to my question she informed me the said debtor had received all letters arriving for him at that address.

4. That I did on the day of 2012 before/after 16.00 hours effect substituted service of the Demand by inserting same in a sealed envelope addressed to the debtor through the letter box of his address...

5. That my letter addressed to the said debtor has not been returned to me through the post or at all and that to the best of my knowledge, information and belief the Demand will have come to the attention of the above-named debtor .... (the date or within 7 days of such insertion thereof) .

(Add paragraph showing efforts made to serve through debtor's solicitor if the debtor is known to be represented.)

6. A copy of the Demand marked 'A' is exhibited hereto.

SWORN at   )
)
in the County of   )
)
this   day of   2012   )

   Before me,
   A Solicitor empowered to administer Oaths.

Filed on behalf of the Creditor
Second Statement of ....
Exhibits "B"
Dated......................
Filed........................

STATEMENT OF SERVICE OF A BANKRUPTCY PETITION

RE...NO:.......................

IN THE MATTER OF A BANKRUPTCY PETITION PRESENTED

(date) ....

I,...................................of.............................in the County of..........................,

Process Server acting in the employ of .... in the County

of .... Solicitors for the Creditors, will state as follows:

1. THAT I did on ....the ...., before/after 1700 hours (*if a Saturday at ....hours*), serve the above named Debtor with a copy of the above mentioned Petition, duly sealed with the seal of the Court, by delivering the same personally to the said.................................at

2. A sealed copy of the said Petition is now produced and shown to me marked "B".

3. I believe that the facts stated in this Statement are true.

Signed......................................

Dated this............... day of 2012

BACK SHEET FOR STATEMENT OF SERVICE
OF A BANKRUPTCY PETITION
(TO BE ALIGNED TO RIGHT HAND SIDE OF PAPER)

                                              Filed on behalf of the Creditor
                                              Statement of ……………………
                                              First
                                              Exhibits "B"
                                              Dated…………………..
                                              Filed…………………….

IN THE …………………………   **COUNTY COURT**

IN BANKRUPTCY   **No** ………………

RE: …………………………………….

IN THE MATTER OF A BANKRUPTCY PETITION
PRESENTED 10.1.2012 (*for example*)

STATEMENT OF PROCESS SERVER

Messrs ……………………………….

…………………………………………,

…………………………………………,

………………………………………….

Tel: ……………………….

Fax: ……………………….

Ref: ……………………….

Solicitors for the Creditors

Filed on behalf of the Creditor
Second Statement of ....
Exhibits "B"
Dated........................
Filed........................

EXHIBIT

"B"

IN BANKRUPTCY   **NO:....................**

RE:..

IN THE MATTER OF A BANKRUPTCY PETITION PRESENTED

(DATE) ....

This is the document marked "B" referred to in the Statement of
....
dated this...................

day of........................2012......

Signed..

APPOINTMENT LETTER FOR BANKRUPTCY PETITION

Dear Sir,

_____

I have been directed to serve you with a Bankruptcy Petition issued under the Insolvency Act 1986.

I have already attended at your address without meeting with you.

I have to inform you that I will attend at your address, as below on.......................... day, the   day of   2012   at   am/pm for the purpose of serving you personally with such Bankruptcy Petition.

Should the above appointment prove inconvenient, I will endeavour to attend any other reasonable appointment you may suggest.

It is my duty to inform you that should you fail to attend the above appointment, or any other made in lieu thereof, application will be made to the Court for an Order for Substituted Service of the said Bankruptcy Petition by way of advertisement in the daily press or in such other manner as the Court may direct.

Yours faithfully,

Process Server

.......Affidavit of........................
Sworn on the ....day of 2012
Exhibit marked 'A'
Sworn on Behalf of the ....

AFFIDAVIT OF PERSONAL SERVICE OF BANKRUPTCY PETITION

IN THE   No.   of 2012

IN BANKRUPTCY

RE:

IN THE MATTER of a Bankruptcy Petition filed on

I, ... of .... Process Server and for the purpose of service instructed by .... of .... Solicitors for the Petitioning Creditor:

MAKE OATH AND SAY AS FOLLOWS:

1. THAT I did on .... the .... day of .... 2012, before/after 1700 hours (if a Saturday at ....hours) serve the above-named debtor with a copy of the above-mentioned Petition, duly sealed with the seal of the Court by delivering the same personally to the said ....at ....(state the EXACT place of service).

2. A sealed copy of the said Petition is now produced and shown to me marked "A".

3. I believe that the facts stated in this Statement are true.

SWORN at   )
)
in the County of   )
)
this   day of   2012   )

    Before me,

    A Solicitor empowered to administer Oaths

..........Affidavit of......................
Sworn on the ....day of 2012
Sworn on Behalf of the ....

SPECIMEN AFFIDAVIT – SUBSTITUTED SERVICE OF BANKRUPTCY PETITION

(Title)

I, ... of ....in the County of .... Process Server in the employ of .... of ....Solicitors for the Petitioning Creditor, make Oath and say:

1. That being directed to effect personal service of the Bankruptcy Petition issued in this matter on the Judgment Debtor James White I did on .... the .... day of .... 2012 attend at the address of the Judgment Debtor James White situate at 10 Blank Street London N and where I saw an adult male who informed me the said Judgment Debtor was not then within and he was unable to say the time of his return or when I might see him. In answer to my further enquiry the said adult male informed me the said Judgment Debtor would receive any letter addressed to him at that address.

2. That I did on ....the ....day of ....2012 send to the Judgment Debtor James White at his address, 10 Blank Street, London N, a letter by first class prepaid post, which letter omitting formal parts ran as follows.
(here quote text of the appointment letter as sent)

3. That I duly attended at the address of the said Judgment Debtor in accordance with my written appointment where I saw an adult female who stated she was the wife of the said Judgment Debtor and who informed me that the said Judgment Debtor was not then within and that the time of his return was uncertain. In answer to my enquiry the said adult female informed me the said Judgment Debtor had received all letters arriving for him at that address and that he had been at the address that morning but no message had been left for me.

4. That I have made reasonable efforts to effect personal service of the said Bankruptcy Petition but I have been unable to meet with the said Judgment Debtor to effect personal service and I verily believe the said Judgment Debtor has received notice of the said Bankruptcy Petition sought to be served upon him and is deliberately evading personal service thereof. My letter addressed to the said Judgment Debtor has not been returned through the post or at all.

5. I crave leave that an Order be made for service of the said Bankruptcy Petition by sending a sealed copy thereof by first class prepaid post addressed to the Judgment Debtor James White at his address, 10 Blank Street London N or in such manner as the Court may direct.

SWORN at   )
in the County of   )
this   day of   2012   )
      Before me,

A Solicitor empowered to administer Oaths

.......Affidavit of........................
Sworn on the ....day of 2012
Exhibit marked 'A'
Sworn on Behalf of the ....

AFFIDAVIT OF SERVICE OF WINDING-UP PETITION AT REGISTERED OFFICE

(Title)

I, ...of.. Process Server and for the purpose of service instructed by .... of .... Solicitor(s) for the Petitioning Creditor MAKE OATH AND SAY AS FOLLOWS:-

1. That I did on .... the .... day of .... 2012 serve the above-named Company with a sealed copy of the Petition now produced and shown to me marked 'A' by handing the same to .... (who acknowledged himself to be) (who is to the best of my knowledge information and belief) (a director) (an officer) (an employee) of the Company at .... the registered office of the said company.

   OR

1. That I did on .... the ....day of ....2012 serve the above-named Company with a sealed copy of the Petition now produced and shown to me marked 'A' by handing the same to .... who acknowledged to me that he was authorised to accept service of documents on behalf of the Company at .... the registered office of the said Company.

   OR

1. That I did on ....the ....day of ....2012 having failed to find any officer, employee or other person authorised to accept service of documents on behalf of the company, deposit a sealed copy of the Petition now produced and shown to me marked 'A' at .... the registered office of the said Company by leaving it ....

SWORN at   )
)
in the County of   )
)
this   day of   2012   )

   Before me,

   A Solicitor empowered to administer Oaths

........Affidavit of..........................……..
Sworn on the ....day of 2012
Exhibit marked 'A'
Sworn on Behalf of the ....

AFFIDAVIT OF SERVICE OF WINDING-UP PETITION OTHER THAN AT REGISTERED OFFICE OR ON AN OVERSEAS COMPANY

(Title)

I .... of .... Process server and for the purpose of service instructed by .... of .... Solicitor(s) for the Petitioning Creditor MAKE OATH AND SAY AS FOLLOWS:

1. That I did on .... the................ day of ....2012, serve the above-named company with a sealed copy of the petition now produced and shown to me marked 'A' by handing the same to ....(who acknowledged himself to be) (who is to the best of my knowledge, information and belief) (a director) (an officer) (an employee) of the company at .... (the company's last known principal place of business in England and Wales) (a place where the company carried on business in England and Wales) . **OR**

1. That I did on .... the .... day of ....2012, serve the above-named company with a sealed copy of the petition now produced and shown to me marked 'A' by handing the same to .... who acknowledged to me that he was authorised to accept service of documents on behalf of the company at .... (the company's last known principal place of business in England and Wales) (a place where the company carried on business in England and Wales) . **OR**

1. That I did on .... the .... day of .... 2012, serve the above-named company with a sealed copy of the petition now produced and shown to me marked 'A' by (leaving it) (sending it by first class post .... the address of ....) whose name has been delivered to the Registrar of Companies as a person authorised to accept on the said company's behalf service of process and any notice required to be served on it (a place of business established by the said company in Great Britain) .

SWORN at   )

in the County of   )

this day of   2012   )

Before me,

A Solicitor empowered to administer Oaths

........Affidavit of...................................
Sworn on the........day of................. 2012
Exhibit marked 'A'
Sworn on Behalf of the ....

AFFIDAVIT OF SERVICE OF DIVORCE PETITION

IN THE DIVORCE REGISTRY   No

BETWEEN

                                                                                                                                     Petitioner
                                                           - and -
                                                                                                                                     Respondent

I, ... of ....
in the County of .... Process Server acting under the direction of
....of.. Solicitors for the above-named Petitioner,
make Oath and say:

1. A copy of the Petition bearing date .... 2012 filed in this Court, issued out of the Divorce Registry (or: issued out of the .... County Court: or .... District Registry) together with Notice of Proceedings and Form of Acknowledgement of Service (add if so: Statement as to arrangements for children) was served by me on .... the Respondent in this case at .... on................... the .... day of .... 2012, by delivering to the said .... personally a copy thereof.

2. At the time of service on the said .... he admitted he was the Respondent in this case and I was able to identify the said .... from a photograph in my possession which photograph is now produced and shown to me marked 'A'.
   or:
   At the time of the said service on the said .... he admitted he was the Respondent in this case and by way of identification he produced to me his Driving Licence issued by the .... Council bearing his name.
   or:
   At the time of the said service the said .... produced to me his Passport No. .... issued in London bearing his name and photograph by way of identification.
   or:
   At the time of service on the said .... the Petitioner was present and pointed out to me the said .... as being her husband the Respondent.

SWORN at   )
in the County of   )
this   day of   2012   )

   Before me,

   A Solicitor empowered to administer Oaths

........Affidavit of..........................
Sworn on the ....day of 2012
Exhibit marked 'A'
Sworn on Behalf of the ....

AFFIDAVIT OF SERVICE OF JUDGMENT SUMMONS

IN THE   No

BETWEEN:

                                                                                                       Petitioner
                                              - and -

                                                                                                       Respondent

I, ... of .... in the County of .... Process Server acting under direction of Solicitors for the above-named Petitioner, make Oath and say:

1. That the Judgment Summons herein issued out of the Divorce (District) Registry on the .... day of .... 2012 was duly served by me on .... the Respondent (or: as the case may be......) in this cause at .... on .... the .... day of .... 2012, by delivering to the said ....personally a copy thereof sealed with the seal of the Court.

2. That a true copy of the said Judgment Summons is now produced and shown to me marked 'A'.

3. That I paid (or tendered) to the said ....at the same time and place the sum of £ to cover his expenses in travelling to and from the Court.

SWORN at   )

in the County of   )

this   day of   2012   )

            Before me,

            A Solicitor empowered to administer Oaths.

………Affidavit of………………..……
Sworn on the …..day of ……… 2012
Sworn on Behalf of the …………………

AFFIDAVIT IN SUPPORT OF ORDER FOR
SUBSTITUTED SERVICE

IN THE DIVORCE REGISTRY   No

BETWEEN:

                     Mary Black   Petitioner

                     - and -

                     Thomas Black   Respondent

I, ………………………………………. of ………………………………………………………………..
in the County of ………………………………….. Process Server acting under the direction of Solicitors for the above-named Petitioner, make Oath and say:

1.   That being directed to effect personal service of the Divorce Petition issued in this cause and bearing date the …………………….. day of ………………………… 2012, together with Notice of Proceedings and Form of Acknowledgement of Service (add any other documents) on the Respondent Thomas Black. I did on ………….. the ……………………... day of ……………………….. 2012, attend at the last known address of the said Respondent Thomas Black situate at No. 10 Blank Street London N. and when I saw an adult female who informed me the said Thomas Black no longer lived at that address and that he left such address twelve months ago. She further stated the said Thomas Black had left behind no forwarding address and all letters were returned to the Post Office marked 'Gone Away'.

2.   On the same day I made enquiries of neighbours in the vicinity of No. 10 Blank Street aforesaid and was informed by an adult female at No. 14 Blank Street aforesaid she recalled the said Thomas Black but that he had not resided at No. 10 Blank Street for at least twelve months and she had not seen or heard of him since he left and had no idea where he was now living.

3.   That I did on …………………… the ……………………… day of …………………… 2012, attend at the address of White & Co at 2 Green Street London N. and when I saw an adult male Manager who informed me the said Thomas Black had left employ of White & Co about twelve months ago and nothing had been seen or heard of him since. He further informed me the only address known for the said Thomas Black was 10 Blank Street aforesaid and that no application had been received for a reference in respect of the said Thomas Black.

                                                                                                                                                                 Cont'd...

4. That I did on .... the .... day of .... 2012, attend at .... the address of John Black, a brother of the said Respondent Thomas Black, and who informed me he had not seen or heard from his brother Thomas Black for over twelve months and he had no idea where he was now living or working. He further informed me that members of the family had tried to locate the said Thomas Black but without success.

5. That I did on .... the .... day of .... 2012, attend at Southern Bank Ltd. 21 High Street London N. and when I saw the adult male Manager who informed me in answer to my enquiry that the said Thomas Black no longer held any account at that branch, it having been closed some twelve months ago and the only known address for the said Thomas Black was 10 Blank Street aforesaid.

6. That as the result of the enquiries I have made I am of the opinion there is little likelihood of being able to trace the said Respondent Thomas Black and that it will not be possible to effect personal service of the said Petition.

7. I crave leave that the Petition issued in this cause be served on the said Respondent Thomas Black by way of advertisement in the press or in such other manner as the Court deem fit.

SWORN at   )
)
)
in the County of   )
)
this   day of   2012)

      Before me

      A Solicitor empowered to administer Oaths

STATEMENT OF SERVICE   **Case number**

Family Law Act 1996

                                    Applicant
                                    Ref.

The Court at which your case is being heard   **Respondent**
                                    Ref.

You must
- **give details of service of the application on each of the other parties**
- give details of service on the mortgagee or landlord of the dwelling house (if appropriate)
- file this form with the Court on or before the first Directions Appointment of Hearing of the Proceedings

You should   if the person's solicitor was served, give his or her name and address

You must indicate the manner, date, time and place of service
                     or where service was effected by post, the date, time and place of posting

Name and address of person served	Means of identification of person, and how, when and where served	Prescribed forms served

I have served [application] [Notice of Proceedings] as stated above.
I am the [applicant] [solicitor for the applicant] [other] (*state*)

Signed: Date:

DECLARATION OF SERVICE

(Form 142 - MC Rules 1981 Rule 67)

I,..of ....
hereby solemnly declare that I did on the .... day of ....
2000 serve .... of .... with the summons of which a true
copy is now shown to me and marked 'A' by delivering the said summons to him.

(or: by leaving the said summons for him with ....)

at .... being the said ....'s last (or usual) place of abode

.... (Signature)

DECLARED Before me the .... day of 2000

Justice of the Peace for the County of ....

CERTIFICATE OF SERVICE

(Form 144 - MC Rules 1981 Rule 67)

I,.. of ....
hereby certify that on the .... day of 2012
I served .... of ....
with the summons (or other documents - as the case may be) of which this is a
true copy by delivering the said summons to him personally.
(together with the sum of £   for costs and expenses)

(or: and that I tendered to him the sum of £   for costs and expenses)

(or by leaving the said summons for him (together with the sum of £   for costs and expenses)

with .... at ....
being the said .... 's last known (or usual) place of abode (or business)

Dated the .... day of 2000

(Signed) ....

SAMPLE AFFIDAVITS

The forms of affidavit of service set out here are either from draft affidavits which have accompanied instructions or copies of affidavits which have been sworn and which appear to have been acceptable. It must be remembered that these affidavits are purely a guide and that from time to time the practice in all Courts changes.

If no affidavit of service is available to suit the process an affidavit should be prepared showing when and where the process was served, specifying the process and headed up according to the original.

IN THE FAMILY COURT OF AUSTRALIA AT ADELAIDE

No   of 2012

IN THE MARRIAGE OF

……………………………………   Husband

            and

……………………………………   Wife

I,   of   in the County of   , England, Process Server, make Oath and say as follows:-

1. THAT I am authorised and empowered to effect service of Process of the Supreme Court of Judicature in England.

2. THAT I did on …………… the ………………… day of …………2012 at ……………o'clock in the ……………noon at …………………… in the County of ………………England, duly serve upon …………………………………the respondent in this cause a sealed copy of the Application for Dissolution of Marriage and Form of Acknowledgement of Service by delivering the same personally to her.

3. THAT at the time and place of service the said respondent admitted her full name as ……………………………… and identified herself from her Australian Passport No …………………………

4. AT my request the said respondent signed the Acknowledgement of Service which is now produced and shown to me marked 'A'.

SWORN at   )

in the COUNTY of   )

England, this   day of   )

                            2012   )

            Before me,

A Notary Public

IN THE SUPREME COURT OF ONTARIO

BETWEEN:

                                                                                                    Petitioner
                                          and
                                                                                                    Respondent

AFFIDAVIT OF SERVICE

I, ... of .... in the County of .... , England, Process Server make Oath and say:

1. I DID on .... day the ....day of .... 2012 personally serve, at approximately ....am/pm the attached Notice of Petition and Petition for Divorce, by delivering true copies of the same to and leaving the same with the said Respondent on the day last aforesaid at ....

2. UPON the said copies so served as aforesaid were endorsed at the time of such service true copies of all the endorsements appearing upon the original Notice of Petition for Divorce and Petition for Divorce.

3. AT the time of such service, I requested the said Respondent to complete and sign the Acknowledgement of Service endorsed on the said Notice of Petition for Divorce and my request was complied with and I witnessed the signature on page 3 of the Notice of Petition for Divorce.

4. MY means of knowledge as to the identity of the person so served was as follows:

    The Respondent acknowledged that she was the person named as Respondent in the Petition for Divorce and used the following method of identification:

    She produced for my inspection her Canadian Passport - or

    I asked in the area and neighbours pointed out the Respondent to me - or
    I recognised her from a photograph supplied to me.

SWORN at   )

in the County of   )

England, this   day of   )

                         2012   )

        Before me,

A Notary Public.

CANADIAN PRINTED FORM OF AFFIDAVIT OF SERVICE

IN THE COURT OF SUPREME/COUNTY

BETWEEN:

                                                                                                   Plaintiff

- and -

                                                                                                  Defendant

AFFIDAVIT OF SERVICE

I, ... of .... in the County of .... England, Process Server make Oath and say as follows:

1. THAT I did on .... day the .... day of .... 2012 personally serve .... the Defendant .... at .... with the .... (name document) by delivering a true copy of the same to, and leaving the same with .... (name and address of person with whom the papers were left)

SWORN at   )

in the County of   )

England, this   day of   )

                         2012   )

        Before me,

A Notary Public.

IN THE CIRCUIT COURT OF THE ELEVENTH JUDICIAL CIRCUIT OF FLORIDA IN AND FOR DADE COUNTY

Case No

GENERAL JURISDICTION DIVISION
CIVIL ACTIONS SUMMONS

....   Plaintiff

- v -

....   Defendants

I, ... of .... in the County of ...., England, Process Server acting under the direction of .... of .... Solicitors for the Plaintiff, make Oath and say:

1. THAT I did on .... the .... day of ....2012 at ....in the County of .... England, personally serve .... and .... each with the Civil Action Summons and Complaint issued herein.

2. THERE is now produced and shown to me copies of each of the Civil Action Summonses so served by me.

SWORN at   )

in the County of   )

England, this   day of   )

                         2012   )

            Before me,

A Notary Public.

IN THE HIGH COURT OF THE STATE OF SINGAPORE ISLAND OF SINGAPORE

                                                                                                            Suit No   of

BETWEEN:

                                                                                                                                Plaintiff

                                                                - and -

                                                                                                 Defendant

I, ... of .... in the County of .... England, Process Server, make Oath and say as follows:

1.   I AM authorised and empowered to effect service of the process of the Supreme Court of Judicature in England.

2.   THAT I did on .... the .... day of .... 2012 , at .... in the County of .... England, duly serve the Defendant .... with a true copy of the concurrent Writ of Summons issued in this action, and bearing date the .... day of .... 2012, the original of which is now produced and shown to me marked 'A'.

3.   THAT I did at the same time and place of service hand to the said Defendant .... a true copy of the Order of Court made in this action and dated the .... day of .... 2012, a sealed copy of which is now produced and shown to me marked 'B'.

4.   THAT at my request the said Defendant signed a form of receipt endorsed on each of the original documents now produced and shown to me marked 'A' and 'B', and which he dated the .... day of .... 2012.

SWORN at   )

in the County of   )

England, this   day of   )

                                  2012   )

              Before me,

A Notary Public.

IN THE HIGH COURT OF ZIMBABWE HELD AT HARARE

Case No   2012

IN THE MATTER BETWEEN:

....   **Plaintiff**

- and -

....   **Defendant**

I,   of   in the County of   , England, Process Server make Oath and say as follows:

1. THAT on the .... day of .... 2012, I effected service of the Citation by Edict, Plaintiff's Intendit, Court Order granting leave to sue by Edictal Citation, and Notice of Set Down for Trial, all in connection with the above matter, by handling copies thereof personally to .... at .... England, at the same time exhibiting to her the originals and explaining to her the nature of exigency thereof.

SWORN at   )

in the County of   )

England, this   day of)

                              2012)

Before me,

A Notary Public.

IN THE SUPREME COURT OF SOUTH AFRICA

(.............................. LOCAL DIVISION)

IN THE MATTER BETWEEN:

                                                                                                                                      Plaintiff

- and -

                                                                                                                                  Defendant

I, ... of .... in the County of .... England, Process Server, make Oath and say as follows:

1. THAT an Office copy of the Edictal Citation issued in this matter and bearing date the .... day of .... 2012 was duly served by me on the Defendant (born) .... at .... England, by delivering the same personally to the said Defendant .... (born) ....

2. THAT at the time such service as aforesaid the said Defendant .... (born) .... admitted to me that she was the Defendant in this action and at my request signed an Acknowledgement of Service upon her and I now produce the said Acknowledgement of Service marked 'A' signed by the said Defendant.

3. THAT the original of the said Edictal Citation is now produced to me marked 'B'.

SWORN at   )

in the County of   )

this   day of   2012   )

      Before me

      A Notary Public.

AFFIDAVIT OF PERSONAL SERVICE (PRINTED FORM) NEW YORK

Family Court

State of New York

County of

Return Date

Part

Docket No

I, ... being duly sworn, depose and say:

1. That I am over the age of 18 years and not a party to the above action, and reside at .... England.

2. On the .... day of ....2012 at .... at (time) .... I personally served the summons (and petition) (or order to show cause) on .... respondent in the above mentioned action, by delivering to and leaving copies of each with .... at said time and place.

3. I knew the person so served to be .... the person named in said summons as the respondent in the action by reason of his admission of identity.

4. Description of person served:

    Sex .... colour of skin .... hair .... approx age .... approx height .... approx weight .... other identifying features (wearing a moustache) ....

SWORN before me this   )

day of   2012   )

       A Notary Public.

COURT OF SESSION (SCOTLAND)

                                                                       Pursuer

                         against

                                                                        Defender

AFFIDAVIT OF SERVICE

I, ...of .... and I, ... of .... both Process Servers acting under the direction of .... Solicitors for the above-named Pursuer, jointly and severally make Oath and say:

        AND I .... for myself say:

1. THAT a true copy of the summons issued herein at Edinburgh on the .... day of .... 2012, together with a Notice of Defender in an action of Divorce where it is stated there has been 5 years non-cohabitation on Form 15C dated the .... day of .... of ....2012, by delivering the same into his hands personally before and in the presence of .... the second Deponent to this Affidavit of Service.
2. THAT the Defender .... so served was identified to me by .... immediately prior to service being effected upon him.
or: produced to me his Driving Licence bearing number ....
(or Passport Number .... expiring on ....)

        AND I .... for myself say:

3. THAT the service effected as aforesaid was duly effected in my presence and I remained present while Mr .... drew the Defender's attention to the contents of all the documents served upon him and I heard the Defender inform Mr .... that he would give the documents to his Solicitor.

SWORN by the first-named deponent   )

at   in the   )
County of   , England, this   )

        day of   2012   )

        Before me,
        A Solicitor empowered to administer Oaths

SWORN by the second-named deponent   )

at   in the   )
County of   , England, this   )

        day of   2012   )

        Before me,

        A Solicitor empowered to administer Oaths.

                                   ***

SECTION 10- GENERAL OBSERVATIONS

Introduction

In preparing these notes the strict practice adopted by the Central Office of the High Court and the Woolf Civil Procedures Rules has been borne in mind. It is appreciated that the practice adopted in the local District Registry and some County Courts is perhaps not as strict or possibly the rules may be interpreted a little differently.

Service Of An Original Claim Form

There is now no need for the original claim form (or second sealed copy) to be in the immediate possession of the process server so the service of an original writ should not occur.

However, should an original document be served in error, immediate efforts should be made to recover the original document and substitute the service copy. If this proves impossible then a further office copy should be obtained. Where photocopies of documents are supplied as copies for service it is often difficult to distinguish the original from the copy at night when outside and especially in sodium-lit-streets.

Marking the documents 'serve' and 'keep' in pencil is sometimes helpful.

Service On A Partnership Firm

Where service is effected on the person in control of a partnership business such service must take place 'at the principal place of business'. It is not good service to serve the Manager in the local café or public house where he is having lunch.

It should be noted the Notice of Service on a partnership which should accompany the claim form should be separate from the claim form and NOT endorsed on the claim form.

Service On Husband And Wife

Where service is required on a man and wife, service must of course be personal on each defendant. On no account should two copies of a document be left with the husband or wife notwithstanding promises made. One should never be persuaded to leave the claim form with a person not the defendant despite any promise or excuse given.

Use Of Envelopes

Process should never be served in an envelope. Letters which are sometimes required to be delivered should not be in sealed envelopes unless the agent has had sight of such letter and holds a copy which can be endorsed as to delivery.

Affidavits

Attention is drawn to the special chapter which has been written in regard to affidavits.

Substituted Service Steps/Service By An Alternative Method

Substituted service steps are available where, according to the rules "it is impracticable for any person to serve a document personally".

Such steps do not usually apply to documents bearing a penal notice.

Where such steps are available it is unnecessary for endless calls to be made at the address of a defendant in an effort to effect personal service. This only tends to increase the cost of the service and waste time.

The subject of substituted service steps has been dealt with earlier but the following points should be borne in mind. When the written appointments are attended, it is important to obtain admissions that letters have been received by the defendant, or that he has been at the address and would have therefore normally received all letters; Or, that none are awaiting collection by the defendant. If it is said that letters have been forwarded to the defendant, whilst it may not be possible to obtain the address, it is important to know whether the letter has been forwarded to an address within the jurisdiction of the Court, i.e. England or Wales. It is advisable to confirm by letter any alternative appointment made by the defendant and any letters received from the defendant, together with the envelope, should be exhibited to any affidavit of attempts.

Service Where The Defendant Alleges The Claim Is Paid

Where a defendant, at the time of service, contends the claim has been paid, and even produces some evidence in the form of a receipt or cheque stub, service should still be effected unless instructions have been received to the contrary. It may be the costs on the claim form are still outstanding or that the defendant's cheque may not be honoured.

If the defendant has paid the amount of the claim since the issue of the claim form, he is normally liable for the costs and credit for any sum paid will always be given. If the defendant claims the debt was paid before the issue of the claim form, then he has a good answer to the claim but service should still be effected. Remember your job is to effect service of the claim form and not to try and decide any issue between the parties. One should not be talked into taking the claim form away unserved. In doing so it is likely that subsequent efforts to effect service, if necessary will present more difficulty since the defendant has received knowledge of the claim form and the process server. On a subsequent attendance the defendant may have 'flown'.

Similarly, when the defendant suggests the claim form should be served on his solicitor and provides the name and address of the Solicitor, service should still be effected upon the defendant and he should be told to send the claim form to his solicitor. It could be the case that the solicitor has not received instructions to accept service of the claim form!

Service Where Defendant Wrongly Described

Where the defendant has obviously been wrongly described in the claim form by way of initials, Christian names or wrong spelling, or in the case of a female whose status as been wrongly given, i.e. married woman, widow, spinster, femme sole; service should not be effected and the claim form should be returned for amendment prior to service.

It is easier for the claim form to be amended before service than after service has been effected. Service on a defendant wrongly described may require an application to amend and the possibility of re-service.

This does not however, apply to an incorrect address which does not require to be amended. The correct address must of course be shown in the affidavit of service.

Place Of Service

It is important that the affidavit of service shows the actual place of service, i.e. "at the corner of Black Street and White Street"; "Outside No 18 Blank Street"; or "in his car outside No 18 Blank Street".

The Bankruptcy Courts have been known to insist on the correct place of service when service is effected in a large complex or office block; i.e. "In room No.702 on the seventh floor of Blank House".

Alterations Of Original Documents

On no account should any original document be altered in any way. The writer has seen names and addresses appearing on original claim forms corrected in ink by process servers. No alteration should be made to any original document unless made by the Court and when it will be appropriately sealed.

Perhaps the only exception to this is in regard to a witness summons. In this eventuality, the copy witness summons can be corrected in ink but the original witness summons must only be amended in pencil. If any obvious error is observed in an original document, it should be returned to instructing solicitors so it may be put in order in the correct manner.

Endorsement Of Service

Whilst a claim form no longer requires to be endorsed as to service, it is useful if other copy documents, not immediately requiring to be proved by an affidavit of service, are endorsed. It assists the solicitors and agents to know when, where and by whom a document was served should it be necessary to prove service of such document at a later date.

Coloured Ink

Coloured ink for the purpose of endorsement and signatures should be avoided. Red, green and violet inks are reserved for making amendments to documents and the Central Office prefer they should be used only for such purposes. Use black or blue/black ink or black typewriter ribbon.

Rubber Stamps

Care should be exercised in the use of rubber stamps when it comes to endorsement of service and in the body of any affidavit. The Central Office do not approve of rubber stamps being used for the name, address and description at the commencement of an affidavit or in an endorsement of service. They are however acceptable where used by a solicitor beneath his signature on an affidavit.

Firms And Limited Companies

Care should be taken to see that a defendant described as a firm is not in fact a Limited Company. If this is discovered, the claim form should be returned for amendment.

Also, when reporting a claim form served on a firm, it should not speak of service on 'a director'. A firm is composed of partners or a sole proprietor and only a Limited Company has directors.

Correct Descriptions

It is important to use correct descriptions when reporting. When Bankruptcy proceedings are taken the Plaintiff becomes the Judgment Creditor and the Defendant becomes the Judgment Debtor. They should always be referred to as such. Similarly, in matrimonial proceedings the Plaintiff becomes either the Petitioner or the Applicant and the other party the Respondent and they too should be referred to as such.

First And Second Class Post

Affidavit of attempts should always refer to First-class post otherwise it will be inferred that second-class post was used.

Finally

Halsbury's Laws of England (Fourth edition, page 288) says, "The object in punishing for contempt where a process server in the execution of his duty has been abused and assaulted is not to vindicate the dignity of the Court but to prevent undue interference with the administration of justice…"

However, slight obstruction or verbal abuse, which does not actually prevent service is not regarded as contempt of Court. It is presumably an occupational hazard!

***

ABOUT THE AUTHORS

Stuart Withers

Stuart was born at the end of the Second World War. He left school at 15 without any academic qualifications and joined the Merchant Navy. Having travelled around the World for four years, he decided that a life at sea was not for him.

Stuart's endeavours to join the Metropolitan Police failed, as he did not reach the minimum height requirement. Being an avid reader of detective stories, Stuart then founded in 1963 a small London based Private Investigation Agency which became Nationwide Investigations Group (www.nig.co.uk) . During Stuarts career as a Private Investigator, he has travelled and worked all over the world having been retained by princes, presidents, governments, politicians and celebrities as well as international corporations, police forces and the national press and broadcasting media.

Stuart is the founder of Nationwide Investigations Group, The Academy of Professional Investigation (www.pi-academy.com) , author of the original NIG Process Servers Guide 2000, contributor to the NVQ in Investigation Level 3 & 4 and founder member of The World Association of Professional Investigation - WAPI (www.wapi.com) .

Helen Withers

Helen joined the Nationwide Investigations Group when it was known as Christopher Robert and Co in 1967 as a lowly investigator having no previous knowledge of the industry, but looking for an interesting and exciting new career.

As a trainee, Helen learnt how to serve process, trace people, do surveillance, take statements and attended court on many occasions with regard to matrimonial cases. At that time, goods were mainly purchased on Hire Purchase, and any default lead to repossession. Helen was involved in the repossessions of televisions, cars, and even a JCB on one occasion!. The unsociable hours suited Helen at the time, and of course are still a very relevant part of any investigators lifestyle. The company expanded to include Security, and during that time Helen also became one of the company's store detectives, during which time she made a considerable number of arrests resulting in the appropriate court cases.

Helen has continued to take part in all the company's activities, working around her family commitments, and in 1998, when the Academy of Professional Investigation was formed, the Distance Learning Course in Private Investigation was written by various practicing private investigators including Stuart Withers, Frank Battes and Helen herself, which has been a successful Course and was upgraded in 2007 to become the Edexcel BTEC Advanced Private Investigation Level 3 Diploma.

Jorge Salgado-Reyes

Jorge moved to the UK at age seven from Chile, where he was born. He is tri-lingual, having lived in the UK and Mozambique, speaking fluent English, Spanish and Portuguese.

Jorge came up through the ranks in various high street retail stores until he became a Security Manager for a leading high street book seller and then various roles as a Senior Retail Loss Prevention Investigator at a national level.

In April 2006, after seventeen years in retail fraud investigations, he started his own private investigator agency, Allied Detectives (UK) and Salgado Investigations (Chile) specialising in corporate investigations, surveillance, process serving and tracing.

Jorge is a founder member of e-Legal Gathering, an online discussion forum for private investigators. He has an Edexcel BTEC Advanced Private Investigation Level 3 Diploma and a BTEC award in Investigative Interviewing. He is currently serving on WAPI's Governing Council in Electronic Media, after having served as General Secretary for a year.

Jorge has also penned a debut Science Fiction novel, "The Smoke In Death's Eye." Available for pre-order from Amazon. The novel features a Private Investigator in a futuristic (2118 AD) London setting :- *"In a dystopian future of nanotechnology and ubiquitous CCTV, a Private Investigator, tortured by the disappearance of his wife, investigates a series of brutal slayings".*

Future books planned are The Zen of Shoplifting and The Zen of Sleuthing, available for pre-order from Amazon.

He also enjoys writing poetry (his works can be found in the poetry section of his writing forum) and is an amateur photographer.

His twitter page is @J_SalgadoReyes.

***

AFTERWORD

I would like to personally thank you for buying and reading this book. Writing this guide for professional Process Servers has been and continues to be fulfilling for us and I hope that it is fulfilling for you to read.

Please consider taking a little extra time to help others find this book by leaving feedback where you purchased it. Your opinion about this book truly matters, both to us and to other readers.

If you have any questions, comments, suggestions or just want to say hi, please visit our publisher's webpage on Indie Authors Press www.salgado-reyes.com and follow our publishers twitter: @Indie__Authors

~Jorge Salgado-Reyes~

INDEX

£

£750 or more, 119

A

a summary of the proceedings, 174
ABOUT THE AUTHORS, 301
Acknowledgment of Service, 141, 142, 143, 235, 236, 244, 248
active service, 148, 150
address, 3, 23, 24, 25, 26, 29, 31, 32, 34, 37, 38, 39, 41, 42, 43, 44, 52, 53, 60, 70, 73, 74, 80, 81, 82, 85, 89, 93, 95, 98, 108, 109, 110, 112, 121, 123, 127, 128, 129, 130, 131, 136, 146, 152, 153, 157, 160, 161, 162, 166, 189, 193, 203, 207, 213, 222, 226, 228, 229, 233, 235, 242, 243, 244, 253, 255, 256, 261, 262, 264, 269, 270, 274, 276, 278, 281, 282, 283, 287, 296, 297
Address, 32, 88, 123
administration of justice, 298
Administration of Justice, 15, 225
Administration Of Oaths, 227
Administration order, 116
Administrations, 75, 81
Administrative Office, 18
Admiralty, 7, 15, 51, 55, 180
ADMIRALTY CLAIMS, 55
Admiralty Proceedings, 51
adoption, 14, 128, 190, 193
Adoption and Children Act 2002, 158, 160
Adoption Section Inheritance Act 1975, 17
ADULTERY, 6
ADVOCATE, 6
affidavit, 53, 61, 73, 139, 142, 143, 144, 168, 173, 211, 221, 222, 223, 224, 225, 227, 228, 231, 232, 262, 285, 296, 297
Affidavit, 51, 53, 66, 142, 143, 169, 173, 222, 223, 228, 234, 235, 236, 237, 238, 239, 240, 241, 242, 243, 245, 246, 247, 248, 249, 250, 256, 257, 258, 259, 260, 261, 263, 266, 270, 275, 276, 277, 278, 280, 281, 293, 298
AFFIDAVIT, 6, 169, 212, 213, 218, 234, 235, 236, 237, 238, 239, 240, 241, 242, 243, 245, 246, 247, 248, 249, 256, 257, 258, 259, 260, 261, 263, 270, 275, 276, 277, 278, 279, 280, 281, 286, 287, 292, 293
AFFIDAVIT OF SERVICE OF PART 8 CLAIM, 248, 263
AFFIDAVIT OF SUBSTITUTED SERVICE OF, 270
affidavit sworn before a judge or registrar, 227
affidavits, 10, 18, 61, 73, 121, 139, 211, 221, 224, 226, 227, 228, 230, 231, 233, 285, 295
Affidavits, 7, 73, 173, 211, 223, 224, 227, 228, 233, 256, 257, 258, 259, 260, 262, 263, 295
AFFIDAVITS, STATEMENTS OF SERVICE AND CERTIFICATES OF SERVICE, 221

AFFIRMATION, 6
Affirmations, 226
affirming of affidavits, 10
affixing, 11
AFTERWORD, 305
ALEXANDER BARON v GERRY GABLE AND OTHERS, 5
all known addresses, 89, 144
Alterations Of Original Documents, 297
alternative method, 22, 23, 26, 27, 28, 35, 40, 41, 44
Alternative method, 30, 35
an application to serve by sending a SMS text message, 41
annulment, 73, 149
anti-social behaviour, 13
any method authorised by the court under rule 6.15, 22
Appeals, 76, 99, 160
Applicant, 5, 255, 264, 266, 283, 298
APPLICANT, 6
Application and interpretation of the rules, 48
Application by defendant for service of claim form, 48
application for an order, 28, 29, 33, 35, 40, 48, 157
application for leave to substitute some other mode, 144
application for relief, 200, 206
Applications, 13, 15, 18, 75, 76, 83, 85, 96, 97, 146
Applications Court, 18
applications for an administration order, 78
applications for an injunction, 78
applications for committal for contempt, 78
applications for the appointment of a provisional liquidator, 78
APPLICATIONS RELATING TO THE REMUNERATION OF APPOINTEES, 76, 100
appointment made by letter, 89
Arbitration Proceedings, 51
Armed Forces Act 2006, 39, 42, 148, 149
Army Officers and other Ranks, 43
arrest the individual without warrant, 151
ARTICLE, 6
Assistance in serving documents on members, 43
attorney, 28, 174
Attorney General, 26, 60
Authentication, 107
Authorised Government Departments, 57
AUTHORISED GOVERNMENT DEPARTMENTS, 57

B

bail, 15, 152
Bailiff, 54, 140
bankrupt, 73, 79, 88, 98, 112
BANKRUPT, 6
bankruptcy, 17, 72, 73, 74, 76, 77, 88, 89, 90, 93, 94, 96, 98, 111, 113, 114, 117
BANKRUPTCY, 6, 79, 267, 268, 271, 272, 273, 274, 275, 276
Bankruptcy Orders, 74

bankruptcy petition, 17, 74, 88, 89, 90, 94, 111, 113
Bankruptcy Restriction Orders, 74
Bankruptcy restrictions undertakings, 76, 98
BFPO, 43
breach of contract, 15, 178
British citizen, 37
British Forces Post Office, 43
British Nationality Act 1981, 37, 181
by agent, 175
by delivering it to the person to whom it is directed, 156
by leaving it for him with some person at his last known or usual place of abode, 156
by post, 11, 31, 38, 43, 51, 52, 106, 130, 132, 136, 137, 141, 144, 146, 156, 157, 255, 264, 283
by way of advertisement in the press, 144, 282

C

calendar month, 50
CANADIAN PRINTED FORM, 213, 287
cargo, 56
CCR Order 7 Rule 3, 48
Central Authority, 174, 203, 204, 205, 207
Central body, 194
Central London County Court, 16, 92
Central Office, 14, 15, 36, 57, 295, 297
certificate, 29, 35, 36, 37, 40, 62, 63, 81, 89, 90, 92, 93, 107, 120, 131, 158, 162, 166, 174, 189, 195, 196, 197, 199, 204, 206, 208, 223, 227
Certificate, 29, 35, 40, 51, 53, 66, 142, 197, 202, 223, 224, 228, 231
certificate of service, 92, 166, 174
Certificates and Statements of Service, 228
Certificates of continuing debt and of notice of adjournment, 76, 93

Ch

CHANCERY DIVISION, 79, 246, 247
Charging Orders, 7, 62
child, 27, 28, 33, 135, 137, 138, 147, 148, 149, 157
Child Support Act 1991, 140
Children Act 1989, 17, 135, 136, 138, 140, 146
church, 51

C

Civil Procedure Act 1997, 19
Civil Procedure Convention, 37, 173, 174, 175
civil procedure rules, 19
Civil Procedure Rules, 7, 3, 5, 15, 19, 43, 48, 77, 175, 228
CIVIL PROCEDURE RULES, 19
civil proceedings, 26, 42, 44, 57, 60
claim form, 21, 22, 23, 24, 25, 26, 27, 28, 29, 31, 32, 33, 35, 36, 37, 38, 40, 41, 47, 48, 49, 51, 53, 54, 55, 56, 80, 111, 121, 132, 167, 168, 175, 176, 177, 178, 179, 180, 254, 295, 296, 297, 298
CLAIM FORM, 6, 47, 121, 234, 235, 238, 239, 248, 249, 251, 256, 265
claim forms, 42, 56, 121, 254, 297
claim in rem, 55
claimant, 8, 15, 21, 22, 23, 24, 25, 26, 27, 29, 31, 40, 42, 43, 44, 47, 48, 54, 55, 56, 112, 121, 167, 168, 176, 177, 178
Claimant, 5, 7, 234, 235, 236, 237, 238, 239, 240, 241, 242, 243, 245, 246, 247, 248, 249, 251, 256, 257, 258, 259, 261, 262, 263, 265
CLAIMANT, 6, 251, 265
Claims in rem, 55
Clerk of the Rules, 17, 18
CLIENT, 8
Coloured Ink, 297
Coming into force, 75, 78
Commercial and Mercantile Actions, 51
COMMONS WRIT SERVER IN CONTEMPT, 5
Companies Act 1985, 51, 123, 124
COMPANIES ACT 1985, 125
Companies Act 1989, 51, 112, 126
Companies Act 2006, 7, 22, 31, 51, 118, 160
Companies Acts, 53, 125
company, 22, 23, 25, 31, 39, 40, 41, 42, 51, 52, 53, 72, 74, 77, 79, 80, 81, 82, 83, 84, 85, 111, 113, 115, 116, 118, 119, 120, 121, 124, 125, 126, 128, 152, 160, 238, 253, 256, 277, 278, 301
Company Directors Disqualification Act 1986, 112, 115, 125, 126
COMPANY DIRECTORS DISQUALIFICATION ACT 1986, 125
COMPANY INSOLVENCY, 75, 81
company's registered office, 51, 52, 82, 84, 120, 160
compensation for loss of time, 65, 66
COMPLAINANT, 6
confidentiality order, 123
consecrated ground, 51
contempt, 5, 161, 260, 298
Contempt of Court, 5
Contempt of Parliament, 5
contempt of the House, 5
Contentious Probate Proceedings, 51
Convention, 7, 167, 168, 173, 175, 176, 177, 189, 190, 192, 200, 202, 203, 204, 205, 206, 207, 208, 209, 210
convention country', 86
Convention on the Service Abroad of Judicial and Extrajudicial Documents in Civil or Commercial Matters, 173
Co-Respondent, 5
CO-RESPONDENT, 6
corporate members and firms, 128
corporation, 23, 25, 39, 40, 156, 160, 161, 239, 253
Correct Descriptions, 298
COUNSEL, 6
County Court, 3, 6, 16, 19, 43, 51, 88, 120, 135, 140, 144, 145, 146, 158, 227, 256, 257, 262, 279

COUNTY COURT, 79, 256, 257, 258, 259, 260, 261, 263, 266, 272
County Courts, 13, 14, 19, 139, 148, 225, 295
Court documents, 75, 79, 226
Court of Appeal, 13, 19, 50, 51, 99
Court of Law, 5, 6, 7
Court of Protection, 17, 28
Court of Session, 8, 118, 165, 166
COURT OF SESSION, 8, 166, 169, 293
court order, 22, 32, 35, 50, 129
court orders, 10, 14, 18, 22, 23, 27, 31, 32, 111, 135, 165
CPR, 7, 3, 15, 19, 38, 51, 55, 57, 66, 73, 74, 77, 80, 86, 99, 100, 106, 111, 112, 121, 122, 132, 135, 144, 145, 177, 221, 227
CPS, 152, 153
creditor, 44, 61, 81, 83, 84, 86, 88, 89, 90, 92, 93, 94, 97, 116, 117, 119, 131
Crime and Security Act 2010, 150
Crime and Victims Act 2004, 147
criminal proceedings, 15
Crown Court, 7, 13, 14, 161
Crown proceedings, 23
Crown Proceedings Act 1947, 57, 60
CROWN PROCEEDINGS ACT 1947, 57
Crown Proceedings Act 1976, 26

D

DATA, 8
Dates for compliance to be calendar dates and to include time of day, 50
debt remaining unsatisfied, 119
Debtors, 7, 61, 73
Declaration as to Service, 170
Deemed Service, 28, 33, 253
deemed unable to pay its debts, 120
DEFAULT, 6
defendant, 3, 21, 22, 23, 24, 25, 26, 27, 28, 31, 35, 40, 44, 48, 51, 53, 54, 55, 56, 119, 120, 121, 147, 167, 168, 174, 176, 177, 178, 179, 191, 199, 200, 206, 244, 247, 262, 295, 296, 297
Defendant, 5, 6, 24, 199, 213, 215, 216, 217, 234, 235, 236, 237, 238, 239, 240, 241, 242, 243, 244, 245, 246, 247, 248, 249, 251, 256, 257, 258, 259, 261, 262, 263, 265, 287, 289, 290, 291, 296, 298
DEFENDANT, 6, 251, 265
delivery of documents electronically, 74
Deponent, 169, 221, 223, 243, 244, 293
DEPONENT, 6
Deponents, 74
deposit, 65, 92, 208, 209, 277
Deposit, 76, 92
Depositions and Court Attendance by Witnesses, 66
deputy, 28

Direction, 7, 15, 21, 23, 26, 31, 32, 34, 38, 50, 54, 55, 57, 65, 66, 69, 70, 75, 76, 77, 78, 80, 100, 121, 159, 177, 221, 229, 231, 232
Directors Disqualification Proceedings, 121
dispense with service, 144
Distribution of business, 75, 78
DISTRICT REGISTRY, 79
Divorce Process, 146
Divorce/Dissolution/Judicial Separation Process, 141
document, 5, 6, 8, 21, 30, 31, 32, 33, 34, 35, 36, 37, 38, 39, 40, 41, 42, 44, 47, 50, 51, 52, 73, 74, 79, 80, 86, 88, 89, 98, 106, 107, 108, 109, 110, 111, 121, 122, 123, 130, 136, 137, 138, 142, 143, 145, 146, 157, 158, 159, 160, 161, 162, 163, 165, 166, 173, 181, 189, 191, 193, 194, 195, 196, 197, 199, 200, 201, 202, 203, 204, 206, 213, 222, 223, 225, 226, 227, 230, 231, 253, 254, 268, 273, 287, 295, 297
document exchange, 21, 30, 31, 35, 38, 47, 136, 137, 161, 162, 253
Document exchange, 33, 253
Documents that must be served by specified methods, 161
Documents to be served, 142
Documents To Be Served, 53
Domestic Proceedings, 147
domestic violence, 147, 150, 151
Domestic Violence, 17, 147, 150, 151, 153
donee, 28
Drawing up of orders, 75, 81
DVPN, 150, 151, 152, 153
DVPO, 150, 151, 152, 153

E

ECHR, 147
EEA state, 24, 32
effecting service, 43
Election Petitions, 15
Electronic delivery, 74, 108, 110
electronic means, 39, 72, 74, 108, 110, 159, 161, 162, 163
electronic transmission, 30, 34, 35, 47
e-mail, 2, 30, 34, 35, 39, 41, 47, 69, 71, 108, 109
ENDORSE, 6
Endorsement Of Service, 297
England, 13, 17, 19, 25, 42, 43, 44, 52, 63, 89, 112, 113, 117, 118, 119, 120, 121, 123, 130, 138, 142, 145, 157, 158, 160, 165, 166, 169, 170, 211, 212, 213, 214, 215, 216, 217, 218, 253, 261, 278, 285, 286, 287, 288, 289, 290, 291, 292, 293, 296, 298
ENGLISH COURT SYSTEM, 13
evidence, 5, 9, 11, 12, 15, 19, 27, 28, 29, 35, 36, 40, 41, 44, 48, 54, 65, 74, 80, 81, 82, 84, 85, 89, 90, 93, 94, 95, 96, 98, 100, 102, 105, 106, 108, 131, 132, 143, 145, 153, 157, 158, 159, 174, 221, 222, 223, 224, 227, 230, 231, 232, 296
Evidence, 75, 80, 158, 221
EVIDENCE, 7, 11

ex parte, 73, 144, 148
Ex parte, 73
exhibit, 222, 225, 226, 229, 230, 231, 232, 247, 259
exhibits, 11, 12, 222, 223, 224, 226, 230, 231, 263
Exhibits other than documents, 226
Ex-parte, 148
Extension of time for serving, 47
Extrajudicial documents, 198, 207
Extrajudicial Documents, 173, 198, 202, 207

F

Family Associates and In-Court Support, 18
FAMILY COURT PROCEEDINGS, 135
Family Law Act 1996, 17, 146, 147, 255, 264, 283
family proceedings, 142, 146, 148
Family Proceedings, 135, 136, 138, 140, 141, 142, 143, 145, 146, 148
Family Proceedings Rules 1991, 136, 138, 141, 145, 146
fax, 21, 31, 34, 39, 41, 47
Fax, 6, 30, 34, 35, 47, 70, 253, 272
Financial Services and Markets Act 2000, 125
Firms And Limited Companies, 297
First And Second Class Post, 298
first class post, 21, 31, 41, 42, 121, 136, 146, 160, 162, 278
Foreign and Commonwealth Office, 36
foreign country, 86, 174
foreign governments, 36, 37
Foreign Judgments (Reciprocal Enforcement) Act 1933, 15
Form 6.4, 89
Form 6.5, 89, 90
Form M 4, 142
Form M 5, 142
Form M 6, 142
Form of Acknowledgement of Service, 142, 211, 234, 251, 279, 281, 285
freight, 56
FURTH, 8

G

gazetted, 82, 83
Gazetting, 75, 82
GENERAL OBSERVATIONS, 295
GLOSSARY OF TERMS, 6
government department, 26, 82
Governor of the prison, 51
guardian, 27, 137, 143
guardians, 27

H

Hague Convention, 86, 175, 181, 192, 200, 202
Hague Service Convention, 173, 174, 175, 202, 210
HAGUE, EU CONVENTION & INFORMAL, 173

Heading, 81, 221, 229
hearing, 11, 12, 17, 18, 49, 50, 61, 62, 63, 65, 76, 78, 82, 83, 84, 89, 93, 94, 95, 96, 97, 98, 102, 131, 132, 137, 138, 139, 142, 144, 145, 148, 150, 151, 152, 158, 161, 226, 259
HEARING, 7
Hearing of remuneration applications, 76, 102
Helen Withers, 1, 2, 301
High Court, 3, 6, 8, 13, 14, 15, 16, 17, 18, 19, 42, 43, 44, 51, 77, 86, 88, 96, 99, 100, 120, 135, 141, 144, 145, 146, 147, 221, 228, 295
HM Courts & Tribunals Service, 13
HM Courts and Tribunals Service, 92
HMCTS, 92
Houses of Parliament, 5
HOW TO START PROCEEDINGS, 47
Human Rights Act 1998, 147

I

identification, 39, 142, 143, 173, 212, 255, 264, 279, 283, 286
Identification Of, 142
in person, 11, 18, 20, 93, 94, 146, 175
IN PERSONAM, 7
in rem, 55, 56
IN REM, 7
IN THE FAMILY COURT OF AUSTRALIA, 211, 285
IN THE HIGH COURT OF JUSTICE, 79, 234, 235, 236, 237, 238, 239, 240, 241, 242, 243, 245, 246, 247, 248, 249
IN THE HIGH COURT OF THE STATE OF SINGAPORE ISLAND OF SINGAPORE, 215, 289
IN THE HIGH COURT OF ZIMBABWE HELD AT HARARE, 216, 290
IN THE SUPREME COURT OF ONTARIO, 212, 286
IN THE SUPREME COURT OF SOUTH AFRICA, 217, 291
Inability to pay debts, 119
Informal Service, 173, 175
INFORMATION, 8
INJUNCTION, 7, 259, 260
injunctions, 10, 147
INSERTION THROUGH THE LETTERBOX, 235
Insolvency Act 1986, 69, 76, 82, 112, 113, 123, 124, 125, 269, 274
Insolvency and winding up, 123
insolvency and winding up of limited liability partnerships, 123, 124
insolvency proceedings, 69, 75, 76, 78, 79, 80, 99, 100, 107, 108, 110, 111, 112, 113
INSOLVENCY PROCEEDINGS, 69, 75
Insolvency Rules, 69, 70, 71, 72, 73, 74, 76, 77, 78, 79, 80, 83, 85, 89, 94, 98, 100, 103, 105, 113
Insolvency Rules 1986, 69, 71, 72, 94, 113
insolvent member, 113, 114, 116
insolvent partnership, 113, 114, 115, 116, 117
INTELLIGENCE, 8

interim application notices, 42
interim applications, 78
Interim Possession Orders, 54
interim third party debt order, 62
INTRODUCTION TO PROCESS SERVING, 5
IPO, 54

J

Jorge Salgado-Reyes, 1, 2, 1, 3, 301, 305
Judgment, 7, 50, 61, 131, 144, 276, 280, 298
JUDGMENT, 7, 280
judgment creditor, 61, 62, 63, 131, 132
judgment debtor, 62
Judgment Debtor., 7, 298
judgment summons, 131, 132, 157
judgments, 15, 50, 176, 200, 207
JUDICATURE, 7
judicial and extrajudicial documents to be served abroad, 202
judicial authorities, 36, 37, 174, 181
JUDICIAL CIRCUIT OF FLORIDA IN AND FOR, 214, 288
judicial documents, 173, 196, 197, 198, 204, 205, 206
Judicial documents, 194
Judicial Documents, 194, 203
Judicial Officer, 174
jurat, 222, 223, 227, 228
Jurat, 222, 226
jurisdiction, 8, 23, 24, 25, 26, 27, 37, 38, 47, 53, 56, 74, 77, 78, 80, 81, 86, 89, 111, 112, 113, 118, 120, 130, 148, 150, 165, 166, 167, 168, 174, 175, 176, 177, 178, 179, 180, 181, 194, 195, 201, 205, 236, 253, 296
Jurisdiction, 17, 23, 75, 80, 142, 149, 166, 175, 176, 177, 178
JURISDICTION, 7, 214, 288
justice of the peace, 156, 157, 158, 170, 224, 227

L

Landlord and Tenant Act 1987, 24
last known address, 146
Leave of the court, 73
leaving it at a place, 21, 31
Legal aid, 200
legal proceedings, 7, 19, 158
legal process, 10
legal representative, 42, 43, 44
legal representatives, 42
Letter of Appointment, 233
letter of request, 174, 181
letter rogatory, 174, 175
Letter Rogatory, 174
Letters Rogatory, 174
libel and slander, 15

limited liability partnership, 22, 31, 77, 122, 123, 124, 125, 126
Limited liability partnerships, 122
LIMITED LIABILITY PARTNERSHIPS, 124
Limited Liability Partnerships Act 2000, 31, 122, 125, 129
Limited Liability Partnerships Act 2004, 22
Limited Liability Partnerships Regulations 2001, 76, 77, 124
Listing Office, 18
litigants, 18, 19, 42
litigation friend, 28, 33

Ll

LLP, 126, 127, 128, 129, 130

L

London Gazette, 73, 74
Lord Chancellor's Office, 44

M

MAGISTRATE'S, 156
MAGISTRATES & CROWN COURT PROCEEDINGS, 156
magistrates' courts, 13, 14, 161
Magistrates' courts, 13
Magistrates Courts, 136, 139
Magistrates' Courts Act 1978, 147
Magistrate's Courts Rule 1981, 156
Magistrates' Courts Act 1980, 158, 161
Matrimonial Proceedings Act 1976, 147
Meaning of 'month', 50
mental disorder, 143
Mental Health Act 1983, 143
Messenger-at-Arms, 165
Messengers at Arms, 165
Methods of Service, 21
Ministry of, 42, 44, 58, 60, 208, 209, 210
minor, 143
Minors, 143
MODERNISATION OF INSOLVENCY RULES, 69

N

National Occupational Standards, 7, 9
NATIONAL OCCUPATIONAL STANDARDS, 9
negligence, 15
New Insolvency Rules for 2012, 71
New insolvency rules for 2013, 70
NEW YORK, 218, 292
nominated person, 74
non-molestation order, 147, 148
non-payment of a debt, 15

Northern Ireland, 3, 38, 43, 52, 58, 118, 120, 130, 158, 160, 165, 166, 167, 168, 170, 179
NOS, 9
NOTARY PUBLIC, 7
Notice, 7, 18, 29, 49, 50, 83, 106, 111, 138, 142, 150, 153, 169, 212, 216, 242, 247, 255, 259, 264, 279, 281, 283, 286, 290, 293, 295
Notice And Certificate Of Service Relating To The Claim Form, 29
Notice of an application, 49, 50
notice of an order, 161
notice of application, 10
Notice of issue of Legal Aid Certificate, 142
Notice of proceedings, 7, 142
notice of registration, 161
Notification Of Outcome Of Postal Service By The Court, 31

O

Occupation orders, 147
Official Receiver, 77, 81, 83, 85, 92, 96
Order, 7, 48, 50, 54, 61, 62, 71, 72, 77, 112, 113, 114, 115, 116, 117, 131, 138, 139, 140, 143, 145, 147, 148, 151, 153, 176, 215, 216, 233, 246, 260, 261, 274, 276, 289, 290
ORDER, 7, 246, 249, 260, 261, 281
order to attend court, 61
Orders available, 147
Orders without attendance, 76, 96
ORIGINATING, 7
Other electronic method, 30, 34, 35, 47, 253
overseas, 42, 43, 51, 52, 53, 160, 181

P

PART 12A OF THE INSOLVENCY RULES 1986, 106
PART 34, 65
Part 49, 51
Part 54, 23
Part 55, 53, 54
Part 6, 7, 3, 21, 38, 47, 73, 74, 80, 86, 106, 111, 112, 121, 122, 177, 253, 254
Part 61, 55
Part 66, 23, 57
PART 7, 47
PART 71, 61
PART 72, 62
PART 73, 62
PART IV, 76, 99, 125
Part VII, 115, 116, 117, 143
particulars of claim, 27, 29, 40, 49, 53, 54, 55, 56, 168, 177, 180
Particulars of claim, 49
Particulars of members to be registered, 127, 128

partnership, 17, 23, 25, 77, 82, 113, 114, 115, 116, 117, 123, 125, 126, 149, 236, 253, 256, 295
PARTNERSHIP, 124, 236
party to proceedings, 31, 32, 180
Patents Court Business and Proceedings, 51
patient, 143
Patient, 143
permission" of the court, 73
Personal delivery, 106
Personal delivery of documents, 106
personal injury, 15
PERSONAL INSOLVENCY, 75, 86
Personal Service, 22, 253
Personal service on a company or other corporation, 39
Persons at risk of violence, 76, 98
persons under disability, 143
persons unknown, 53
petition, 17, 21, 73, 74, 75, 76, 81, 82, 83, 84, 85, 88, 89, 90, 91, 92, 93, 94, 95, 96, 97, 106, 110, 111, 113, 116, 117, 118, 119, 120, 141, 142, 143, 144, 218, 278, 292
Petition, 141, 142, 143, 212, 271, 274, 275, 276, 277, 279, 281, 282, 286
PETITION, 7, 271, 272, 273, 274, 275, 276, 277, 278, 279
petitioner, 17, 81, 82, 83, 84, 85, 93, 94, 116, 117
Petitioner, 5, 141, 142, 143, 212, 260, 279, 280, 281, 286, 298
petitions, 10, 16, 74, 75, 76, 78, 81, 83, 90, 92, 94, 96, 97, 111, 117
Place Of Service, 297
PLAINTIFF, 7
possession claim against trespassers, 53
Possession Claims, 7, 53, 54
Possession claims relating to mortgaged residential property, 54
possession of land, 15
Postal delivery of documents, 106
postcode, 23, 32
postcodes, 23, 32
Power Of Court To Dispense With Service Of The Claim Form, 29
practice direction, 21, 22, 31, 32, 33, 35, 38, 39, 42, 49, 50, 86, 110, 223, 226, 232, 253
Practice Direction 5C, 50
Practice Direction 6a, 7, 38
Practice Direction 6A, 21, 23, 31, 34
pre-action application notices, 42
principal place of business, 23, 52, 118, 119, 130, 236, 253, 256, 278, 295
Principal Registry, 17, 42, 139, 144
prison, 51, 260
proceedings against the Crown, 22, 26, 60
Proceedings for divorce, 42
proceedings in the Family Courts, 42
process, 1, 3, 7, 9, 10, 37, 48, 52, 72, 100, 111, 119, 130, 142, 145, 148, 149, 150, 158, 165, 166, 168, 173, 174, 175, 211, 215, 228, 243, 246, 278, 285, 289, 295, 296, 297, 298, 301, 302

PROCESS, 1, 2, 5, 7, 9, 156, 165, 166, 173, 272
process papers, 9, 10
Process Server, 1, 2, 5, 140, 165, 211, 212, 213, 215, 216, 217, 228, 233, 234, 235, 236, 237, 238, 239, 240, 241, 242, 245, 246, 247, 248, 249, 251, 257, 258, 259, 260, 261, 263, 265, 266, 267, 269, 271, 274, 275, 276, 277, 279, 280, 281, 285, 286, 287, 289, 290, 291
Process Serving, 7, 5, 9
Proof of sending, 107
Proof of Service, 66
Proof Of Service, 139
proofs of service, 10
Protected information, 129
protected party, 27, 28, 33
protection from disclosure, 129
PROTECTION FROM DISCLOSURE, 129
Protection Notices, 150
Protection of Children, 135
PROVISIONS APPLICABLE TO APPLICATIONS UNDER SECTIONS 7(2) AND 7(4) OF THE ACT, 121
public authority, 42
pursuer, 8

Q

QUEEN'S BENCH DIVISION, 234, 235, 236, 237, 238, 239, 240, 241, 242, 243, 245, 249

R

Reason For Non-Service Of Document, 189
Receipt of documents by receiving agency, 195
RECORDS, 8
Refusal to accept, 196
Register of Companies, 83
REGISTER OF MEMBERS, 126
registered company, 39, 40
Regulation (EC) No 1393/2007 of the European Parliament and of the Council of 13 November 2007, 190
Relationship with agreements or arrangements to which Member States are party, 200
Relevant criteria and procedure, 76, 102
remuneration application, 78, 100, 101, 102, 104, 105
Remuneration of Appointees, 76, 100
Rescission, 75, 83
residence of the Sovereign, 51
Respondent, 5, 6, 138, 141, 142, 143, 212, 255, 260, 264, 266, 279, 280, 281, 282, 283, 286, 298
RESPONDENT, 7
Revoked by Magistrates' Courts, 157
Right of witness to travelling expenses and compensation for loss of time, 65
Rogatory Letter, 173
Royal Air Force Officers and Other Ranks, 43

Royal Courts of Justice, 13, 14, 15, 16, 36, 77, 79, 81, 83, 85, 86, 92, 93, 96, 99, 144, 160, 181
Royal Navy and Royal Marine Officers, Ratings and Other Ranks, 43
Rubber Stamps, 297
Rule 7.4, 40, 144
rule 7.5, 28, 47, 48
Rules Modernisation Update with Stakeholder Commentary – March 2010, 71
rules of civil procedure, 19
Rules of the Supreme Court, 3, 19

S

SAMPLE AFFIDAVITS, 168, 256, 285
Scotland, 3, 8, 38, 43, 52, 60, 72, 112, 118, 120, 123, 125, 126, 130, 158, 160, 165, 166, 167, 168, 170, 179, 187
Second Respondent, 5
SECTION 10, 295
SECTION 2 – SERVICE OF CLAIM FORMS, 47
SECTION 3, 65
SECTION 4, 69
SECTION 5, 135
SECTION 6, 156
SECTION 7, 165
SECTION 8, 173
SECTION 9, 221
Secure Accommodation Orders, 135
Securing the property, 54
Senior Master, 15, 36, 37, 181
SERVE, 7, 166
serve a document, 22, 31, 32, 39, 53, 130, 137, 162, 166, 296
serve legal documents, 42
served on the Crown, 57, 60
served out of, 26, 47, 80, 86, 142, 145, 180
served personally, 22, 23, 32, 34, 41, 61, 131, 141, 142, 228, 253
service, 4, 3, 5, 9, 10, 11, 14, 18, 21, 22, 23, 24, 26, 27, 28, 29, 30, 31, 32, 33, 34, 35, 36, 37, 38, 39, 40, 41, 42, 43, 44, 47, 48, 49, 50, 51, 52, 53, 55, 56, 57, 60, 62, 63, 65, 66, 74, 75, 76, 77, 80, 82, 86, 88, 89, 90, 92, 94, 101, 106, 107, 108, 109, 111, 112, 119, 121, 127, 128, 129, 130, 131, 132, 136, 137, 138, 139, 140, 141, 142, 143, 144, 145, 146, 148, 149, 150, 157, 158, 159, 160, 161, 162, 163, 165, 166, 168, 169, 170, 173, 174, 175, 176, 177, 180, 181, 190, 191, 192, 193, 194, 195, 196, 197, 198, 199, 200, 203, 204, 205, 206, 207, 211, 212, 215, 216, 217, 221, 226, 227, 228, 236, 241, 242, 243, 244, 245, 247, 253, 254, 255, 261, 262, 264, 269, 270, 275, 276, 277, 278, 279, 281, 282, 283, 285, 286, 289, 290, 291, 293, 295, 296, 297, 298
SERVICE, 4, 47, 121, 158, 159, 166, 169, 212, 213, 218, 221, 234, 235, 236, 237, 238, 239, 240, 241, 242, 245, 246, 247, 248, 249, 251, 255, 256, 258, 259, 260, 261,

263, 264, 265, 267, 270, 271, 272, 275, 276, 277, 278, 279, 280, 281, 283, 284, 286, 287, 292, 293
Service abroad of, 75, 86
Service abroad on a Sunday, 48
Service addresses, 51, 53, 130, 131
Service by an alternative method or at an alternative place, 35
Service by another method, 162
Service by diplomatic or consular agents, 198
Service by leaving, 160
Service by person in custody, 162
Service by postal services, 198
Service in a Commonwealth State or British overseas territory, 181
Service In Claims Against Trespassers, 54
Service may be effected, 141
Service of a claim form in a Royal Palace, 51
Service of a summons issued by a justice of the peace, 156
Service Of An Original Claim Form, 295
Service of application notices in disqualification proceedings, 121
Service of claim form or other document on a State, 36
Service of claims against trespassers, 53
Service of court documents, 74, 75, 80
Service of Court Documents, 111
SERVICE OF DISQUALIFICATION ORDERS, 121
Service of documents, 51, 52, 130, 196, 254
Service of Documents, 7, 21, 31, 57
Service of documents on company, 51
Service of documents on directors, secretaries and others, 52
Service of interim order, 62
Service of orders staying proceedings, 111
Service of proceedings, 149
Service of Process in Maintenance Proceedings, 148, 149
Service of the claim form by contractually agreed method, 26
Service of the claim form in proceedings against the crown, 26
Service of the Claim Form in the Jurisdiction, 21
Service of the claim form on a defendant in a Convention territory outside Europe, 177
Service of the claim form on a defendant in a Convention territory within Europe or a Member State, 176
Service of the Claim Form on a Solicitor within the Jurisdiction or in any EEA State, 23
Service Of The Claim Form On Children And Protected Parties, 27
Service of the claim form relating to a contract on an agent of a principal who is out of the jurisdiction, 27
Service of the claim form where the defendant does not give an address at which the defendant may be served, 24
Service of the Claim Form where the Defendant gives an address at which the Defendant may be served, 24
Service of the claim form where the permission of the court is not required – out of the United Kingdom, 167
Service of the claim form where the permission of the court is required, 177
Service On A Partnership Firm, 295
Service on children and protected parties, 33
Service On Husband And Wife, 295
Service on joint office-holders, 112
Service on Members of the Regular Forces, 7, 42
Service on members of the Regular Forces and United States Air Force, 39
Service on person acting in, 146
Service Out Of, 142, 145
Service Where Defendant Wrongly Described, 296
Service Where The Defendant Alleges The Claim Is Paid, 296
serving a witness summons, 65
serving the document, 39, 41
Setting aside a statutory demand, 75, 89
shall be of no effect, 149, 150
Sheriff, 8, 15, 54, 158, 165, 166
Sheriff Court, 8, 165, 166
SHERIFF COURT, 8
Sheriff Courts, 8
Sheriff Principal, 8
Sheriff's Officers, 165
solicitor, 3, 21, 23, 24, 26, 32, 38, 39, 56, 60, 88, 89, 97, 106, 107, 122, 131, 136, 137, 141, 152, 227, 228, 253, 255, 264, 270, 283, 296, 297
Solicitor, 5, 23, 24, 26, 57, 59, 60, 81, 82, 88, 143, 153, 169, 170, 227, 228, 234, 235, 236, 237, 238, 239, 240, 242, 243, 244, 245, 246, 247, 248, 250, 257, 258, 266, 270, 275, 276, 277, 278, 279, 280, 282, 293, 296
SOLICITOR AND ADDRESSES FOR SERVICE, 57
Solicitors Act 1974, 225, 227
Special provision on account of expense as to website use, 109
Specialist proceedings, 51
State, 6, 23, 36, 37, 53, 58, 60, 77, 80, 98, 112, 116, 149, 168, 173, 176, 180, 181, 189, 191, 192, 193, 194, 195, 196, 197, 198, 199, 200, 203, 204, 205, 206, 207, 208, 209, 210, 218, 292
State Immunity Act 1978, 36
statement, 2, 6, 19, 37, 39, 73, 74, 80, 82, 83, 84, 85, 89, 90, 94, 95, 97, 98, 103, 105, 108, 109, 122, 123, 137, 139, 161, 221, 222, 227, 229, 230, 231, 232
Statement, 10, 11, 12, 51, 53, 66, 138, 139, 142, 228, 229, 230, 251, 265, 267, 268, 271, 272, 273, 275, 279
Statement of arrangements for children, 142
STATEMENT OF SERVICE OF A BANKRUPTCY PETITION, 271
statement of truth, 73, 230, 232
STATEMENTS OF CASE, 232
statutory demand, 74, 86, 87, 88, 89, 90, 92, 97, 107
STATUTORY DEMAND, 88, 267, 268, 269, 270
statutory demands, 10, 75, 86, 88
Statutory demands, 75, 86
Stop Notices, 7, 62
Stop Orders, 7, 62

Stuart Withers, 1, 2, 301
SUBPOENA, 7
subpoenas, 10, 144
substituted, 11, 84, 86, 88, 89, 92, 94, 157, 269, 270, 296
Substituted Service, 143, 233, 274, 296
Summons, 7, 144, 145, 156, 158, 168, 170, 214, 215, 280, 288, 289
SUMMONS, 7, 214, 241, 258, 280, 288
summonses, 10
SUSPECT, 8
swearing, 10, 18, 221, 228

T

Taking Possession Of Mortgaged Property, 54
Technology and Construction Court Business, 51
tenant against a landlord, 24
the 1985 Act, 124, 125, 126
the 1986 Act, 124, 125, 126
the 2000 Act, 125
The Administrative Court, 13
the Chancery Division, 14, 15, 16, 99, 100
The Chancery Division, 13, 15
The Child Support Act, 140, 146
THE CHILDREN ACT 1989, 135
THE CIVIL PROCEDURE AMENDMENT RULES 2008, 21
The Criminal Procedure Rules 2011, 159
The European Parliament And The Council Of The European Union,, 190
the Family Division, 14, 17, 139, 141
The Family Division, 13, 17
The Family Proceedings Courts, 136
The Family Proceedings Rules, 135, 142, 146
The Hague, 173, 174, 175, 208, 210
THE INSOLVENCY ACT 1986, 79
The Insolvency Service, 69, 71, 74
the precincts of Parliament, 51
the Probate Service., 13
the Queen's Bench Division, 14, 15
The Queen's Bench Division, 13, 14
The Smoke In Death's Eye, 302
The Witness Rule, 165
The Zen of Shoplifting, 302
The Zen of Sleuthing, 302
third party, 5, 62, 73, 143
THIRD PARTY, 7, 8
Third Party Debt, 62
THIRD PARTY ORDER, 7
Time, 48, 49, 50, 65, 132, 138, 139, 140
Time limits may be varied by parties, 50
TORT, 7
Transitional Provisions, 150
translation, 36, 37, 180, 191, 195, 196, 225, 231
Translation, 36, 195
Transmission and service of judicial documents, 194
Transmitting and receiving agencies, 193

Travelling expenses, 61, 66

U

United Kingdom, 7, 21, 31, 32, 38, 42, 44, 52, 53, 63, 69, 118, 127, 148, 149, 150, 156, 157, 160, 165, 167, 168, 174, 175, 193
United States Air Force, 39, 44
United States authorities, 44
unregistered company, 113, 116, 117, 118, 119, 120
Urgent applications, 75, 81
Use Of Envelopes, 295
Use of websites by office-holder, 108
usual place of abode., 156

V

Validation orders, 75, 76, 84, 94
victims of domestic violence, 147
violence against the debtor, 98
Voluntary arrangement of insolvent partnership, 115
Voluntary Arrangements, 74, 96
Voluntary arrangements of members of insolvent partnership, 116

W

Wales, 13, 17, 19, 25, 42, 43, 44, 52, 58, 60, 63, 89, 99, 112, 113, 117, 118, 119, 120, 121, 123, 130, 138, 142, 145, 157, 158, 160, 165, 253, 278, 296
Where To Serve The Claim Form, 23
Who is to serve, 31, 65
Who Is To Serve The Claim Form, 22
WINDING UP AND INSOLVENCY, 125
Winding up of unregistered companies, 118
Winding Up of Unregistered Companies, 118
winding up order, 75, 82, 83, 84
winding up petition, 81
winding-up, 81, 85, 86, 111, 113, 116, 118, 119, 120
without notice, 27, 28, 29, 33, 35, 48, 73, 144
Without Notice Applications', 18
without notice to any other party, 73
witness, 6, 12, 53, 54, 65, 66, 73, 80, 83, 84, 89, 90, 94, 98, 121, 144, 145, 158, 161, 165, 166, 210, 224, 229, 230, 231, 232, 297
witness statements, 53, 54, 121, 144, 230, 231
WITNESS STATEMENTS, 229
witness summons, 65, 66, 144, 145, 158, 161, 297
Witness Summons, 7, 144, 145, 241, 258
WITNESSES AND DEPOSITIONS, 65
WRIT, 5, 8
writ of summons, 145, 199, 200, 206
writs, 10, 165